POSTCOMPOSITION

POSTCOMPOSITION

Sidney I. Dobrin

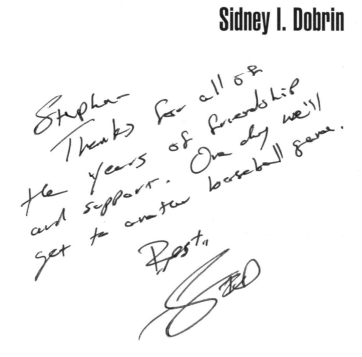

Stephen—
Thanks for all of
the years of friendship
and support. One day we'll
get to another baseball game.

Post,,

[signature]

Southern Illinois University Press
Carbondale and Edwardsville

14 13 12 11   4 3 2 1

Library of Congress Cataloging-in-Publication Data
Dobrin, Sidney I., 1967–
Postcomposition / Sidney I. Dobrin.
    p. cm.
Includes bibliographical references and index.
ISBN-13: 978-0-8093-3041-6 (pbk. : alk. paper)
ISBN-10: 0-8093-3041-5 (pbk. : alk. paper)
ISBN-13: 978-0-8093-8788-5 (ebook)
ISBN-10: 0-8093-8788-3 (ebook)
1. English language—Rhetoric—Study and teaching.
I. Title.
PE1404.D637 2011
808'.042071—dc22   2010040311

*This one is for Gary A. Olson,
my mentor and friend;
with much gratitude and respect.*

We call ourselves what we are, but also what we wish to be. This is inspiring and this is corrupting. For the ambiguity allows us to see the one in the other, to mistake what we wish to be for what we are. Since the satisfaction of an ideal is so hard to attain, it is easy to imagine. But the reality of an ideal must not blind us to its unreality, which is the source of its enticement to action, and of its usefulness as a measure of progress. A good rule is: we are never already what we should be.

—Leon Wieseltier, *Against Identity*

If I surround an area with a fence or a line or otherwise, the purpose may be to prevent someone from getting in or out; but it may also be part of a game and the players be supposed, say, to jump over the boundary; or it may show where the property of one man ends and that of another begins; and so on. So if I draw a boundary line that is not yet to say what I am drawing it for.

—Ludwig Wittgenstein, *Philosophical Investigations*

Contents

Acknowledgments

I would be foolish to pretend that this book was solely the product of my work; it is collaboration in the truest sense. Without the conversations, feedback, taunting, prodding, and encouragement from many, this book would have taken a much less useful or interesting shape. To each of you who, in whatever way, has contributed to this effort, I offer my genuine thanks and acknowledge your contributions.

I am grateful for the phenomenal colleagues with whom I work, whose intellectual rigor, dedication, and passion are the reason the University of Florida Department of English is so successful. I am humbled by the opportunity to work with such remarkable scholars, colleagues, and friends; I am better at what I do because of the examples you all set. Without question, the conversations I have with my colleagues have deeply influenced the content of this book; I acknowledge and sincerely thank Roger Beebe, Marsha Bryant, Kim Emery, Terry Harpold, Susan Hegeman, Scott Nygren, Amy Ongiri, Robert Ray, Leah Rosenberg, Jodi Schorb, Malini Schueller, Stephanie Smith, Chris Snodgrass, Robert Thompson, Maureen Turim, Greg Ulmer, Phil Wegner, and Ed White for all they have taught me. I am especially grateful to Pam Gilbert, Kenneth Kidd, and John Leavey for their wisdom, guidance, friendship, and institutional savvy.

My gratitude also goes to Friedrich Ferdinand Runge and Hermann Emil Fischer, whose work often makes it possible for me to do mine.

I thank the Southern Illinois University Press reviewers who provided substantial feedback on the manuscript for this book. I thank the entire editorial and production staff at SIU Press for their work in bringing this project to fruition. My sincerest gratitude goes to Karl Kageff for his dedication to this project and his insightful guidance throughout the review and editorial processes.

This book would not be what it is without the never-ending friendship and deeply detailed suggestions at every stage of my reading, thinking, and writing by Joe Hardin, Julie Drew, and Raúl Sánchez. I can never thank the three of you enough—for all of it. Corn.

Finally, there is no point to any of what I do without Teresa, Asher, and Shaia. You are my motivation, my inspiration, and my pride. I love you. Always.

POSTCOMPOSITION

Introduction: On the Occasion of Becoming Postcomposition

> Our existence today is marked by a tenebrous sense of survival, living on
> the borderlines of the "present," for which there seems no proper name
> other than the current and controversial shiftiness of the prefix "post."
> —Homi K. Bhaba, *The Location of Culture*

> Don't Panic.
> —Douglas Adams, *The Hitchhiker's Guide to the Galaxy*

Don't panic. I am not calling for the end of composition studies or even
identifying something as dramatic as the death of composition studies,
despite the way that many may read the title of this book. The rumor of the
death of composition studies has been greatly exaggerated. What the field
was and is, is still likely to be—at least for a while. Though, to be honest,
there really isn't anything wrong with the idea of the "end" of composition
studies. In fact, parts of this book will address the possibility of such ends,
just as other books, like David W. Smit's *The End of Composition Studies*
and Gary A. Olson's *Rhetoric and Composition as Intellectual Work*, have
addressed them. Composition studies, of course, can end, will end at some
point. All phenomena with histories necessarily must end. All progress of
life is toward death. That which has beginning requires (at some point) an
ending, or, more accurately, a re-categorization, a redefining. Ends and
deaths are merely moments of new formations, hybrids, and mutations. One
category may appear to end, but its components move on in new formations.
The idea of an end is frightening as an acknowledgment of termination and,
more so, as a question of accomplishment: what has been done in this time
before the end? But, an end of composition studies as a discipline does not
really mean that much. Its end will likely not initiate the end of the American
university system; it will certainly not launch the end of civilization, the end
of culture, the end of existence (though their ends would likely bring about
the end of composition studies); and it won't cause or signify the end of writing (or even writing instruction), nor do those who talk about an end of the
discipline even really suggest such a thing. However, the end of composition

studies, should such a thing ever actually occur in some notable, codifiable manner, will likely go unnoticed by most of the world, and even by most who have considered themselves to be compositionists, to be of composition studies. What will likely occur, what has already occurred numerous times over, is that composition studies' end will merely mean its mutation into something more adaptable to the time of its end, its new hybrid formation, a formation dependent upon cultural demands and manifestations of what the field is and should be. And, as we know from Jean-François Lyotard's *Peregrinations: Law, Form, Event,* "any narrative whatsoever begins in the middle of things and . . . its so called 'end' is an arbitrary cut in the infinite sequence of data" (2). Composition studies becomes/continues to be fractal.

In his foreword to Smit's *The End of Composition Studies,* Doug Hesse makes an interesting distinction between "writing" and "composition":

> Understanding what is at stake begins with the distinction between "writing" and "composition." The two are not synonymous. The former term is the larger and, mostly, loftier. We call people who publish books and articles writers (or authors), reserving composer for musical production. Except for fairly snooty usages (one's "composing a text" is rather akin to one's "penning a letter"), written composition belongs almost strictly to the college freshman classroom. (ix)

This distinction is an academic distinction, one that only brushes the deep differences between composition and writing. This book, *Postcomposition,* underscores these differences, identifying composition (studies) as an academic discipline and composing as an act that is chained by that discipline to an understanding of student subjects performing that act (often only as academic performance). Writing is a phenomenon that requires the attention of intellectual and scholarly inquiry and speculation beyond composition. Writing is more than composition (studies).

Postcomposition works to create tremors in composition studies' ground, with the intent of violence. It works within what Victor J. Vitanza would call the "terrorism of theory" specifically against the "will of the field" (143). It is a work of disruption and discomfort; it is a work against the discipline's pedagogical imperative toward the contingency of writing. This is not work toward the death of the field but to its passing. That is to say, it is an attempt to figure what comes next, what comes after composition studies. In a revealing discussion of what might be implied by the "post" of academic "post-isms," Judith Halberstram and Ira Livingston explain that posthumanism takes up the "post" of postmodernism, poststucturalism, postcolonialism, and postindustrial capitalism because "post" indicates the "regrettable failure to imagine what's next" (2), and, turning to Jacques Derrida, what will appear must do so as "the as yet unnamable which is proclaiming itself and which can do so, as is necessary whenever a birth is in the offing, only under the species of the non-species, in the formless, mute, infant and terrifying form of monstrosity" (*Writing and Difference* 293). This is the "post" of postcomposition: a reaction to the field's regrettable failure to imagine what comes next and an attempt to catch a glimpse of the monster.

So, why postcomposition? Simply, the disciplinary imperative is not enough. There is an (ethical) imperative beyond the boundaries of composition studies' field that demands that work be pursued that theorizes writing beyond the disciplinary limit-situation. Embedded within that imperative is a need to call to question composition studies' conservative allegiance to subject and administration and the strictures that such allegiances have imposed on the field. This isn't just about composition studies; it is about writing. The field's historically imposed prohibition on theory inflicts a constitutive blind spot that limits what may be known about writing. *Postcomposition* works to extend that field of vision so that should composition studies end (again)—an end I have already indicated as meaningless—its passing becomes more significant than its presence. Composition studies, you see, does not matter; writing does.

Simply put, what I argue for in these pages is that composition studies requires (or perhaps is already witnessing) a shift from the disciplinary focus upon (writing) subjects and pedagogy to a more explicit focus on writing itself. The danger for composition studies in the argument I unfold here is that it removes the ethical guarantor, the safety net, to what the discipline does. Without the solidity of student subjects and administration, of seeing this as a teaching field, there is no certainty for the field; the posts have been taken down. In order for composition studies to adhere to its mythologies, there must be a guarantor, but, à la Slavoj Žižek, we must know there never is a guarantor. The guarantor is merely a deferred position. For composition studies not to have a tangible guarantor is a frightening contingency, but contingencies are precisely the possibilities of writing.

Raúl Sánchez, in his important book *The Function of Theory in Composition Studies*, contends that composition studies and composition theory have been distracted in their attention to writing by focusing on the "something else" of writing (20)—an argument that Michael Carter points out that I have similarly made previously, calling it the "thingness" of writing (xi)—rather than upon the text. I argue in *Postcomposition* that composition studies' distraction comes not from an unnamed "something else" but from a very specific something else: subjects and administrations of those subjects. That is to say, composition studies' primary object of study is not writing or even the teaching of writing, as the field often claims; the field's primary object of study is the (student) subject. Such a focus greatly limits, as I hope to show, what can be known about writing. I do not seek an explanation of writing beyond writing; I look to understand writing as writing. But, to do so, I attempt to look beyond composition studies.

In order to initiate moves beyond the limits of the discipline, I take an approach that blends disciplinary critique with an attempt to unfold (the beginning of) an ecological/networked theory of writing that does not rely upon subjects as a principle tenet of the theory. In the first chapter, I consider the (e)state of composition studies, examining particularly the central importance of subjects and program administration to the missions of the field. Likewise, I regard the ways in which the disciplinary nuzzling up to subjectivity and administration has fostered an anti-theoretical climate within the field and has influenced the overall direction of what can be considered legitimate research within the field. After situating my argument within and against composition studies, I develop in the second chapter a spatial understanding of writing, one that exceeds the metaphoric approaches to space already appropriated by the field. My consideration of space examines the historical construction of images as spatial and writing as chronological and works to rethink writing as spatial. To this end, I develop a theory of occupation as a beginning point for ecological theories of writing that I forward later in the book. At the same time, I consider how the very idea of occupation has been a disciplinary force within composition studies.

Following these first two context-setting chapters, I examine the obsolescence of subjectivity and subject formation as a central feature to theorizing and understanding writing. Moving instead to a posthumanist approach to subjectivity, I work to remove the idea of the subject from the arena of writing theory. With my objection to subject/subjectivity as fundamental to writing studies in mind, the fourth chapter levels a critique against the ever-growing importance of writing program administration to composition studies' identity. This critique addresses the very idea of administration as well as the professional organization of the Council of Writing Program Administrators. To move postcomposition requires that administration be abandoned as a useful part of the field.

The two chapters that follow my critique of administration begin the work of developing one form of writing theory free of subjectivity and administration. Chapter 5 reconsiders ecocomposition as a location from which productive theories about writing might evolve. This chapter also begins to examine how network theory and systems theories might influence our understanding of writing. The penultimate chapter continues this effort, by laying the groundwork in establishing a networked theory of writing.

It is commonplace for works in theory in composition studies to conclude with an address of pedagogy, to show how the presented theory might be of "use" to the field by situating it in what is assumed to be the field's raison d'être: teaching. Thus, the final chapter of *Postcomposition*, "Pedagogy," takes up a familiar position, but to the end of disrupting the field's pedagogical imperative, rethinking the very idea of pedagogy.

Finally, I provide a postscript. The postscript comes first. That is, the postscript contends with the very idea of what it means to be "post." In many ways, concepts like "post" and "beyond" are tired metaphors; they are not new ideas; they have been used by scholars in numerous ways over a long period of time. My push throughout *Postcomposition* to get past the constraints of composition studies, thus, is limited by the metaphors I employ to make such a push. Later in this book, I contend that the field lacks the vocabulary necessary to talk about writing as writing to any useful degree and that finding such a vocabulary would require some hard work. Yet, seemingly, I then fall prey to this very entrapment, not seeking out the new vocabulary needed, instead embracing the discursive tools just lying about already available. But, my use of the prefix "post-" is intended to embrace its traditional use and twist it a bit. The postscript, then, is a discussion of how I came to the idea of post and why, even in its tiredness, I find it to be valuable.

Ultimately, the occasion of *Postcomposition* is one of a desire for disruption, a sense of frustration with the conservatism of composition studies, and a need to tear at the field's seams a bit. It is an occasion of change.

1. Disrupting Composition Studies

> The field has been working at theory for too long to have gotten so little out of it.
>
> —Raúl Sánchez, *The Function of Theory in Composition Studies*

Composition studies, as a field, doesn't talk much about its intellectual future and only minimally considers its institutional future (the notable exception is the September 2010 special issue of *College Composition and Communication* that takes up composition studies' future). Perhaps this is the case because it has been enamored with its own history. A substantial amount of the field's "research" has been geared toward understanding why (and how) it became an academic discipline. That same research often embraces a narrative of oppression that empowers the field's self-sustained image, as Susan Miller has put it, as "the sad women in the basement" (*Textual Carnivals* 121). Much of the field's self-reflective narrative has focused on validation of the work that it does. But, much of the work that examines composition studies' history and its evolution into an academic field presents that evolution as a primarily epistemological endeavor, as a development of intellectual and pedagogical need. Rarely do such historical assessments account for a bureaucratic history, beyond, perhaps, narratives of how writing instructors were and are treated as labor and devalued in relation to those who taught literature. Those conversations, however, are usually cast in terms of the power struggle between rhetoric and literature; that is, those conversations, despite their evidence of labor issues, are presented as representative of larger epistemological power struggles. As an academic effort, the field has followed an economic, bureaucratic, and organizational trajectory as much as it has followed theoretical and pedagogical/pragmatic lines of development. In order for composition studies to become an academic field, those doing the work of composition studies had to persuade administrators that the teaching of rhetoric and writing was important enough to secure funding. With this funding (minimal as it may have been, at times) came efforts to ensure tenure lines in the field and provisions for developing a labor class within the field, as well. From these positions, then, composition studies could justify funding for journals, professional organizations, graduate programs, and all of the trappings that make and validate a discipline as disciplinary to its members and others in the academy. This bureaucracy, like any other, then, attains a state of self-perpetuation by creating its own audiences and need for publication and conferences as well as a system of self-replenishment through PhD programs in which the field replicates itself through disciplinary standards, core knowledge, and professional doctrine and lore. Pedagogy and epistemology do not exist outside of corporate/bureaucratic systems; to evaluate either without the other is to ignore a primary context of the other. In many ways, we might think of the division of epistemology and bureaucracy as a division between the philosophical and the political. To deny this facet of composition studies' history is, first, to accept a disingenuous history that portrays the field as strictly an epistemological effort and, second, to risk condemning composition studies to a future bound to the very academic bureaucracy it has failed to acknowledge historically. With this absence of bureaucratic history, composition studies has painted a vision of its research agendas that entrap the field as a service industry.

In the pages that follow, I argue that the possibility of this future for composition studies demands disruption, epistemological and bureaucratic. I argue that the nexus for disruption lies at the center of the field's intellectual focus upon (writing) subjects and the teaching and management of those subjects rather than upon writing itself. Such disruption, I believe, is necessary at this moment in the discipline's evolution in order to avoid the possibility of an intellectual stagnation brought about by an over-attuned focus on student subjects and the administration of those subjects rather than on a disciplinary concentration upon writing itself. How and why such disruption might occur is at the center of this book and the agenda of what we might think of as a shift postcomposition.

The (E)state of Composition/Theory

The introduction to Stephen North's 1987 book *The Making of Knowledge in Composition* addresses the "methodological land rush" that composition has experienced since the 1960s and its move to "really *become* a field," despite its inability to articulate any coherent methodology (2, 3, emphasis in original). *The Making of Knowledge*, of course, is concerned a good deal with the role teachers played in that becoming-of-field, in developing methodologies that helped push composition studies into its field-ness. North identifies part of the liability of composition studies' move to field as the ways it has "ignored, discounted, or ridiculed" practitioners' role in knowledge-making, disenfranchising them within their own field (3). But within this critique,

North does not call for composition studies' becoming-field to be driven by methodologies based in classroom inquiry. He argues that the "modes of inquiry" in the field's research agenda "should not be confused with the various research *techniques* their practitioners might use" (1–2, emphasis in original). North argues that "investigators often seem unreflective about their own mode of inquiry, let alone anyone else's," and that an "absence of critical consciousness capable of discriminating more carefully the various kinds of knowledge produced by these modes have been piled up uncritically, helter-skelter, with little regard to incompatibilities," resulting in "an accumulated knowledge of a relatively impressive size, but one that lacks any clear coherence or methodological integrity" (3). Robert J. Connors's *Composition-Rhetoric*, in reaction to North's claim, identifies that "we are already pursuing research paths so disparate that many thoughtful people have feared the discipline may fly apart like a dollar watch" (18). Now, nearly twenty-five years since North proclaimed that "the work of the first six decades of the century have been pathetic" and suggested the same about the work since 1963, little seems to have changed for composition studies (17). In fact, North expresses a concern that "if Composition research is to scientific inquiry what alchemy was to chemistry, then presumably current practice must be to 'scientific' practice what 'real' medicine is to witch doctoring. A practice based on 'dreams, prejudices, and makeshift operations' is quite capable of doing as much harm as good" to the burgeoning field (17). Careful not to discount the work of practitioners, North nonetheless argues that "practical knowledge, the stuff of teachers' rooms, how-to articles, textbooks, and the like, doesn't count as research" (17). If composition studies cannot develop a coherent research agenda, North warns, then composition studies itself is "in serious trouble indeed" (17). North goes on to proclaim a new era of research, an era in which "the dominance of practice and sloppy research would have to end" (17). Unfortunately, the new era for which North called has not been achieved.

Instead of North's "land rush" of methodology, the past twenty-four years of scholarship in composition studies has largely served to institutionalize the inflated claims that classroom-based research counts as the primary form of disciplinary knowledge and to marginalize theory except as a way to explain or support what happens in the classroom. In saying so, however, I do not wish to adhere to an either-or proposition regarding classroom-based research as the only valid form of research within the field. In fact, such insistence on separation and denigration has impoverished the field because once a field establishes such either-or thinking in terms of what counts as disciplinary knowledge, many within the field stand to lose out on validation. Likewise, little critical reflection regarding composition studies' modes of inquiry has been forwarded outside of a rubric that works to revalidate those very modes of practice-based inquiry. This is not to imply that the elevation of pedagogy, narrative, and practice as viable disciplinary concerns is inherently detrimental. In fact, composition studies has masterfully exploited its feminized and "othered" place in the academy to expose the biases of traditional forms of research, to draw attention to the possible disciplinary value of teacher-based knowledge, and to make anecdote and narrative accepted forms of presentation for some scholarship. However, work to engage in research that does not rely upon or even mention classroom practice or application as either a source of or a goal of theory has often run up against resistance with a missionary zeal to minimize "theory for theory's sake." Composition studies casts the classroom and the classroom compositionists as heroic figures and construes research as useful only if it reports on or has application to classroom practice. Consider Smit's *The End of Composition Studies*, which proclaims that

> the past forty years have seen research and scholarship in the field proliferate in so many different directions that composition studies, which never had a common methodology, has lost touch with its primary reason for being—the teaching of writing—and I want to argue that composition studies needs to go back to basic questions, such as these: What is writing? How is writing learned? Can writing be taught, and if so, in what sense? And if writing can be taught, how should it be taught? (2)

These questions reckon a nostalgic connection to the process era's desire for easy answers to such queries in order to solidify skills-based writing curricula. It is interesting to note that Smit does not take up the question of "What is writing?" in *The End of Composition Studies* in any way other than directly tied to how students learn to write and, more often, how writing teachers teach writing. The book, in fact, argues that writing as phenomena cannot be studied independent of the local contexts in which it is taught and learned (166). According to Smit, then, the question of "What is writing?" is more a question of how (student) subjects write, and the disciplinary goal of composition studies is one of developing better methods for teaching and learning how to write. This focus offers a determined agenda for how composition studies must proceed, since as Smit contends, "further research on these questions will not substantially alter the broad outline, the substantial picture of what we already know" (181). In fact, Smit goes so far as to argue for a re-envisioning of the merit of faculty work, not only to emphasize the teaching of writing over research but to alter the condition under which research is produced and disseminated, contending that a primary objective of composition studies research should be the spreading of the field's knowledge to fields outside of composition (198–99). While Smit's move beyond composition studies' disciplinary boundaries is applaudable, his stagnating claim enshrines the field in the composition classroom and binds all research and service to that classroom.[1]

Smit's push to codify the field and its research agendas within a rubric of classroom and student prevents any advances (or any movement) in understanding the phenomena of writing outside of or beyond the pedagogical scene. As I hope to show throughout this book, by developing complex ecological understandings of writing, we gain a greater access to understanding writing; this is specifically a move away from composition research that looks to identify parts of writing in favor of more systemic theories of writing. In chapters 5 and 6, I address ecologic theories, systems theories, and complexity theories in order to move in this direction. And while Smit argues that composition studies must spread its knowledge of writing instruction beyond the composition classroom, this move is little more than an attempt to create larger populations of composition students in order to enlarge and to further justify composition studies' territorial hold over "student."

Interestingly, Susan Miller's "Writing Theory: Theory Writing" identifies that in working to grant composition studies with the status of "field," several scholars (North, Lester Faigley, James Berlin) pose as the field's central question "How do writers write?" (69). This question is very different from the one Smit asks in posing "What is writing?" The difference in these two questions is critical, as it seems that the field has been more willing to ask the "how do writers write" question and that even Smit's follow-up question about learning and teaching redirect the focus of the inquiry from writing to writer, a shift that directs attention away from writing and toward a more manageable subject: writer. What such a shift allows, then, is the formation of a narrative of inquiry, an approach that becomes entrenched in the discipline's master narrative as the appropriate way to conduct research in the field. Ingraining such an approach in the field's population can be likened to Donna J. Haraway's critique of scientific inquiry, which she contends is so dramatically dominated by a patriarchal system of inquiry that it disavows any inquiry that breaks with the approved "scientific method," let alone any that might critique knowledge acquired through that method (*Simians*). Inquiring as to the function and/or phenomena of writing absent of any inquiry that inherently links the possible outcomes of that inquiry to issues of writer or writing-subject risks negation within composition studies as not being part of the field's research agenda. The seven questions that frame Lynn Z. Bloom, Donald A. Daiker, and Edward M. White's *Composition Studies in the New Millennium: Rereading the Past, Rewriting the Future*, for instance, echo Smit's questions, establishing the entire objective of composition studies in relation to students by asking in part, "What do/should we teach when we teach composition?," "Where will composition be taught and who will teach it?," and "What languages will our students write, and what will they write about?" (vii–viii).

These kinds of inquiries identify composition studies' entrenchment in inquests of undefined methodologies, methodologies that, according to North, did little if anything to forward the work of the field. These questions also imply that it is specifically and only through classroom application that research in composition studies will be able to find value. Not through research (theory), Smit posits, will advances be made in composition studies, but through action (practice) and, more specifically, classroom practice.

David Bartholomae's "What Is Composition and (if you know what that is) Why Do We Teach It?" makes a similar argument, contending that work in theory does not have any real, positive effect upon what it is composition studies does: "The essays on Mikhail Bakhtin or Hélène Cixous in our journals make only the faintest connection to the history paper (even the 'composition' paper). This is partly an intellectual problem—what *is* the connection?" (15). Bartholomae additionally points out that "composition . . . is concerned with how and why one might work with the space on the page, and, in this sense, it is not the same thing as Theory" (21). There is a litany of texts that make similar arguments regarding the disconnect between theoretical work and the essentialized understanding that work in composition studies is inherently classroom-based. Again, little has changed.

Post-Student

Even much of what is touted as composition theory is not theory about writing but theory about how writers write—or more often about writers themselves, issues of identity. Sharon Crowley's "A Letter to the Editors" explains that "writing teachers began to theorize about the writing process. And, lo and behold, a new professional category emerged: composition theory. As used in this phrase, however, *theory* meant something like generalizing about what writers do—intellectually, emotionally, ritually, whatever—when they compose" (319). This distinction is important as it identifies a difference of attention between writer and writing, whether the act or object. Composition studies' methodologies—even those identified as *theories*—have maintained a focus on writers, not on writing. To this end, then, composition studies has been less of a chaotic mix of research methodologies than its historians have professed. Despite its self-professed inability to define a unified research agenda, the field has been rather single-minded in its overall research path. Composition studies has rallied under the question of not "How do writers write?" but "How do student writers write?"—or, to be even more specific, "How do we teach students to write?" This restriction on composition studies' theoretical economy has not only segregated theory work in the field but has limited the kinds of theory work that can be allotted capital: that which can be directly secured to the pedagogical.

Composition studies' allegiance to research methodologies grounded in the classroom and the experiential/anecdotal have maintained such a strong foothold for three primary reasons: simulacra improvement, institutional validation, and ease. Composition studies has always proclaimed that it works to improve student writing, to make students better writers. Crowley's *Composition in the University* details the history of the role of FYC in helping make better students; the field has claimed much of its disciplinary identity from its association with FYC. Composition studies, then, stands as a purveyor of betterment and enhancement. However, such improvement is false, a simulated notion of improvement that functions primarily to make compositionists "feel" as though they are working with their students' best interests at heart. Such "improvement" operates only under a guise of making students' writing better, serving, instead, as purveyor of institutional politics.

On the surface, the field works toward improvement, but such "improvement" might be better interpreted as "civilizing" or even "humanizing" or, more accurately, "colonizing." As Crowley so rightly points out, this "improvement" is also a veil for creating a universal student subjectivity and for institutionalizing the parameters of what that subjectivity is to be—or to be more precise, for actually producing that subjectivity (as product) based on institutionally set parameters. To this end, composition studies' work toward improvement is, of course, sanctioned by the institution because it operates as an institutional control mechanism. No matter the standard that composition studies flies proclaiming critical consciousness, liberatory learning, literacy, or other "emancipatory" practices, these "methods" are confirmed by the institution as valid methods of initiating students into institutional discourses. This is said not to cast that sanction as the catalyst for the simulacra of improvement; there is nothing inherently wrong with such a sanction. What is wrong, however, à la Gilles Deleuze and Félix Guattari, is that such "improvement" serves not to emancipate students but to "reterritorialize" them into positions more easily controlled (note, too, that such a reterritorialization is, at its heart, a move of spatial positioning).

What is even more bothersome—if not ethically abhorrent—is composition studies' masking of its institutional missions as agendas of improvement and doing so with little, if any, critical examination of the work toward improvement. Casting such work as positive, as helping students become "better," allows compositionists to divest themselves of the responsibility of having to take into consideration in any critical way their own roles in colonizing students, since such approaches are, compositionists tell themselves, methods for resisting the very system in which they operate. This is, of course, an easy way to rationalize the field's role in such institutionally colonizing acts. As Kenneth Burke so plainly puts it: "The shepherd, qua shepherd, acts for the good of the sheep, to protect them from discomfiture and harm. But he may be 'identified' with a project that is raising the sheep for market" (27). After all, institutional support for composition studies will always be there—departments will continue to hire compositionists and students will be required to take composition courses—as long as composition studies research remains devoted to its pedagogical methods, methods that simply cheer on the institutional mission, no matter what compositionists tell themselves. Theory attached to classroom practice is necessarily, always already co-opted and cannot, by definition, be emancipatory since classroom practice is sanctioned by the institution. Thus, any hope of real emancipatory work in theory, in composition studics, must be disassociated from the classroom. To this end, too, investing in research methods that derive from classroom practice, composition studies is able to avoid doing the difficult work of theory in favor of doing the easier work of the institution, work that is funded and sanctioned and that provides objects of study—students—at the ready. All of these factors contribute to composition studies' resistance to theoretical work. Because composition/writing theory does not always (immediately) work toward improving students' writing in any easy, identifiable manner, many compositionists do not see theoretical work as having any bearing on the mission of the field's research. Composition theory is resisted because it does not work to the end of "improvement" in any tangible way.

The focus, then, of composition studies has been one directed not at writing but at subjects and the administration of those subjects. Composition studies is more interested in issues of subjectivity and agency than in writing. While many may argue that the field's focus has been the teaching of writing or helping students improve their writing, it might be more accurate to identify that such a focus has drifted even from the teaching of writing to the teaching of students, the emphasis here moving from "writing" to "student," placing writing and the teaching of writing in service of the subject and improvement from better writing to better student, better subject. In composition studies, the notion of subject is reduced not to writing-subject— as books like Susan Miller's *Rescuing the Subject* and Raúl Sánchez's *The Function of Theory in Composition Studies* argue might be the appropriate method for addressing the relation between subjects and writing—but to student-subject, and more specifically to college-student-subject. That is, in a discipline that focuses primarily on classrooms, writing-subjects are (re) formulated as student-subjects, the implication being that these are novice subjects, not-yet-fully-formed subjects, inexperienced subjects, subjects in need of training, in need of making. "Student" also implies a formal relationship with an educational institution, an enrollment indicating a particular position and occupation, a placement in rank. These distinctions are crucial in that they signify the field's desire to foreground its work not in issues of writing or even writing-subjects, or even student writing, but in the work of student subjectivity, of producing student-subjects.

Composition studies' attention to student-subject not only shifts attention away from writing as its central object of inquiry but also provides compositionists the opportunity to address subject formation and ways in which subjectivity is formed as primary objects of study. This work becomes the work of analysis, of interpretation, allowing compositionists to redirect their attention to better understanding what forces affect subject formation. Concepts such as culture, ideology, discourse, and language all become central to the composition studies conversation as the vehicles through which subjectivity is formed/produced. The work of the field becomes both an examination of and a pedagogy of reading how those forces play upon student subjectivity. Often in the name of rhetorical analysis, this is the work of interpretation of texts/artifacts in order to better see how those texts affect individual subjectivities so that those subjects might be better empowered to react to those forces. Sánchez's work and Susan Miller's "Technologies of Self?-Formation" make clear that such an approach to understanding subject-formation is essentially the work of interpretation and that such approaches deny students—or at least deny that students have—the power to write the very artifacts of their own subjectivities.

Miller rightly identifies that the central focus of composition instruction—and, in turn, all of composition studies—is "managing students' interiors" ("Technologies" 498). Miller works away from this focus of composition instruction by placing language at the center of composition teaching in order that students are better able to act through language. "By teaching texts rather than their making," Miller explains, "by teaching awareness rather than rhetoric, and by teaching the power of meanings rather than the making of statements, we inadvertently reproduce a politics that is aware but passive." "Reading," that is, "is not writing" (499).

Many may now begin to hear me calling for a concept of writing devoid of student-subjects or even writing-subjects, but such a reading would be inaccurate. Rather, in the pages of *Postcomposition* I do not forward a no-student approach but instead a not-only-students or a writing-without-students position, not grounding writing in *student* or even in *subjectivity*. Certainly, the idea of postcomposition that I develop here is post-student, or at least post-student as student is currently conceived, and it is certainly postpedagogy. This redirection away from student serves two primary purposes: the first, and most obvious, is to argue that the work of theorizing writing is not the work of a teaching subject nor dependent upon the role students play in making writing an object of study. Second, the work of theorizing writing is—and must be—bigger than the idea of students.

In the United States in 2001, 58 percent of the population enrolled in college upon graduation from high school, though 25 percent of those will never complete their degrees (Carey 2). As Kevin Carey's "A Matter of Degrees: Improving Graduation Rates in Four-Year Colleges and Universities" of 2004 indicates, "The United States has long had and continues to have the best-educated, most productive workforce in the world" (1), emphasizing not only the elite nature of American education but its inseparable link to developing a workforce. The report also indicates that while American college enrollments are rising, the rate for noncompletion is also rising. For instance, the report, using a US Department of Education survey, shows that only 54 percent of low-income students who begin college finish; 46 percent of African American students finish, as do 47 percent of Latinos, 59 percent of men, and 66 percent of women (2). Perhaps more telling, though, are enrollment rates of the world population. Worldwide, there has been tremendous growth in the numbers of students enrolling in tertiary educational programs—including colleges, universities, "technical institutes, polytechnics, community colleges, distance education centers, nursing schools, teacher-training facilities, and many more" (UNESCO 7). The UNESCO Global Education Digest 2006 identifies that in some countries—China and Malaysia, for example—"entry ratios have doubled in the five-year period between 1999 and 2004" and that in 2004 there were more than 132 million students enrolled in tertiary education institutes worldwide (7). Despite such significant growth globally, we must also identify that given the United Nations Population Division's medium variant estimate for world population in 2005 of 6,514,751,000, just over 2 percent of the world population enters into tertiary educational programs.[2] Tracking graduation ratios is difficult, but UNESCO cites ratios ranging from a high of Finland reporting 56 percent of its tertiary students graduating and Australia reporting 47 percent. The lowest ratios are reported from sub-Saharan African countries: "Burundi (0.6%), Kenya (2%), Lesotho (2%), Sierra Leone (6%), and Uganda (2%)" (12). UNESCO is also clear, via data from the Organization for Economic Co-operation and Development, that tertiary education is directly tied to economic development (11). College, as we would assume, is a marker of privilege.

The American academic institution supports a tradition of exclusivity. If composition studies relegates understanding of the act of writing—of the power of writing—to a context driven by that minimal (and elite) population, it reduces the very scope of what can be known and/or theorized about writing. And, as works like Richard M. Ohmann's *English in America* and Crowley's *Composition in the University* have shown, composition studies' role in the American university has been to reinscribe a rhetoric of privilege and (military) dominance in that population. To that end, it should be noted that a primary argument of "A Report by the Education Trust" is to show how earning potentials of college graduates is superior to that of those who either never attend or never complete higher-education degrees. If composition studies is to embrace an understanding of writing in relation to agency and the often-articulated agenda of emancipation or liberation of the student-subject, then such work in composition classrooms is undertaken to liberate the most elite, most privileged portion of the world population. Without this address, the way that composition studies encounters students is limited.

Part of this limit grows from the fact that it is only through the manufactured subjectivity of students that (composition) teachers are able to create their own subjectivities and claim an authority over a discipline. This is the "phantom scenario of pedagogy" that Jean Baudrillard raises in *Simulacra and Simulation* (156). Without students, the discipline disappears. However, removing the student subject as the origin of need and authority of the discipline and resituating student subjectivities as a by-product or function of a discipline invested first in the idea of writing refigure the work of the (post)compositionist as gaining its authority from a less fleeting object of study: writing. While essays like Gary A. Olson's "Ideological Critique in Rhetoric and Composition" may claim that the reason the work of composition studies is so crucial is that compositionists are training students who "will help determine the future shape of our culture" (82), wedding the need for and the intellectual impetus for writing studies to students does a serious disservice to that study as well as to the very potential of informing the future shape of culture(s).

Certainly, it is difficult work to think/talk/write about writing without the intrinsic concepts of subject and agency; in fact, it may be downright impossible. Postcomposition does not argue opposed to or devoid of notions of subjectivity, only that the composition studies approach of foregrounding thinking about writing in terms of subjectivity and agency be moved beyond into theories that foreground writing (an argument Sánchez lucidly forwards). Only then can subject/subjectivity be better understood—or, more accurately, only then can *becoming* subject be understood—as a function of writing, of the producing machine. Likewise, as I hope to show, the traditional humanist and postmodern notions of subjectivity that composition studies has adopted have been rendered obsolete, and part of the move beyond the confines of composition studies includes a refiguring of the subject as posthuman, non-autonomous agent. Composition studies' focus on empty signifiers like "ideology" and "culture" and on how those concepts affect subjects allows composition studies to embrace a conversation that foregrounds reading the effects of texts (or more to the point, *writing*) upon subjects rather than on how, as Sánchez has shown, those signifiers are a result of writing-subjects writing. Composition studies' focus permitted the burgeoning field to maintain a command over subjects while invoking a discourse of cultural interpretation already favored by colleagues in literary criticism rather than working to develop a rhetoric and grammar that centralized writing as the field's focus. Failure to work toward such a writing-centered disciplinary focus displays in many ways composition studies' self-loathing and willingness to succumb to a disciplinary history that has cast writing and production as second-class citizens to reading and interpretation. Chapter 3 takes up the role of subject and subjectivity in composition studies in greater detail toward the end of disrupting the very idea of student subject and of recasting subjectivity in light of posthumanism.

An Academic Field

There is little question that a good deal of conversation in composition studies over the past forty years has been specifically about trying to figure out exactly what composition studies is, about questions of identity, about validation as a discipline.[3] Robert Connors's "Composition History and Disciplinarity" labels this "time in our historical development the 'Era of Disciplinarity'" (4), and Lester Faigley's *Fragments of Rationality: Postmodernity and the Subject of Composition* calls it the "disciplinary period" (77). As Susan C. Jarratt's "New Dispositions for Historical Studies in Rhetoric" tells it, "one distinguishing feature of this recently reinvented field is its instability, producing a continual need for definition" (65). Gary Olson's "The Death of Composition as an Intellectual Discipline" echoes this claim: "Since the beginnings of composition as a field, we have all been struggling over how to define it, over its heart and soul" (30). Tom Fox's "Working Against the State: Composition's Intellectual Work for Change," likewise, identifies that "one of the most distinctive features of intellectual work in composition is a focus on the relationship of the discipline of composition to the academic institutions in which it is housed" (91). And Richard H. Haswell's telling article "NCTE/CCCC's Recent War on Scholarship" identifies the view of composition studies as a non-discipline from both within and outside of the field. Smit sums up the work regarding composition studies' identity rather succinctly: "Despite the heightened status of composition studies in the academy, just what composition studies *is* remains a matter of some dispute" (5). That meta-conversation has itself become a central part of composition studies' identity, though certainly not all of its conversation. Composition studies is a "field" (a spatial term that requires a bit more unpacking, which chapter 2 will attempt in light of Nedra Reynolds's examination of the concept of "field") that tries to understand what exactly the field is.[4] As Joe Marshall Hardin's "Writing Theory and Writing the Classroom" explains so well, much of that work to identify composition studies' identity is also an argument about whether composition studies *can be* defined as a discipline, whether it is or is not a field. "For most academics," Hardin contends, "rhetoric and composition would seem to be either a subdiscipline of English or an interdisciplinary activity that might, at best, warrant the status of academic 'program'" (37).

Much of this discrepancy over composition studies' legitimacy as a field results from/in an inability to articulate an intellectual focus beyond the training of teachers, an activity set in service of the continued management of student bodies rather than in pursuit of understanding of writing in the formation of the signifier "student." Composition studies, if it is a field, is a field that has little vision of its own frontiers beyond its reliance upon management of students, but at the same time has rampant fear of losing what little territory it has gained, clinging tightly to its academic territory. In protecting that field, composition studies is excessively conservative. Faigley's *Fragments of Rationality* rightly identifies composition studies' conservatism, but that conservatism has expanded into a defensive conservatism as well. Jeff Rice, in his absolutely brilliant critique of the Council of Writing Program Administrators in "Conservative Writing Program Administrators (WPAs)," identifies a deep-seated conservatism among WPAs, explaining that conservatism means "the desire to preserve and conserve very specific administrative and pedagogical stands *as is*" (2, emphasis in original). While Rice's critique of the WPA is dead on—I address WPA work further in chapter 4—it is also an argument that must be considered as microcosmic of the discipline at large, not just its administrative arm. Composition studies has identified—though tenebrously—its little bit of space in the American academy and has developed a conservatism that does as little as it can to risk that space, to actually test its borders, borders that are in desperate need of disruption. Postcomposition, in response to composition studies' conservative and defensive positioning, works against—here "against" invokes a sense of buttressing, as I will explain shortly, as this move requires the establishment of composition studies' position in the academy—and beyond composition studies in its becoming postdisciplinary. This is specifically the difference that books like Olson's *Rhetoric and Composition as Intellectual Work* can help make between the academic role of composition studies and the potential of the intellectual and theoretical work of, as many contributors to *Rhetoric and Composition as Intellectual Work* would call it, "writing studies."

This difference between academic work and intellectual work and the conservatism that academic work produces is critical, as Lynn Worsham's "Coming to Terms: Theory, Writing, Politics" distinguishes between the two efforts:

> Academic work is inherently conservative inasmuch as it seeks, first, to fulfill the relatively narrow and policed goals and interests of a given discipline or profession and, second, to fulfill the increasingly corporatized mission of higher education; intellectual work, in contrast, is relentlessly critical, self-critical, and potentially revolutionary, for it aims to critique, change, and even destroy institutions, disciplines, and professions that rationalize exploitation, inequality, and injustice. (101)

Such moves postcomposition—or more specifically postcomposition-theory—are maneuvers to reposition writing theory beyond the normative restraints that composition studies inherently imposes in its acceptance of its academic positioning with the specific agenda of disruption, or as Worsham puts it, "revolution" (101). This is not to suggest that the work of composition studies is strictly only academic. As Worsham and Fox each make clear, the boundaries between academic and intellectual work are difficult to discern: some academic work lends to intellectual work; some intellectual work can become neutralized by becoming too academic. Susan Miller's "Composition as a Cultural Artifact: Rethinking History as Theory," in fact, moves away from thinking of composition studies as intellectual, instead looking at it as a cultural practice whose cultural purposes need to be questioned (21). While I agree with Miller's assessment and the need for a critical questioning of composition studies' purpose, it seems that composition studies is an academic field and that its purpose is one of academic proportions. Take, for instance, Joseph Harris's claim in "The Rhetoric of Theory" that "most theories of composing gain interest only when they are linked to teaching" (145) and that "ideas are usually interesting precisely to the degree that they are meant to have practical consequences" (147). What Harris sums up in these claims is a stock position in composition studies: intellectual work is of little interest without an academic justification.

Composition studies is normative. Its roles in managing students, in pedagogy, and in the teaching of writing all work toward a normalization of student, of writing program, and of writing. Saying that composition studies is normative invokes a question as to whether normalization is to be seen as a negative or a positive, and the tone of the invocation here appears to be a negative association. Norms can be oppressive, as the claim here seems to imply and as chapter 4 details. Normalization is rationalized, however, as a necessary step in disciplinary validation—something that composition studies has sought for more than forty years now. Composition studies accepts its normative politics under an illusory doxa that normalizing the discipline is necessary in order to lay claim to disciplinary status. The argument seems to be that composition studies' normative demeanor is acceptable because it allows for freedom of movement within the normalizing umbrella. But what this normalization does is create the perception of safety in place; composition studies' place in the academy, identifiable through its normative structures and boundaries, encapsulates its field, placing its posts around its borders, keeping the hordes out, but more important keeping its populations tied (by a short leash) to the post of field. Composition studies likes to boast a cross-disciplinary/interdisciplinary agenda, but this is a boast of false proportions. Composition studies is perhaps one of the most conservative fields in its willingness to explore its contingent borders. Protective of its own orthodoxies, composition studies seeks the safety of being ensconced within the small spaces it has eked out in the academy, spaces limited by its attachment to students rather than to theory or research. Theories that have opened new frontiers for composition studies have been virtually shut down, appeased in assimilations that grind radical thinking and unprecedented thinking into impotent versions that safely fit within composition studies' established posts. The normative aspects of composition studies will undercut its potential, will level its rise to the detriment of its future, relegating the field to nothing more than an academic, administrative entity permitted the space of FYC and little more. Postcomposition is actively an abolitionist position, and much of this book will work in support of such positions, heralding Crowley's and other abolitionist texts as critical in the move beyond composition studies. No matter how composition studies claims it is open and encouraging of difference, any move to incorporate that difference under academic disciplinary borders is specifically a move away from difference. Primary attention to subjectivity, to students, to classrooms, to pedagogies, even if called attention to multiple subjectivities, heteroglossias of students, divergent classrooms, or varying and radical pedagogies, is still a focus on little more than a homogeneous notion of composition studies, a leveling of composition studies, a razing of composition studies. Chapter 2 takes up the spatial aspect of composition studies' desire to protect its limited borders; chapter 4 addresses the normative qualities of composition studies in greater detail.

Of course, the immediate critique to this claim is that in order to declare and retain its academic authority, composition studies must establish, define, and defend disciplinary norms. Composition studies needs its fields, its safety in field and in numbers. Composition studies must protect the minimal (e)statehood it has achieved. Normative functions in composition studies are necessary, one might say, in order for composition studies to be composition studies at all, to be at all. Composition studies requires the authority that the normative provides. Composition studies requires that authority in order to fight the very authorities that have imposed unjust boundaries, unjust subjectivities upon it. Composition studies must maintain disciplinary authority over its field in order to be able to defend against unjust working conditions of its populations, against the questions of composition studies' integrity as a boundaried territory, against incursions into its field and raidings of its resources. Composition studies can defend against invasive powers only by falling back to a position of orthodoxy. Unfortunately, composition studies has decried that its field is to be a field devoted to subjectivities (students) and to administration (classrooms). Openly, the population and leadership of the composition studies body have consistently disavowed the potentials of theory by providing it minimal space within the field and questioning the very value of it altogether. Composition studies' "Theory Wars" have never been about theoretical questions but only about the value of theory. Inherently, then, they have also been about the value of teaching, a line of questioning that invites less damage, since teaching will always be sacrosanct while theory is every pragmatist's and conservative's punching bag. In an increasingly anti-intellectual world, we cannot aid the destruction of intellectualism within our own discipline by insisting that theory must serve teaching. Theory, for composition studies, can have only one end: the classroom. Hence, even the minimal space for theory in composition studies is normalized back into the shallow pool of what can be composition studies.

Such a position, of course, is academic, and, as I have begun to show, there is a distinct difference between the academic work of composition studies and the intellectual potential that theory can provide postcomposition. In presenting these distinctions, Worsham makes the critical observation that "the sine qua non of intellectual work is theory; thus, the primary way to make the work of composition more seriously intellectual is to make it more seriously theoretical" ("Coming to Terms" 103). Worsham articulates a need for theory and the political nature of theory to perpetually disrupt and reorganize the very understanding of what composition studies is and does while also taking into account what those disruptions and reorganizations render and the effects of their executions. Writing theory, at all times, subverts composition studies' agenda as an academic discipline. It is the potential of revolution that postcomposition must feed, not remanding work to the academic but striving beyond the limit-situation the academic imposes, not exerting energy into the tired debates about the role of theory in composition studies but in making theory that has the potential to demolish the very idea of institutions that create a need for things like disciplines, like the academic, like composition studies.

Only through continued theorizing about the phenomena of writing can such demolition occur for/within composition studies. Only when the intellectual work of writing theory supersedes the disciplinary focus of teaching and managing students will the field of composition studies have achieved the momentum to exceed itself. Stuart Hall's "Cultural Studies and Its Theoretical Legacies" provides an opportunity "of self-reflection on cultural studies as a practice, on its institutional positioning" (277). It is a moment of self-inflicted critique that terminates in a serious question about the role that theoretical work has played in cultural studies. Hall's final paragraph encapsulates the importance of the distinction between the intellectual and the academic and the powerful need for the intellectual work of theory and the potential of political change within that work of theory:

> I come back to the deadly seriousness of intellectual work. It is a deadly serious matter. I come back to the critical distinction between intellectual work and academic work: they overlap, they abut with one another, they feed off one another, the one provides you with the means

to do the other. But they are not the same thing. I come back to the difficulty of instituting a genuine cultural and critical practice, which is intended to produce some kind of organic intellectual political work, which does not try to inscribe itself in the overarching metanarrative of achieved knowledges, within the institutions. I come back to theory and politics, the politics of theory. Not theory as the will to truth, but theory as a set of contested, localized, conjunctural knowledges, which have to be debated in a dialogical way. But also as a practice which always thinks about its intervention in a world in which it would make some difference, in which it would have some effect. Finally, a practice which understand the need for intellectual modesty. I do think there is all the difference in the world between understanding the politics of intellectual work and substituting intellectual work for politics. (286)

Composition studies has failed to see the potential in the intellectual work of theory. As Worsham makes clear,

> the technical and professional authority of composition has already been established and . . . is not now in jeopardy. . . . If we persist in allowing the "theory-practice split" to govern the social relations of the field—and ultimately the way we articulate our own role in the university and its relation to society—then we do so because we prefer to misperceive the nature of the task at hand: we must make the academic work of composition studies more vigorously, more resolutely intellectual. ("Coming to Terms" 103)

The work that postcomposition(ists) must address is work away from critique—difficult as it may be—of self, of discipline, away from the tradition of the theory-practice debates. Critique is always a look back; postcomposition must be work ahead, or better: work away. But such work is difficult, and often work beyond requires glances back. This is no hypocrisy; it is strategy. The critiques I offer throughout this book are generally grounded in a spatial sense of composition studies, one less concerned with the temporal, though the two are tangled. The specific attention away from the temporal works to avoid the implication that postcomposition is a call to a new *era* of composition studies. Eras tell little about the objects they ensconce; they are arbitrary assignments leveled to justify a particular politic within a simplified parameter—a maneuver that allows a language of simulacra origin to form. To be in the time from the beginning until before the time of the end is to be granted legitimacy. Both Jacques Derrida and Fredric Jameson, of course, have been extensive in their discussions of origin and periodization; I will not rehash those positions here. Postcomposition is neither a new era nor a move toward identifying a composition studies period; it is a position critical of composition studies' refusal to move on. It is also an attempt to move onward beyond the academic terrain that composition studies inhabits. "Rather than pressing forward and taking flight into the future," Baudrillard explains in *The Illusion of the End*, "we prefer retrospective apocalypse, and a blanket revisionism. Our societies have all become revisionistic: they are quietly rethinking everything, laundering their political crimes, their scandals, licking their wounds, fueling their ends" (22). Postcomposition works away from such revisionism and toward a new vision. Composition studies' revision is without merit; no matter the work done within the limit-situation that is composition studies, the field itself may grow and expand, but it does not develop.

Thus, the primary agenda of *Postcomposition* is to argue for a move beyond the academic work of composition studies in favor of the revolutionary potential of the intellectual work of writing studies, specifically the work of writing theory, an endeavor likely best removed from the academic work of pedagogy and administration. While *Postcomposition* reverts to critique in order to move beyond composition studies, it also works to invest in an ongoing postdisciplinary effort to forward writing theory, to present theories of writing in order to better understand the possibilities of writing, to move beyond seeing writing, to borrow from Roland Barthes, as "an activity" and instead also see writing as phenomena, the results of which are other phenomena like ideologies, politics, subjectivities, agencies, identities, discourses, rhetorics, grammars, and, as Sánchez makes clear, theory itself. These phenomena stand as functions of writing, not precursors to them, Sánchez shows. "Turning the field's intellectual and disciplinary gaze back to writing," Sánchez explains, "gives composition studies the ability to articulate writing in new ways" (*Function* 10). Writing theory is not—should not be—theory made to describe/explain things like ideologies, politics, subjectivities, agencies, identities, discourses, rhetorics, or grammars, nor are writing theories descriptions/explanations of the relationships between writing and other phenomena like ideologies, politics, subjectivities, agencies, identities, discourses, rhetorics, or grammars; instead, such theories describe/explain writing as phenomena that are sorts of producing machines through which other phenomena manifest. The frustration here, of course, is the difficulty in trying to identify writing as independent from other phenomena and the dangers in trying to essentialize writing as a scientific (positivist) thing devoid of ecological/textual/network connection to other phenomena. This frustration grows from a discursive encampment in the boundaries of composition studies.

Composition studies lacks a discourse to talk about writing as phenomena precursory to the phenomena it writes. Finding such a vocabulary would be hard work, and in composition studies, often, doing that kind of hard work is shunned in favor of doing the work that is easy, already spread out before us on the bodies of students. Likewise, there are many in composition studies who would see a danger in not talking about things like ideologies, politics, subjectivities, agencies, identities, discourses, rhetorics, and grammars because talking about those things gives composition studies links to talking about the things that other theorists in English studies talk about, gives claim to legitimacy, as Susan Miller argues. Similarly, many will see talking about writing as phenomena before phenomena like ideologies, politics, subjectivities, agencies, identities, discourses, rhetorics, and grammars as potentially dangerous because it suggests that writing *can be* talked about devoid of the very things that composition studies has come to be so invested in. I am in favor of such dangers. My argument here isn't that the phenomena of writing can be/should be identified in an a-contextual, vacuous state not related to other phenomena but that in order to examine those relationships with any effectiveness, theories of writing must first work to understand what the phenomena of writing are and, in turn, how writing functions to produce other phenomena, like those I have identified as central to the composition studies project. Inherently, this requires that writing theory not revolve around theories of student subjectivities or around writing pedagogies, programs, or administrations.

Charles Bazerman's important essay "The Case for Writing Studies as a Major Discipline" identifies that given the overall importance of writing in the daily lives of most people, it is disheartening to realize that there is no discipline in the American university that seriously addresses writing as a primary object of inquiry. Given that writing is a "fundamental matter of the constitution of our world," Bazerman argues, "the organization of research and of the university itself remains consistently blind to this fact" (33). While compositionists may bristle at this accusation, wanting to testify to the field's dedication to studying writing, Bazerman is dead-on in pointing out that "only the relatively young field of composition has paid primary attention to writing, but our core attention has tended to be narrow: on students and classes in a few courses in universities in the United States over the last several decades, with particular attention to the underprepared student" (33). In fact, Bazerman may be a bit generous in this assessment by allowing that composition studies' focus has been on writing and not specifically on the teaching of writing within the constraints it identifies. But even so, Bazerman forwards the idea that "of all disciplines, composition is best positioned to put together the large, important, and multidimensional story of writing. We are the only profession that makes writing its central concern" (33), a claim echoed by Sánchez: "*Writing* is almost exclusively our field's term, in ways that *discourse, language,* and *signification* are not" (*Function* 10). Composition studies, Bazerman claims, "is as good a standpoint as any from which to view writing at this juncture in history" (33–34). "It is time," he continues, "for us to rise above the accidents of disciplinary history that have kept our truly significant subject only minimally visible and that have blinded us to the enormity of the material we have taken to instruct our students in" (34). Amen. But, to do so, composition studies requires a dramatic shift postcomposition, beyond the very disciplinary constraints that have, arguably, blinded (or, perhaps more accurately, hobbled) composition studies. And while Bazerman sees a need for further student-driven research "because learning to write will remain a major imperative in education and society for the foreseeable future" (34), I want to push for a more radical position that contends that such research still only limits what we can possibly know about writing within a particular political context. To be clear, this argument does not deny the value or importance of student-centered research within specific local contexts. Such efforts are important in that they attract the attention of local resources, garner support from local administrations, and often solve local problems. However, what must be resisted is the insidious creeping in of the insistence that *all* work in composition studies must be context-specific and about students/ teaching and that such an insistence serve as the primary parameter as to what it means to work in composition studies. To this end as well, Bazerman frames the writing studies approach around the idea of writing lives and "life spans of writing," tying writing to subjects. These are shackles that must be shaken before any substantial consideration of writing can occur.

Other attempts at developing the "writing studies" model for the future of composition studies also fall short of providing the field any radical new avenue of departure in developing revolutionary possibilities in understanding writing. John Trimbur's "Changing the Question: Should Writing be Studied?," for instance, does little toward proposing methodologies or departures for studying writing. Instead, Trimbur proposes a shift away from the practical workshop-focused writing classroom to a seminar approach in which writing is studied as a subject rather than taught as an activity. While such a proposal may have curricular value, it still falls prey to the same pitfalls into which composition studies has fallen and been unable to extract itself.

Susan Miller's "Writing Studies as a Mode of Inquiry" opens in the familiar terrain of composition studies' methodological scramble and inability to pinpoint a definitive object of study and recognizes that it is not easy "to assume that 'writing practices' are in fact the objects of study that unite the field's current favored questions" (41). Miller proposes amid composition studies' muddling that there is a need for a "strategically calculated descriptor that can assure its further development, as well as general agreement over the particular set of intellectual questions that such a descriptor entails" (41). Writing studies, Miller argues, is said descriptor. What makes the writing studies Miller proposes so appealing is the emphasis that writing must be analyzed within the specific historical, social, material, and personal contexts in which that writing was produced. Ultimately, Miller contends that "the situated writing subject is the focus of writing studies" (47), again emphasizing the role of the subject as producer of writing. While Miller's is the most tempting of the many proposals regarding the methodological unification of composition studies, it places undue emphasis on the role of the subject as producer of writing rather than upon writing and the subject as function of politically, historically, socially, materially mediated contexts for writing.

Ultimately, *Postcomposition* proposes a form of writing studies, one that moves beyond composition studies' subject-distracted view of writing and theorizes about writing. But, in doing so, *Postcomposition* does not intend to forward the idea of a noncontextual, essentialized notion of writing. Instead, *Postcomposition* works toward a buttressing of writing theories against the work of composition studies in order not to strengthen the work of composition studies but to disrupt it, as its nominalized codification has rendered the field paralyzed. Susan Miller's "Writing Theory: Theory Writing" explains the need for buttressing writing theory against composition studies by identifying that "theories of writing are significations embedded in a signifying system of writing, and their value (or meaning) is more or less apparent in particular contexts" (67). She goes on to say that "without the field of composition, . . . composition theory could not claim institutional time for its writing or reading, could not be published (as many remember too well), could not be critiqued, could not be recognized in professional rewards systems, or could not, finally, be applied" (67). While *Postcomposition* contends that it is institutional space that theory occupies, not (only) time, it is true that any agenda postcomposition forward is dependent upon its signification within composition studies. As Gary A. Olson's preface to *Rhetoric and Composition as Intellectual Work* makes clear:

While many compositionists insist that all research, all inquiry in the field, should serve the sole purpose of furthering and refining the *teaching* of composition, many of us contend that although we all desire to learn more about the teaching of writing or about our own writing processes, these are not the *only* intellectual concerns we should have as a discipline, that constituting rhetoric and composition as a discipline whose raison d'être is the teaching of writing is dangerously and unacceptably narrow and even, in some people's eyes, anti-intellectual. (xii)

Postcomposition contends that the field's narrow-minded attention to teaching, to subjects, and to the management of those subjects has not only created an anti-intellectual condition but has given rise to the need to cast aside composition studies as an intellectual endeavor, bequeathing it to its own powerful position as a service entity and training ground for professionals in education and midlevel management (more on this in chapter 4).

Composition studies research has always orbited the imperative of a pedagogical enterprise. Because of composition studies' historical foundations as an educational initiative—one more closely akin to the work of schools of education than other humanities disciplines, generally, and English, specifically—research that breaks orbit and ventures into other spaces has always been seen as suspect, as not championing the imperative. Historically, composition studies' research has been inherently applied research, and embedded in that mandate is a history resistant to theoretical work. Writing theory must move beyond composition studies' neurosis of pedagogy, must escape the shackles of classrooms, students, and management.

2. The Space of Writing

If things endure, or if there is duration in things, the question of space will need to be reassessed on new foundations. For space will no longer simply be a form of exteriority, a sort of screen that denatures duration, an impurity that comes to disturb the pure, a relative that is opposed to the absolute: Space itself will need to be based in things, in relations between things and between durations, to belong itself to the absolute, to have its own "purity."
—Gilles Deleuze, *Bergsonism*

The ways in which we imagine space and place have a direct impact on how we imagine writing and acts of writing as well as the inhabitants of composition studies—and its outsiders, real or imagined.
—Nedra Reynolds, *Geographies of Writing: Inhabiting Places and Encountering Difference*

The thin film of writing becomes a movement of strata, a play of spaces.
—Michel de Certeau, *The Practice of Everyday Life*

Because of the more popular use of "post" as an indicator of chronology, many may hear postcomposition to indicate an issue of time, a marker of a shift in era, a time after composition studies. However, as I hope I have indicated thus far, I intend "post" primarily as a spatial indicator. Separating the spatial from the temporal is a tricky maneuver, and I do not mean to suggest the possibility of an essential—or even necessarily possible— bifurcation between the two; instead, I emphasize the role of the spatial, turning to the temporal only when unavoidable, conveniently placing time aside until invoking it becomes strategically useful. I do this because time is the more familiar approach (think: process); space, in its unfamiliarity, offers potential for theorizing writing in ways not yet put forward and not confined by chronological thinking. Space and time are inseparable, but they are also politically loaded terms of demarcation.[1] As W. J. T. Mitchell's *Iconology: Image, Text, Ideology*, explains it, space and time "take on different ideological roles and relationships at different moments in history" (98). The explanation continues: "The categories of space and time are never innocent . . . they always carry an ideological freight" (98). My separation, too, of space and time in this discussion is conducted without innocence; it is strategic, for as Mitchell points out, "the terms 'space' and 'time' only become figurative or improper when they are abstracted from one another as independent, antithetical essences that define the nature of an object. The use of these terms is, strictly speaking, a concealed synecdoche, a reduction of the whole to the part" (103). I will add to this configuration of space-time that not only can they not be separated but neither can they be removed from an intrinsic relationship to writing, and like any other (problematic) metaphor, they ultimately can be understood as functions of writing.

My intention here is to emphasize the spatial over the temporal as a method for disrupting the traditional sense of writing as temporal in favor of a spatial understanding of writing, of the act of writing, of the function of writing, and, in turn, of a spatial conception of the discipline of composition studies. To do so, I bring spatial theory not to bear *upon* writing but instead bring the two together in such a way as to elucidate a reciprocal relation between the two toward the end of conceptualizing writing as spatial and casting space not as that which must be in the beginning before creation, as Plato's *Timaeus* suggests it must, but as a function of writing. Of course, by separating the two, I am reducing space to metaphor, thus limiting how space can be addressed in terms of my larger argument. I return often in this book to the idea of a will to metaphor but for now must acknowledge that despite my wish to not reduce space to metaphor, I am in some ways trapped by being able only to do so.

In order to make such a distinction between writing as temporal and writing as spatial, it is important to note how the tradition of literature and literary analysis—and, in turn, the relationship between writing and literature—embraces the temporal. Given the history that binds writing to reading, that binds production to interpretation/consumption, that binds a concept of a written product to the idea of a literary work, that binds the value-judgment of a piece of writing to the relational value assessed to a piece of literature, that binds the morality of rhetoric (good men speaking well) to the morality of learning literature (great books), and that binds the discipline of composition studies to the discipline of literature (forming English departments), it is important to understand the tradition of the temporal in writing and literature as inextricably bound in such a way that any understanding of writing is fettered by a tradition of literature as temporal. Composition studies' disposition toward its object of study, the (teaching of the) production of writing, has been dominated by the disposition of literary studies to its object of study, the interpretation of written text. Despite the many tactical maneuvers composition studies has made to separate itself from its ties to literature (perhaps a separation that is no more possible than separating time and space, except in the form of metaphor for strategic purposes), writing—as an institutionally professed and promoted act and in the many ways in which scholars in composition studies have forwarded ideas as to what the teaching of writing is—is seen as a temporal act alongside its literary predecessor. Rhetoric and literary studies have tussled over the right to stand upon the dais, and with the few exceptions in which contemporary departments and programs of composition/rhetoric have seceded from the union between literary studies and rhetorical studies (most often merely as a political/bureaucratic move to better control the FYC territory—resources and curriculum—and, ultimately, the student subject), literary studies has remained dominant in its control over the ideologies and methodologies for understanding writing and reading.[2] These histories are well documented, so I will not rehash them here (see, for instance Susan Miller's *Textual Carnivals*, Sharon Crowley's *Composition in the University*, and Stephen North's *The Making of Knowledge in Composition*, especially parts 5 and 6).[3] Despite composition studies' adoption of social science methodologies in the 1970s to begin to explain the processes through which student writers produce texts, literary studies methodologies have maintained a grip on how writing is understood—even within composition studies. The historical tension between rhetoric/writing and literature is not likely to ease any time soon. In fact, given the changes to the economic situation that universities face at the beginning of the twenty-first century and the commodification of information, it stands that these tensions will only increase. Debates regarding the position of composition studies within English departments (should there be secession?), the content of FYC courses—particularly the second part of a two-semester sequence, which often includes a literary component—tenure and promotion requirements, hiring emphasis, administrative and other service requirements, and the value of research emphasis will likely continue ad infinitum. Ultimately, such debates, both of and about disciplinary positioning and ideological control, are insignificant. What is significant is understanding how composition studies has come to accept writing as temporal and the willingness to disrupt that tradition toward the ends of disrupting composition studies' faith in its mythologies of chronology as it shifts postcomposition.

Gotthold Ephraim Lessing's monumental *Laocoon: An Essay upon the Limits of Painting and Poetry* (1766) is one of the most significantly influential works in fine arts theory, arguing that confusing the role and possibilities of various art forms—for example, painting and descriptive verse—would result in aesthetic chaos. Instead, Lessing works to categorize the "nature" of painting and verse into the temporal and the spatial, identifying poetry as a temporal art and painting as a spatial art. Lessing reacts against Johann Winckelmann's interpretation of the Hellenistic sculpture *Laocoön and his Sons*, which depicts the scene in book 2 of Virgil's *Aeneid* in which the Trojan priest Laocoön and his two sons, while making sacrifice at Neptune's altar, are strangled by sea snakes sent by Greek gods angered by Laocoön's attempt to warn the Trojans not to bring the wooden horse inside the Trojan walls. Through his rejection of (most of) Winckelmann's reading of the sculpture, Lessing shifts the discussion of reading sculpture to a more broadly directed understanding of art, particularly painting, which Lessing explains must depict spatial proximity because it depicts a single moment—what Lessing calls the most expressive moment—in a narrative. Lessing explains: "Since painting, because its signs or means of imitation can be combined only in space, must relinquish all representations of time, therefore progressive actions, as such, cannot come within its range. It must content itself with actions in space; in other words, with mere bodies, whose attitude lets us infer their action. Poetry, on the contrary—" (90). On the other hand, Lessing argues, poetry depicts entire events in temporal sequence, not merely individual moments: "Nothing obliges the poet to concentrate his picture into a single moment. He can take up every action, if he will, from its origin, and carry it through all possible changes to its issue" (21).

The essence of painting, according to Lessing, then, is spatial, whereas the essence of poetry—and in turn all literature—is temporal, the representation of movement in time. Mitchell summarizes Lessing's position: "Reading occurs in time; the signs which are read are uttered or inscribed in temporal sequence; and the events represented or narrated occur in time. There is thus a kind of homology, or what Lessing calls a 'convenient relation' (*bequemes Verhältnis*) between medium, message, and the mental process of decoding" (98–99). Though some literary critics have identified exceptions to Lessing's principles of temporality, literary criticism embraced the "primacy of the temporal" as the nature of literary medium.[4] For literary critics, via Lessing, to claim that literature is a temporal art is to account for concepts of reception, medium, and content of given literary works. Lessing's assessment of poetry set the standard for inquiry for aesthetic and literary principles and bound literature to the temporal (and painting to the spatial).

This traditional division is, of course, problematic. Space and time are not easily separated. Paintings are as much temporal as they are spatial. The historical/temporal moments in which they are produced affect a chronological difference from the historical moments in which they are viewed, interpreted, and understood. Literature is as much spatial as it is temporal, and as I hope to show, writing is spatial in character, as well, particularly when considered in terms of its visual components, as current shifts from page to screen seem to make immediate.

Fortunately, composition studies has recently begun to embrace (though only minimally) ideas of spatiality when addressing writing. Unfortunately, most of the moves to adopt a spatial understanding of writing have been limited to using spatial metaphors—most often geographic or cartographic—as a means of talking about relationships between subjects (students) and locations; note, for instance, Rhonda C. Grego and Nancy S. Thompson's *Teaching/Writing in Thirdspaces: The Studio Approach*. In addition, most spatially motivated work in composition studies either conflates metaphors—like those of space and place—or simply accepts spatial metaphors without understanding or unpacking their metaphoric qualities (or their spatial dimensions). Composition studies' attachment to subjects and administration of those subjects—and its minimal attention to writing as an object of study—has limited composition studies' ability to examine the spatial dimensions of writing beyond the metaphors that can be employed to better articulate the relationships between student-subjects and the space they inhabit: classrooms, cyberspace, discourse communities, campuses, workplaces, public spheres, and so on. As an example, consider this claim from Julie Drew's "The Politics of Place": "Students pass through, and only pause briefly within, classrooms; they dwell within and visit various other locations, locations whose politics and discourse conventions both construct and identify them" (60). Spatial/place-based metaphors have been useful to composition studies in this way. Yet, the problem of metaphor is in its limits. Nedra Reynolds's important study of place and writing pedagogy, communication, and literacy, *Geographies of Writing: Inhabiting Places and Encountering Differences,* works to understand composition studies' use of spatial metaphors. In the opening chapter, "Between Metaphor and Materiality," Reynolds tends to the issue of spatial metaphor in composition studies, identifying that composition studies "has been drawn to the metaphorical and imaginary" (12) and that "because space is so abstract and intangible, language to describe it tends toward the metaphorical and the narratable" (13). Most important, though, Reynolds makes clear that "space, at least as it is represented metaphorically, hides consequences from us" (27).

Metaphor, of course, is deeply problematic, particularly in terms of developing theory. Louis Althusser's often cited "Ideology and Ideological

State Apparatuses (Notes towards an Investigation)" makes an interesting comment regarding the relationship between metaphor and theory when discussing spatial metaphors. Metaphors, Althusser contends, are limited simply because they operate at the level of description. All theories, Althusser continues, must pass through a metaphoric phase, a transitional phase that is "necessary to the development of theory," identified as the "descriptive phase" (138). However, the term "theory," Althusser identifies, "'clashes' to some extent with the adjective 'descriptive'" (138). Yet, Althusser makes clear that the transitional descriptive phase of theory is a necessary part of theory, though it can be only the beginning of theory. For theory to fully develop, it must go beyond description, beyond metaphor. If we are to accept the relationship between metaphor and theory that Althusser forwards, then three maxims apply to composition studies' development of spatial theory in terms of writing:

1. Space and spatial concepts (including place and location) have been used only metaphorically by composition studies.
2. Composition has not developed any of its own spatial metaphors to describe writing—or even subjects and the space they inhabit. Instead, it has only appropriated established (and accepted) spatial metaphors to its own needs.
3. Because of #1 and #2, composition studies has limited (eliminated) its own transitional moments into developing theories of writing, instead settling for descriptions of how students write or, more accurately, descriptions of how we believe to best instruct students how to write.

These maxims, of course, hold true only if we accept the relational premise of metaphor and theory that Althusser establishes, and to do so strictly would be reductive, as the problems of metaphor strain beyond the relationship between metaphor and theory. Nonetheless, these maxims and relationships between metaphor and theory that Althusser present are useful in initiating an understanding of the role of the spatial in writing.

But to suggest that we can get beyond metaphor and into a more informative (and perhaps more accountable) form of theory is to imply that, well, we can get beyond metaphor. As Derrida's "The *Retrait* of Metaphor" so elegantly puts it:

> *Metaphora* circulates in the city, it conveys us like its inhabitants, along all sorts of passages, with intersections, red lights, one-way streets, crossroads, crossings, patrolled zones and speed limits. We are in a certain way—metaphorically of course, and as concerns the mode of

habitation—the content and the tenor of this vehicle: passengers, comprehended and displaced by metaphor. (102)

The discussion continues:

> I am trying to speak *about* metaphor, to say something proper or literal on this subject, to *treat* it as my subject, but through metaphor (if one may say so) I am obliged to speak of it *more metaphorico*, to it in its own manner. I cannot *treat it* (*en traiter*) without *dealing with it* (*sans traiter avec elle*), without negotiating with it the loan I take from it in order to speak of it. I do not succeed in producing a *treatise* (*un traité*) on metaphor which is not *treated with* (*traité avec*) metaphor which suddenly appears *intractable* (*intraitable*). (103)

Derrida goes on to say, "Any statement concerning anything that happens, metaphor included, will be produced *not without* metaphor. There will have been a meta-metaphorics consistent enough to dominate all its statements. And what gets along *without* metaphor? Nothing, therefore, and rather it should be said that metaphor gets along without anything else" (103–4). This echoes the groundwork Derrida established in "White Mythologies: Metaphor in the Text of Philosophy" that identifies that we cannot conceive outside of the metaphoric, that only one metaphor exists outside of metaphor: that of the metaphor of metaphor, the extra metaphor, which ultimately is not removed from being metaphor. Paul de Man's "The Epistemology of Metaphor" likewise identifies that "metaphor gives itself the totality which it then claims to define, but is in fact the tautology of its own position" (17).

Theory itself is reduced/elevated to nothing more than metaphor, despite distinctions between theory acting as describer of phenomenon and informer about phenomenon. Nonetheless, my point here in placing Althusser's relational position of metaphor and theory in dialogue with the encompassing views of metaphor Derrida and de Man express is to acknowledge that to employ metaphors of space to simply describe conditions of subjectivity in relation to writing or writing pedagogy is to reduce the potential for what we can ultimately come to know about the phenomena and function of writing. Of course, to say so is to admit to a disingenuous argument in this chapter: one that relies upon spatial metaphors—and metaphors in general—in order to disrupt composition studies' reliance upon the spatial metaphor in favor of more rigorous development of spatial theories of writing. There is no linguistic, discursive, rhetorical, grammatical theory outside of metaphor; there can be no theory outside of metaphor. But there can be use of concepts like "space" to do more than merely offer descriptions of phenomena—like students' relationships to classrooms—and to work to theorize beyond description toward informing. And so while I criticize composition studies for limiting its use of the spatial as metaphor for describing particular situations, really composition studies can employ the spatial only as metaphor and any call—mine or otherwise—for an other-than-metaphoric employment of space would be ill-informed. However, I do find it reasonable to call for a more-than-metaphoric approach to considering the spatial properties of writing. Ultimately, then, when talking about space, we must acknowledge that we cannot escape space as metaphor, escape all representation as metaphor.

The Idea of Space

I write: I inhabit my sheet of paper. I invest it, I travel across it.

I incite blanks, spaces (jumps in the meaning, discontinuities, transitions, changes of key)

—Georges Perec, *Species of Spaces and Other Pieces*

I write
in the
margin

When we evoke "space," we must immediately indicate what occupies that space and how it does so.

—Henri Lefebvre, *The Production of Space*

Places, geographer Yi-Fu Tuan tells us in *Space and Place: The Perspective of Experience*, offer security; space, Tuan says, is freedom. Space is marked and defended; places have "felt value": they have been given identity (3, 4). Places are divisions of space to which meaning and organization have been attached because, as Tuan explains, "'space' is more abstract than 'place.'" Segments of space become places as that space is endowed with values, for space and places depend upon one another for definition (6). Tuan again: "The ideas of 'space' and 'place' require each other for definition. From the security and stability of place we are aware of the openness, freedom, and threat of space, and vice versa. Furthermore, if we think of space as that which allows movement, then place is pause; each pause in movement makes it possible for location to be transformed into place" (6). That pause, that transformation, is a function of writing. To write is to give pause, to take up space and endow it with place-ness. Writing occurs out of space. In theorizing the spatiality of writing, I pause to consider how composition studies moves from space to place and the dangers in doing so, to consider how the field has (seemingly) become complacent in the safety of the places it has acquired in the American university without acknowledging the possibilities held in its spatial freedoms and the limits it has imposed upon the very idea of writing by couching its methodologies in places rather than in space. More specifically, in light of the postcomposition project, I consider the occupation of composition studies, the places it occupies, and the methods and manners in which it has attempted (and likely failed) to conquer space in the American academic territory in order to find a safe place—I use the singular "place" here intentionally, identifying a move toward homogenization, normalization within the field, an issue I address more fully in chapter 4. Working from the understanding that space is made up of infinite places, this chapter works toward an understanding of place and space from the perspective of composition studies. As recent work in spatial theory in composition studies bears witness, the spatial dimension of composition studies is of crucial importance. As Edward W. Soja notes, "The spatial dimension of our lives has never been of greater practical and political relevance than it is today" (1); so, too, is this true for the "life" of composition studies.[5] In the space allotted to me in the following pages (writing, after all, is bound by material conditions not always imposed by the writer), I address the spatial and place-ial positioning of composition studies, not in an attempt to codify that space—and certainly not in the attempt to make it safe—but instead to examine the idea of space as it pertains to composition studies and to begin to understand the role of space in theorizing writing.

Tuan, as I have noted, distinguishes between space and its phenomenological counterpart place, identifying the safety of places and the freedom of space. Distinguishing between space and place may seem confusing, contradictory, yet seeing the two as distinct yet enmeshed is crucial to understanding the role of space in formulating a spatial concept of writing and in the occupation(s) of composition studies. We might think of this as similar to John Dewey's "nesting dualisms." Like Tuan's *Space and Place*, other theoretical works move to distinguish space from place. Such discriminations are pivotal in formulating an understanding of space, though space must be considered both in terms of place and independently. It would be impossible to summarize all that has been written about space—the centuries-old debate about the relationships between space and time and the endless discussion of the differences between space and place. However, I will attempt to provide a general overview of key ideas regarding space in order to devise both a space and a place on and in which to base my consideration of writing as spatial and from which to level critique within composition studies postcomposition. Space—in various conceptual forms—has been addressed from a wide range of disciplinary and discursive positions, including philosophy, theology, psychology, astronomy, mathematics, and physics, to name but a few. The majority of my comments here in summary will be directed toward the history of an epistemology of space forwarded through philosophy and rhetoric, though in places I will turn to other sources.[6]

Interestingly, the concept of space, as we now address it, has roots set distinctly in Greek thinking; the word itself a Latinate derivative. Concepts that predate the Greek concept of space are more directly tied to articulations of place. For instance, the Torah introduces the concept of place through the invocation of the word מקום (*makom*, literally translated as "place").[7] *Makom*—which we might understand in the same vein as "topos," though chronologically topos appears later (*Parmenides*)—denotes a larger concept than just a physical location; it alludes to the manner in which space is politically arranged in province, is occupied by subjects, is occupied and arranged by placement of objects, and is defined by its subjects. *Makom* leans toward the metaphoric, which, given its origin in the Torah, makes sense, allowing the word to fulfill a variety of theological uses that give significance to the named *makom*—a place of cultural value. Likewise, in the early attention to space in Greek writing, "Chaos" is applied as the designation for space (see, for instance, Aristotle's *Physica*, book 4, chapters 1–5, and Hesiod's *Theogony*). Chaos, though, does not designate space in the way we currently understand it; rather, chaos is relational to space, often indicated in theological approaches to space as that which occurs before space, space not yet made. This concept of space is central to Plato in *Timaeus* as he explains how creation brought order. Homer, of course, attempts to give order to chaos, as well, through his use of "cosmos." I take up chaos again in chapter 6, arguing that from the perspective of complexity theories, writing is situated just beyond "the edge of chaos." For now, though, it becomes important to make evident that in space, in chaos, there is a lack of arrangement.

Timaeus offers an important unfolding of how space has been conceptualized, presenting Plato's understanding of the formation of the universe and the beauty and order ascribed to it by a "divine Craftsman." *Timaeus* is Plato's creation story. It introduces the concept of *chora*, a word closely related to "topos," though used in less-specific contexts. The space of *Timaeus*, Edward S. Casey explains in *The Fate of Place: A Philosophical History*, "is what *must* be there in the beginning, even before the act of creation occurs" (32, emphasis in original). This concept of space invokes an assumption of a preexisting space, space as a priori. According to Plato, whatever comes into existence "comes into existence and vanishes from a particular place," and "everything that exists must be somewhere and must occupy some space" (52a). Plato expands this notion of occupation by describing space as a receptacle, which "provides a position for everything that comes to be" (52a). The metaphor of the receptacle allows Plato to give form to space. The receptacle is not empty in the way that space is; rather, emptiness can occur within the receptacle as there is no space outside the receptacle. Form, in this explanation, though, is not physical form; rather, it is regional form. The receptacle, shaking the forms within it, separates the forms into regions (*Timaeus* 53), but the receptacle does not take the forms itself. Derrida has explained this in "Khōra": "Khōra receives, so as to give place to them, all the determinations, but she/it does not possess any of them as her/its own" (239). What we gain from Plato in *Timaeus*, then, is the understanding that region, that definitions within space, are formulated through occupation. As Casey puts it, "A region is not just a formal condition of possibility. It is a substantive place-of-occupation" (34).

Diverging from Plato's wide-sweeping conception of space, Aristotle's *Physica* introduces the concept of topos, a concept richly ingrained in composition studies' understanding of writing. Topos provides constraint, whereas *chora* was cosmologically boundless. The topos of *Physica* is cast as a boundary for that which is contained. This definition of topos has provided two directions in understanding space: as an account of physical space, topos has informed physics and classical mechanics through Sir Isaac Newton's work. Likewise, topos has clearly evolved into a rhetorical understanding of topic.[8]

Ultimately, what Plato and Aristotle provide is the idea of an a priori concept of space—space as the ontological. Contemporary philosophic approaches to space have been bogged down in argument as to whether or not space is a priori or a discursive framework necessary for understanding. This consideration is most notably forwarded by Immanuel Kant's *Critique of Pure Reason*. I won't take the space here to recount all of Kant's argument about space other than to say that it explains space as an ordered framework that provides a system through which we can comprehend experience. To rehash all of what is said in *Critique of Pure Reason* would be to tread into the long familiar, though later I will address out of necessity some concepts found in "Principles of Pure Understanding." So, too, would it be tedious to revisit all of the well-worn contributions to philosophical discussions of space, including those of Arthur Schopenhauer, Emmanuel Levinas, and Newton. Instead, I want to move forward to some more contemporary theories of space that drive more toward my argument in distinguishing space from place and ultimately in working toward a spatial understanding of writing.

In Michel de Certeau's *The Practice of Everyday Life*, place is the "order (of whatever kind) in accord with which elements are distributed in relationships of coexistence" (117). It is this ordering of places that makes them familiar, accountable. De Certeau's ordering of place echoes Tuan's concept of place as safe in that the places that can be ordered can be secured in that order. The security of order elicits safety. Like nearly all who write about space, de Certeau cannot escape the relationship between the spatial and the temporal, and as compositionists, we must also acknowledge that there is an equivalent relationship between the spatial and the rhetorical. For de Certeau, when (time) two objects are understood to be in the same place at the same time, they are, in fact, adjacent to each other in different places, unable to occupy the same space at the same time; they are "*beside* one another, each situated in its own 'proper' and distinct location, a location it defines" (117). "A place is thus an instantaneous configuration of positions" (117). What is most important about this understanding of place is that for de Certeau, places are produced by those "things" that occupy them, and occupation of places is limited. Locations/places are occupy-able and dependent upon those occupations for their definitions. Strikingly, too, de Certeau is clear that the configuration of places by their occupying elements "implies an indication of stability" (117). This moment of stability is a moment of meaning, a moment of rhetorical understanding. Of course, that order is relative and is rhetorical. Order is imposed through power, and though one body orders a space to a particular end, that order is not necessarily recognized or obeyed by all who enter that space. Yet, stability, order, safety are all inscribed upon the pause of place in writing the meaning of that space. Introduce meaning and you give it safety; you make it a place.

Space, on the other hand, is not stable; it lacks meaning. "Space," de Certeau explains, "is composed of intersections of mobile elements. It is in a sense actuated by the ensemble of movements deployed within it. Space occurs as the effect produced by the operations that orient it, situate it, temporalize it, and make it function in a polyvalent unity of conflictual programs or contractual proximities" (117). This is specifically why we cannot conveniently sever time from space, because the very notion of the pause inherent in space is its pre-arrangement, pre-order, pre-meaning, which is always produced/given by power. The moment of possibility exists in the moment prior to space becoming place, the moment before arrangement and meaning. As I will show in chapter 6, this moment in space, the moment prior to order and arrangement, emerges from the edge of chaos. This is where writing—not text, but writing—occurs. We write *in* that space and *at* that time. Possibility, then, is not an instantaneous change but one that can accommodate (endless) revision, (re)circulation, remixing, and readers, who, of course, are also writing, inscribing meaning, and ordering space, despite the increasing limits to possibility that arise as texts are received and ordered and assigned meaning and space is made place. For de Certeau, then, space is ambiguous, not given location by context, by meaning. It is undefined. Space stands in contradistinction to place specifically because of its lack of stability, its lack of meaning. According to de Certeau, space is produced by practices of particular places; by inscribing meaning onto and through places, space can be read by the places within them. Like place, the very idea of space is dependent upon the "things"—in this case, the practices, the meanings—that occupy the places of space. What is central to de Certeau's definition of space is that it is *produced*.

Space, then, is ambiguous in that it is freedom; it may be bordered or identified by means of places within its borders, but space is unstable, uncertain because of the possibilities it contains for occupation. Space is yet-to-be written. It is potential; it is imagination; it is the possibility and means of every discourse to disrupt every discourse, to disrupt its own discourse. Space is yet-to-be written because space has not (yet) been given meaning; it awaits occupation. Space itself does not then occupy a different location than place but the same locations, only as locations yet-to-be written, yet-to-be produced. Place is a (temporal) moment when space is defined, defined through and by its occupiers and occupations. Place is the temporal instance of observation of a site of ideological struggle and is written by whomever is winning the struggle at that moment. The production of space, the writing of place, is the inscription of power onto the freedom of space in order to embed the safety of an order onto/into a place. There is, after all, security in definition. Space is where hegemony is trying to happen but where counter-hegemonies still have footholds. Space is where inequity and suffering happen; space is where struggle occurs to take place. Space is the ever-present trace of possibility that the meaning of a location—whose interests are represented by the social as natural, as right, as in the best interest of who has written the meaning of the place—might be changed. Place is where consent has been achieved.

Like de Certeau, Henri Lefebvre, in *The Production of Space*, identifies space as the result of production. "To speak of 'producing space' sounds bizarre," Lefebvre contends, "so great is the sway still held by the idea that empty space is prior to whatever ends up filling it" (15). For Lefebvre, the concept of production of space is inseparable from power, and his spatial theories grow from critique of representations of power. As Soja explains, Lefebvre links difference and otherness with spatial theory. Lefebvre does so by "insisting that difference be contextualized in social and political practices that are linked to *spatio-analyse*, the analysis, or better, the knowledge (*connaissance*) of the (social) production of (social) space" (*Production* 34–35). The very concept of the social, of the dialectic, is no longer bound to temporality but to space and spatiality (Lefebvre, *Survival* 17).

For Lefebvre, space can no longer be considered as merely "a pre-existing void, endowed with formal properties alone," or as "a container waiting to be filled by a content—i.e. matter, or bodies" (170). Rather, space is produced socially, dialectically, just as place is produced socially, dialectically. From Lefebvre, then, we can say that space is that which within every discourse has the potential to disrupt that discourse; place is the discourse. Space is the site of ideological struggle; place is the result of that struggle. Place is hegemony made visible, readable. Space is where bodies combat to make meaning and, in doing so, make place, produce the location of hegemony. Space is social space or, as Lefebvre puts it, "(social) space" (73). Everywhere that place can be identified, so too can space be identified in the same manner (and for the same reasons) that, as Michel Foucault explains, everywhere that discourse is found, so too is the means to dismantle that discourse. The relationship between space and place is never linear, never progressive. It is always fluid, always overlapping, always simultaneous. Space and place are not either/or. Space and place coexist and co-constitute. Place is space given temporal meaning through social practice and hegemony by whichever ideological position happens to have gained an upper hand in the struggle for making meaning at any given moment when a place is identified. Thus, to speak of place is also to invoke the temporal, as there can be no place out of time. For composition studies to speak of space, then, it must do so with the acknowledgment that composition studies itself is a place and time of hegemony.

The Idea of Occupation

I wouldn't be happy if I were occupied, either.
—President George W. Bush, April 13, 2004

To address any notion of space requires that we also address the idea of occupation. As Lefebvre notes, when we speak of space, we necessarily speak of what and how that space is occupied, for "space considered in isolation is an empty abstraction" (12). The simple follow-up to this would be to say that space is defined by its occupation and that the identities of those occupiers/occupations—here I am speaking both in terms of subjectivity and physical occupation—are defined by the space they occupy. However, such a simplistic formulation fails to fully examine the role of occupation in/of space and traps/limits/misunderstands definitions of space, fails to discern between the *definition of space* by occupation and the *production of space* by occupation.

In beginning to examine the idea of occupation, it is necessary to understand the very idea of occupation from four inseparable, yet distinct, positions.[9] First, "occupation" refers to the act of occupying or being occupied, the taking possession of a space. Conceptually, "taking possession" means social and political practice; it means imbuing space with meaning, producing a place. More often than not, this use of occupation refers to an action, an active taking—often a kind of violence and often a military action—in which a space is gained by force: liberation, invasion, intrusion, intervention, transfer, relocation. In this way, occupation is militant; vying for space is combative. Because vying for meaning is combative, and since occupying space creates its meaning (and our own, which together make place), occupation, then, is clearly a struggle of power, an ideological struggle to inscribe meaning. This notion of occupation may also carry a temporal meaning: the length of time in which a space is occupied. Here we see the metonymic "the occupation" referring to both the act of the violent takeover of a space and the duration of that occupation. This metonym is never innocent or apolitical, securing its own political/ideological/spatial occupation, as its speaker invokes a sense of invasion, of unjust violence *against* the speaker's position; for instance, "the occupation" might be uttered by an opponent of Israel's presence in the West Bank, the Gaza Strip, and East Jerusalem. Even such a position occupies varied ideological space—say, the difference between the Palestine Liberation Organization's use of "ending the Occupation" as leading to an "end of Israel" versus the "US Campaign to End the Israeli Occupation." While it is easy to see the violence attributed to occupations of geopolitical space, this understanding of occupation occurs in all notions of space. All occupations are political; all considerations of the spatial must account for the political. All occupations are discursive, rhetorical, hegemonic. Through its occupations, space is not merely social; it is political. It is precisely the political occupation of a space that imbues that space with its place-ness. Conflict for control over naming a place, for controlling the power to say what can and cannot occupy a space, is often a fight to change the way in which that place has been named by other occupiers who held power in a different temporal moment. Occupations may change over time, but inscribed meanings may not be erased for all who know a place. A place may be Palestine to one subject and Israel to another, no matter who names that place in any specific moment.

The second understanding of "occupation" derives from the first and refers to the state of being subject to the action of occupation. In this instance, we think of occupation not in the active/invasive sense as in the previous definition but as the result of that action, as the direct object of that verb form. An example: New cultural apparatuses (the ban of one kind of literacy and the promotion of another) enforced the occupation.

Third, "occupation" refers to the taking up or filling up of space. In the previous understandings of occupation, the term carries not only spatial meanings but temporal ones as well in referring to the length of time a space is occupied. Place, we recall, is the temporal occupation of space. This instance of occupation refers to the very act of holding a position within a space, to the hegemonic writing of a place. This definition emanates from Archimedes' Principle of Displacement: any object, wholly or partly immersed in a fluid, is buoyed up by a force equal to the weight of the fluid displaced by the object—the principle de Certeau relies upon. Archimedes identifies that an object displaces a volume of liquid equivalent to the volume occupied by the object that displaces the liquid. Derived from this is a basic principle of physics: no two objects can occupy the same space at the same time. Again, the temporal becomes critical in understanding the spatial. From this, we understand that things occupy space—not only physical things but all objects, events, ideas, phenomena, and utterances. As de Certeau clarifies, however, objects occupy adjacent places, not the same place. In chapter 6, I extend a theory of saturation to further address how writing occupies network space. In doing so, Archimedes' principle becomes useful in considering how fluid saturation occurs, seemingly allowing multiple objects to occupy the same space, though actually changing the very constitution of those objects toward the end of spatial occupation.

The fourth degree of "occupation" is more problematic in its transcendence of the spatial into the realm of the temporal. The fourth understanding of occupation refers to the manner in which individuals occupy their time through engagement or the pursuit of an activity. This may refer to employment/work (those terms distinctly different), a profession, or a calling. Certainly, here the idea of the temporal comes into play as occupation refers to how one fills one's time; however, occupations should be seen as primarily spatial in that they distinguish particular *positions* in time held by individuals, often, in fact, referred to as such.

From the rhetorical tradition, we understand that the idea of occupation is derived from *occupatio*. For Cicero's *De Officis*, *occupatio* identified both the acquisition and ownership of property by taking possession of—that is, by occupying—that which had no previous owner (I, 7). This notion of ownership and property leads to concepts of *res nullius*: physical things that do not have or never had owners. A thing that is *res nullius* may be physical, but it cannot have an owner; it cannot be property. For example, light is *res nullius*, but a rock found by a river or an object captured in battle is not. Such distinction became crucial to concepts of Roman law as this early understanding of *occupatio* distinguished between things lost or abandoned out of necessity. Cargo abandoned by a sinking ship could not be repossessed by a new owner because it was abandoned out of necessity. However, a thing abandoned not out of necessity could be possessed, understood as *res derelictae*, property abandoned by an owner. For Justinian, *occupatio* became the method for acquiring property that was to be accepted by nearly all people as *adquisitiones naturales*.

For Kant, space is an inseparable condition of the objects that occupy it (85). Space, he explains, cannot be perceived by itself. Objects—or, using his term in "Principles of Pure Understanding," "materials"—that occupy space give representation to space (80). Without occupation, space is a nonentity. This same notion can be found in a number of philosophers' concepts of space, most notably Gottfried Wilhelm Leibniz's, who argued that space is necessarily occupied in order for it to be identified. What occupies space, then, are bodies: specific bodies that mark and identify segments of the space they occupy. According to Lefebvre, that occupation provides orientation to the space; space without orientation has no identifying characteristics (170, 169). Space requires content. Bodies occupy places within space, giving parts of space orientation and discernible boundaries. Space is infinite; bodies are finite. Only through such occupations can fractions of space be demarcated. Space—infinite, indiscernible—defies the grasp of identity through the movement of perpetual transformation, what we will see in chapter 6 might be understood as "flow." Only the pause of place, the moment of orientation and of identity, permits momentary identity of space's perceived boundaries. This can be seen in the (not so) simple production of maps: the actual terra firma we stand on and measure exists spatially and temporally. It is only the identity of country, of state, that becomes place. So, Istanbul is not Constantinople, and as the song says, "No, you can't go back to Constantinople / Been a long time gone, Constantinople" because places on maps appear only when a discourse emerges, however briefly, victorious for long enough to inscribe meaning to Istanbul or Constantinople, the moment of orientation and identity in which the land can be named a place, given identifiable boundaries. The map will change as new occupiers, new occupations and practices, create new meaning, new identity, produce new places. It is that instability of space—the possibility for changing meaning—that exists in countersignature with place. This is why Lefebvre's claim that space is infinite is so important. Recognizing/imagining space is critical and is the first step toward counter-hegemony, toward creating new meanings through occupation, to producing new places through occupation. Identifying the use of space in any given moment—the *occupation* of space in any given moment—provides the opportunity to reveal contrasting, contradictory uses of space, to identify the very ideological struggles that look to inscribe meaning.

This does not, however, translate into the simple formula that bodies define the space they occupy. As Lefebvre explains:

> Can the body, with its capacity for action, and its various energies, be said to create space? Assuredly, but not in the sense that occupation might be said to "manufacture" spatiality; rather, there is an immediate relationship between the body and its space, between the body's deployment in space and its occupation of space. Before *producing* effects in the material realm (tools and object), before *producing itself* by drawing nourishment from that realm, and before *reproducing itself* by generating other bodies, each living body is space and has its space: it produces itself in space and also produces that space. (170)

Gilles Deleuze and Félix Guattari's *Kafka: Toward a Minor Literature* explains that "we know nothing about a body until we know what it can do, in other words, what its affects are" (13). It is specifically the effect of occupation by the/of the body that becomes central in thinking about spatial occupation. As Foucault accounts in *The Archaeology of Knowledge*, subjects take up positions in space, that is, occupy space. Granted, Foucault does not address what space *is* in the way that Lefebvre does, but attention to occupation can be seen in much of Foucault's writing.

Once given orientation through occupation, parts of space have particular functions. Those functions—as well as that space—are dictated by social convention, by inscribing meaning. What space we may occupy and in what manner we may occupy is socially dictated. Georges Perec's *Species of Spaces and Other Pieces*, in discussion of the function of rooms, identifies the manner in which functions are defined by the occupations of those rooms: "A bedroom is a room in which there is a bed; a dining room is a room in which there are a table and chairs, and often a sideboard" (27).[10] The architect of space—and by "architect," here I do not mean the occupation (job) of being an architect but the very power structures that design, delineate, and produce what space may be—produces space with an eye toward how the places of that space will be occupied. For instance, when preserves/parks/habitats are set aside by governing bodies (bodies that occupy authority), there is an underlying idea of how that space will be occupied that drives how it is constructed. Likewise, the metaphoric distinction commonly articulated between a classroom space and, say, a writing "lab" space distinguishes occupational value. While these are concrete (pun intended), easily defined/defended examples, the same holds true with all space, abstract or concrete: space on a page, space in culture, imagined space, third-space. That is, whether considering first-space or second-space, the occupation of that space produces that space. Gregory L. Ulmer's notion of apparatus in *Heuretics: The Logic of Invention* becomes crucial in understanding the idea of occupation. For Ulmer, apparatus refers to "the matrix of a language machine" composed partly of the technological and partly of the social that functions in any give time—though I would argue in any given space as well—to make meaning. Apparatus is not merely the technology of language—a pencil, ink, a typewriter, the alphabet—but the institution and that institution's methods and practices that evolve with the technology, what Jody Berland in "Angels Dancing: Cultural Technologies and the Production of Space" refers to as "cultural technologies." Apparatuses are the means through which knowledge is named. Through Ulmer's apparatus, we come to see occupation, then, not as a mere case of functionality, of function-ability, of the possibility of how space may be *used*. "Use" suggests that the occupation of space produces space only through its usability. When and how space is occupied extends beyond use to the apparatus of space: its technological and social practice. How space is made through its technological and social functions defines how, when, and by whom space can be occupied. As we will see in later chapters in this book, this aspect of understanding space opens the doors to employing systems theories and complexity theories as ways of theorizing writing.

Can there be space, then, without use, that is unusable, that is without occupation? Seemingly, such a question presupposes a binary answer: space is infinite, the site of chaos, freedom, and struggle, and when it is ordered it becomes place while *at the same time* space is produced by way of its places, not an a priori condition. Yet, this seemingly conflicting answer provides the possibility of chaos as the location from which order emerges, and part of that ordering comes from the attempt to name space as usable or unusable. The very move to identify space as usable or without use, as occupied or unoccupied, or as occupiable or unoccupiable, is itself a use-function, an attempt to identify unusable space as used for the unusable. Basic Derridean otherness. Unused space can be seen as other than the used and thus serving the use of being unused. "Serving the use" implies an agent for whom the use has value, who enacts the use, even if only passively. However, as I hope to show later in the book, this implied agent should not be understood as an autonomous agent but rather as an integrated part of the networks that occupy a space. Perec, too, lets us consider unused space by identifying that language does not allow us to articulate the unused space as space. Perec, in trying to convey what the unused space might be, says: "A space without a function. Not 'without any precise function' but precisely without any function; not pluri-functional (everyone knows how to do that), but a-functional. It wouldn't obviously be a space intended solely to 'release' the others (lumber-room, cupboard, hanging space, storage space, etc.) but a space, I repeat, that would serve no purpose at all" (33). There is unusable space and space that is not used but not space without use—not even imagined space. There is space that is unoccupiable and space that is unoccupied but not space that cannot be occupied. The use-function of space is bound up with how space is occupied, even in its unoccupation. This echoes Lefebvre's concept of spatial orientation and unoccupied space. Space requires occupation. However, constructing unused space as Other space affords the dominant occupier of space, those who write meaning in place, the opportunity to make the Other the same, to turn the unused into the used.

Occupation imposes "partition" (Perec, *Species* 37); partitions/borders/boundaries become/are political, are rhetorical, are discursive. Without demarcated partitions, there is no space, no space to occupy, no formation of place. Space is defined by the boundaries imposed by its occupiers. To make the partitions/borders/boundaries appear natural—nonexistent, if possible—and nonpolitical is the ultimate goal of use: to identify occupation as appropriate, as natural, as correct. This is my space; it always has been. This is the manufacture of consent; this is hegemony. This is how space is used; this is how it has always been used. Then space can be seen as a factor in constructing the occupier's identity, not the opposite—though, of course, this is an illusion. The relationship becomes eventually reciprocal in that those who come to occupy a space—say, the space of the university—must mold their identities to fit the space as defined by previous occupiers/occupations. This is also Soja—via Lefebvre—asking us to think not only about how occupation demarcates space but also about the manner in which space demarcate the occupiers.

For Perec, partitions, from the political perspective of dividing geopolitical regions, thus giving name/identity to the idea of country, are marked by divisions of frontiers, unnamed, unoccupied space that marks boundaries within and between space(s). Perec, in an interesting maneuver, identifies that some space is uninhabitable, but when listing what uninhabitable space might be, he does not mean to suggest that uninhabitable space is uninhabited (for instance, he identifies shantytowns, towns that smell bad, the out-of-bounds, the corridors of the Métro, and so on), only that that space should not be inhabited. Though not explicitly, Perec moves to a distinction between habitable and occupy-able. For Perec, there is space that has been occupied in such a fashion that renders it no longer habitable. This is specifically the moment in which the primary occupier of space can shift the non-use, the uninhabit-ability of space, into used space, habitable space. The primary occupier of space can construct the uninhabitable shantytown as used space, as place, positioning the occupants of that place in the ranks of the hegemony that defines the place. In such a case of Other space, of unused space made use of, there is little difficulty in seeing how a dominant discourse imposes occupation, imposes order to maintain its own safety. Remember, places may be safe, but they are safe only for those who make them. For composition studies, this is crucial, as we shall see.

The ordering of occupation can also be seen as an ecology of storage, of how space is occupied. Occupation itself is a spatial storage. Places to put things, to occupy, to be occupied, to keep occupied. Places to save, to be saved; places to cage, to be caged. Occupying a field and guarding its borders keep the invaders out but also keep the (e)state in (power) by writing those borders as containing what can safely be contained and what can be excluded safely. As Roland Barthes's *Image, Music, Text* puts it, "What can be separated can also be filled" (120); this is what Lefebvre refers to as the "logic of container *versus* contents" (*Production* 3).

To invoke writing, to name a thing, to consider knowledge (that is, by thinking/talking about anything) is to deploy all of these into space, thus naming/writing space by its occupying force. Perec asks, "What does taking possession of a place mean? As from when does somewhere become truly yours?" (24). These are questions of identity, of a place's identity, and ultimately of the occupier's identity. Identity is the attempt to mark a container (both as a container and in terms of its use) by naming its contents. Unoccupied containers are unmarked space. I'm thinking here of the kind of unmarked space found in Italo Calvino's "A Sign in Space" in *Cosmicomics*. Space, Calvino notes, is not definable until that space is occupied by sign: "Space, without a sign, was once again a chasm, the void, without beginning or end, nauseating, in which everything—including me—was lost" (35). What Calvino is getting at are points of reference, the ability to identify what is occupied, to demarcate, to mark:

> In the universe now there was no longer a container and a thing contained, but only a general thickness of signs superimposed and coagulated, occupying the whole volume of space; it was constantly being dotted, minutely, a network of lines and scratches and reliefs and engravings; the universe was scrawled over on all sides, along all its dimensions. There was no longer any way to establish a point of reference: the galaxy went on turning but I could no longer count the revolutions, any point

could be the point of departure, any sign heaped up with the others could be mine, but discovering it would have served no purpose, because it was clear that, independent of signs, space didn't exist and perhaps had never existed. (39)

To make a sign in space is to give signification. To signify is to assign meaning, to produce a place, to occupy that place. To occupy a place is to produce that place; to produce a place is to occupy it, to write it in the script of hegemony, to make it safe in a glimpse of time.

The Occupation of Composition

Once composition could be named a field, a concept reflecting absolute space, then it could wield power.

> —Nedra Reynolds, *Geographies of Writing: Inhabiting Places and Encountering Difference*

The present epoch will perhaps be above all the epoch of space. We are in the epoch of simultaneity; we are in the epoch of juxtaposition, the epoch of the near and far, the side-by-side, of the dispersed. We are at a moment, I believe, when our experience of the world is less that of a long life developing through time than that of a network that connects points and intersects with its own skein.

> —Michel Foucault, "Of Other Spaces"

Out of a need for vocabulary, composition studies has (reluctantly) adopted spatial metaphors—classrooms, writing environments, sites of conflict, and so on. Nedra Reynolds, in her article "Composition's Imagined Geographies: The Politics of Space in the Frontier, City, and Cyberspace" and her book *Geographies of Writing: Inhabiting Places and Encountering Difference*, argues that "spatial metaphors have long dominated our written discourse in this field ('field' being one of the first spatial references we can name) because, first, writing itself is spatial, or we cannot very well conceive of writing other than spatial" ("Composition's Imagined Geographies" 14) and that "space is usually described or represented by making comparisons with familiar objects or ideas—like an academic discipline being called a field (giving it the boundaries of absolute space)" (*Geographies* 13). But, unlike these two works, which are two of the most substantial contributions to composition studies' discussion of space and spatial theory, most work in composition studies embraces such metaphors only half-heartedly—and in ways that are often inattentive to the implications of the spatial dimensions of those metaphors—as an easy way to talk about composition studies, and generally just composition pedagogy. I have already noted the problems of relying simply upon the metaphoric as well as the impossibilities of operating outside the metaphoric.

Much more so than its embrace of the spatial, composition studies has entrenched itself in concepts of the temporal. As I noted earlier, much of composition studies' attention to the temporal notion of writing can be attributed to its historical shackling to literary studies. In the next section, I begin to unpack composition studies' relegation of writing to the temporal in an attempt to begin to theorize writing as spatial and space as a function of writing, but before doing so, I want to take a bit of space to consider composition studies' disciplinary devotion to the temporal and the way in which it straps its own identity to that temporality. Talking about what composition studies is/does is so much a prevalent part of what the discipline does/is that having such conversations *is* what composition studies does: composition studies *studies* composition studies. Despite its relatively recent inception, composition studies spends an immense amount of time attempting to place itself historically.[11] Much as Soja demonstrates of historians and sociologists, compositionists have privileged historical placements in culture and, for the most part, have rendered spatial determination and occupation nearly insignificant. To claim history is to order validation.

To see composition studies' attachment to the temporal, one need look no further than those whose scholarly work has been heralded as the most important in/of composition studies: Stephen North's *The Making of Knowledge in Composition*, Susan Miller's *Rescuing the Subject* or her essay "The Feminization of Composition," James Berlin's "Contemporary Composition: The Major Pedagogical Theories," Richard Fulkerson's "Four Philosophies of Composition." These are attempts to tell the (his)story of composition studies. More recent histories such as Robert J. Connors's *Composition-Rhetoric*, Joseph Harris's *A Teaching Subject*, Thomas P. Miller's *The Formation of College English*, Lynn Z. Bloom, Donald A. Daiker, and Edward M. White's *Composition in the Twenty-First Century*, John C. Brereton's *The Origins of Composition Studies in the American College, 1875–1925*, and Sharon Crowley's *Composition in the University* are all works of temporal placement—though I might argue that Crowley's *Composition in the University* (one of the most important books in composition studies in the last fifteen years) is actually a book of spatial dimensions despite the fact that it does not approach its argument as such.[12] Composition studies, it seems, is determined to find a foothold in temporal placement, in history.

What composition studies might now consider, beyond its initial importation of spatial metaphors, is its own occupation. Such an avenue of self-reflexive critique might provide insight into the condition and functions of composition studies' places in the academy. This inquiry, I would argue, is likely to reveal that the tenuous comfort the discipline has found has resulted in an anxiety about the actual safety of those places. This anxiety might emerge because what we have accepted as the place of composition studies—manifest in places like FYC, writing program administration, and subject formation/management—lacks the freedom and possibility of space. What composition studies might begin to recognize is that its attempt to find even temporal ground is dependent upon not its histories but its occupations and its abilities to continually produce counter-hegemonies that question the field's places. Composition studies should become attuned not to spatial metaphors as a method for speaking *about* its work but rather to the dynamics of the very production and occupations of space in order to elucidate the complexity of composition studies' (ever-shifting) position(s): historically, institutionally, territorially. Composition studies' identities and histories can "no longer be sought (as they once were) simply in the abstract realms of 'ideology' or 'discourse,' but very precisely in the grounded and interanimating practices of the . . . bodies whose organised everyday life reproduces the spaces in question" (Murphet 204). That is, composition studies should become more attuned to its own occupations. Or, to borrow from Foucault, I believe that the anxiety of the composition studies era has "to do fundamentally with space, no doubt a great deal more than with time" ("Of Other Spaces" 23). It is specifically because of this that I posit postcomposition, the move beyond composition studies, as a spatial positioning rather than as an era-marking historical or temporal maneuver.

Gaston Bachelard explains in his landmark book *The Poetics of Space* that we do not live in empty space, in homogeneous space. Space, he claims, is filled by quantities, with occupations (though for Bachelard, these occupations may be "fantasmatic"). Composition studies is, we might say, social space, cultural space, occupied space, or, more accurately, as we will see later in this book, a network. Its bodies and boundaries are produced by the occupiers of that space, and the occupations are the defining forces of those spaces. Understanding the spatiality of composition studies thus allows for producing new places and new ways to occupy the places of the field, a new opportunity to define not only places and boundaries, territories and fields, but the very politics of those places and boundaries; it allows for recognizing the hegemonies that mark those territories and the counter-hegemonies that necessarily must question and resist those hegemonies. Composition studies, in many ways, has become complacent in the safety of the pause, in the safety of the place of the field. That complacency has left composition studies defending the illusions of borders, not of spaces, but of places. Composition studies might consider exploring more actively its contingent frontiers, contingencies that may be adverse to the "field," frontiers that can be riddled with the possibility of disorder and violence to the stability of the field. Frontiers, we discern from G. W. F. Hegel, always involve violence. Occupation is often violent; occupation is a maneuver toward new frontiers, a passing into the beyond.

Composition studies' simulacra of safety of place rests on its desire to claim disciplinary status, its desire to be seen as field. But fields are demarcated by boundaries, generally discernible, claim-able boundaries. As composition studies has witnessed in its "history," its field is often penetrated by occupying forces (think Minnesota, think Florida, think Brodkey).[13] Fields with defendable borders are also exclusionary, not only in terms of territoriality but also in terms of identity. Hegemonic discourses maneuver (within) disciplinary borders to protect the places within those borders, to protect the field's rights to construct those places, to protect its own safety. In composition studies, the safety of the home field risks becoming exclusionary, guarded against incompatibility with ideologies and (perhaps incursive) missions of other field boundaries, guarded against counter-hegemonies, guarded against space. Composition studies is hegemonic—and as I said in the previous chapter, deeply conservative and active in promoting and protecting its hegemonies. Despite its self-congratulatory discourse of openness and diversity, of freedom and emancipation, composition studies is adamant about its fields, about its places. Composition studies guards its places by presenting a discourse of inclusiveness, by making that discourse seem a natural part of the field's discourse. But that diversity, that openness to dissent, must share occupation within composition studies places, and as we have seen, the Other residing in an occupied space has little voice in naming that space.

To move beyond the safety of composition studies' place requires first an acknowledgment of composition studies' heterotopic space. "Heterotopias," Foucault pronounces in "Of Other Spaces," "always presuppose a system of opening and closing that both isolates them and makes them penetrable. In general, the heterotopic space is not freely accessible like a public space. Either entry is compulsory . . . or else the individual has to submit to rites and purification. . . . To get in, one must have certain permission and make certain gestures" (26). Heterotopias resemble the open and closed systems of systems theories, upon which I elaborate in chapters 5 and 6. Heterotopias, too, Foucault explains, may "seem to be pure and simple openings, but that generally hide curious exclusions. Everyone can enter into these heterotopic sites, but in fact that is only an illusion: we think we enter where we are, but by the very fact that we enter, are excluded" (26). This is the power of occupation.

"The political synthesis of social space," Michael Hardt and Antonio Negri's *Empire* tells us, "is fixed in the space of communication" (33). From this we understand that it is the very language of composition studies' occupation—the manner in which that space is occupied—that protects composition studies' places in safety, protects composition studies in its places, not casting more than a glance beyond its places to the frontiers of its spaces, to the territorial occupations, accepting its exclusions and its being excluded. This is why the very metaphors of "conversation" as well as the increased role of heterotopic conversations (think WPA-L, which I address in greater detail in chapter 4) are powerful producers of composition studies' space, of defining and defending composition studies' occupation. Communicative entities not only are able to impose controlling structure over the composition studies place but also give credence and validation to that occupation. As Hardt and Negri put it, "Power, as it produces, organizes; as it organizes, it speaks and expresses itself as authority. Language, as it communicates, produces commodities but moreover creates subjectivities, puts them in relation, and orders them" (33). I take up the problematic notion of subjectivities in the next chapter but for now acknowledge that for composition studies, a central question of its spatial inquiry, in its move postcomposition, must be a question of the powers that produce and organize the (social) spaces of composition studies, which organize the relative safety of composition studies' places. Composition studies can no longer afford to rest in the safety of recirculated conversations of temporal/historical identity, of imposed subjectivities, of self-validation. Composition studies should move to occupy other places in order to move beyond its simulacra of safety, its artificial safety, to explore the horizons of its contingent frontiers in order to produce its own counter-hegemonies, in order to not accept the "natural" (or naturalized) boundaries of composition studies' field. The occupation of composition studies is not merely an occupation of the fourth order—that of a task to occupy time—it is an occupation that requires critical attention to the very space it occupies/produces, its occupation of particular, produced places, because it is in those occupations that we see composition studies' places as written demarcations, as dependent upon the meaning inscribed on them, and from which those meaning-full places are the result of ideological struggle. Composition studies is an occupied territory and in its occupation risks creating a homogeneous composition studies space, a naturalized place. And as Jean Baudrillard explains in *Simulacra and Simulation*, "Homogenous space, without meditation, brings together men and things—a space of direct manipulation. But who manipulates whom?" (76). Composition studies is in need of spatial disruption.

Ultimately, composition studies must acknowledge its spatial positioning but in doing so must also initiate a move to counter-spaces. Counter-spaces, as Lefebvre defines them, are "spaces of resistance to the dominant order arising precisely from their subordinate, peripheral or marginalized positioning" (*Production* 68). Composition studies should deterritorialize, give up the safety of its places—places that claim occupational/disciplinary authority yet constrict the domain of that authority to limit-situations such as "the teaching of writing." Composition studies needs Baudrillard's polyvalent space, a space of mass participation in its occupation, in which the occupiers become the writers of the cultures that occupy that space. In polyvalent space, occupiers "participate and manipulate so well that they efface all the meaning one wants to give the operation and put the very infrastructure of the edifice in danger" (Baudrillard, *Illusion* 66).

The questions, of course, that this short consideration of space begs are who occupies (or what bodies occupy) composition studies? Is composition studies occupied? Or is composition studies otherwise occupied, distracted by its occupations? Does composition studies occupy its own (social) space, or has it become satisfied/complacent (put) in its own place? To what (governing) bodies does composition studies bow in its occupation, and to what bodies does it stand adjacent? Who determines the content, the orientation, the direction of composition studies' occupied spaces? How long will this occupation last? There are questions to be posed of composition studies' freedom in the occupation of its places and questions that should not be ignored about the complacency and conservatism composition studies has adopted in its settlement of/with safe places.

Writing Occupation

At this level of volume, it's almost quaint to think that the main purpose of writing is to carry some content from one place to another.
—Raúl Sánchez, "The Ideology of Identity and the Study of Writing"

In *The Function of Theory in Composition*, Raúl Sánchez argues that theory is a function of writing, not a precursory mechanism for describing the activity of writing. Writing, I contend, is an attempt to occupy space, to name and to make areas of space into places. As I will argue in chapter 6, writing saturates space. In so doing, writing's power comes not from temporal moments but from occupations in space, occupations that we must immediately come to recognize as endlessly deferred in the same ways the *différance* of writing endlessly defers meaning. Space is occupied and defined in relation to other occupations, lack of occupations (emptiness), and potential occupations. In this way, space has most often been accepted as a site of emptiness, a receptacle, à la Plato's *Timaeus*, in which objects give form and function to space by a means of referential demarcation. Space has no meaning, no shape, but is instead imbued with its dimensions. Thus, space is seen as an a priori universal and writing as providing shape to space. Yet, such a view of the relation between space and writing fails to acknowledge the spatial dimensions of writing itself, condemns and empowers writing in the same breath to the position of mechanism that shapes space without considering the powerful ways in which writing is itself space, a spatial phenomenon. In the same vein, it can be said that a reciprocal argument could be made that space is itself a phenomenon of writing, shaped and encrypted with meaning through grammatological processes.

To claim that writing gives or can give shape to space, provides structure to the shapelessness of space, is to suffuse writing with power over space. We know that writing is not power; to say that writing *is* power is to conflate writing into an essence, an absolute, that is limited. Instead, we know that writing and power work together systemically, that some writing is powerful—the adjectival form granting the potential of characteristic and the possibility of function rather than the reductive encumbrance of pith—some more powerful than some other. We also know that "writing and power never work separately" ("Scribble" 117). Derrida's "Scribble" also makes clear that "writing does not come to power. It is there beforehand, it partakes of and is made of it" (117). Derrida continues to explain that "*struggles* for *power* set *various* writings up against one another" (117–18, emphasis in original). In such struggles, writing works to occupy—specifically in the first degree of occupation via violence—space, specifically space *against* other writing, keeping in mind that these are positional struggles of occupation. They are also, at all times, political.

Writing requires space. Writing requires the material space onto/into which writing is inscribed, and it requires cultural, historical, political space to occupy. In both of these instances, writing sets up occupancy within or saturates a particular space. Such an occupation not only sets in motion the alteration of the space occupied but also authorizes the writing in varying degrees of distance to the occupied space. Occupation and distance are established in form and content; it is the *content* in which writing finds its power. Content is, of course, spatial; it is that which fills writing, which occupies writing, which empowers writing to occupy. Content is that which is contained; content is limited by its container. Content is contained by writing;

writing is the spatial boundaries of that which is contained. Content is limited by capacity. Content limits space, limits possibility. Content is subject matter, the matter of the subject, denoting both power of the subject over the matter/the content and the makeup of the subject. The matter of the subject, the subject's matter, is that which composes the subject, and too often in composition studies, writing is understood in this way, as matter of subjects, as materials or substances of subjects, but as I hope to show throughout this book, the very ideas of subjectivity and writing subject require critique in light of the current hyper-circulatory, networked condition of writing.

The problem with content, though, is volume—the amount of space taken up by content. As Raúl Sánchez's 2007 Conference on College Composition and Communication presentation "The Ideology of Identity and the Study of Writing" pointed out, "There's far too much of it—too much writing, that is. . . . There's too much text being produced, too much writing in circulation. Everywhere you look there is writing. And if you expand what you mean by writing to include various forms of inscription, other forms of textual production, then there is even more writing. It is a question of volume." A volume is, of course, a collection of writing, a division, a spatial demarcation of content. Volume is also a measurement of space, of how much space is occupied, a quantity of mass. Interestingly, the spatial condition of writing has undergone a shift since the "invention" of writing. Early writing occupied a great deal of space, both materially and politically. Early writing required lots of space to contain limited content. As content expanded, writing had to adjust to accommodate increasingly complex amounts of content. In order to do so, writing necessarily had to take up less space, both material and symbolic space. Early writing shifted from pictograms and ideograms to alphabetic forms in order to more efficiently/ economically account for increasing volumes of content. Material developments in writing have accounted for and fostered this shift as well. Methods of storing writing have evolved to account for and contain the increased volumes of content. Methods of production have developed on the backs of the methods of storage, rendering methods of production chained by the storage space available, by the space that can be occupied.

If there is, as Sánchez claims, too much writing, it is because the technologies of storage and circulation have exceeded the possibilities of production. Production has taken a backseat to circulation and storage. It is not that there is more space in which to store writing; it is that writing moves (or flows) in more efficient ways. Thus, circulation, the movement of writing, takes center stage in understanding the current spatial characteristics of writing. Issues of system—closed and open—become the central force in occupation dictated through circulation. Circulation is systemic and so is itself spatial. Circulation, particularly in a new-media, computer-mediated enhanced system of circulation, shifts the focus of writing away from the producer of writing to the writing itself and the systems in which it circulates. Such a move allows us to sidestep the disciplinary trap of subject, allows us to begin to theorize writing neither as process nor product but as occupying circulating spaces within space.

3. Beyond the Subject of Composition Studies

> Classically, the subject outshines the object.
>
> —Jean Baudrillard, "Photography, or the Writing of Light"

> We have always lived off the splendor of the subject and the poverty
> of the object. It is the subject that makes history, it's the subject that
> totalizes the world. Individual subject or collective subject, the subject
> of consciousness or of the unconscious, the ideal of all metaphysics is
> that of world subject; the object is only the detour on the royal road of
> subjectivity.
>
> —Jean Baudrillard, *Fatal Strategies*

> The production of a student subject is a chief outcome of a course in
> composition.
>
> —Lester Faigley, *Fragments of Rationality:*
> *Postmodernity and the Subject of Composition*

To begin to shift focus from subject toward a greater attention to writing, I propose reconfiguring how we think about the subject, the writing-subject, and the student-subject in composition studies. Undoubtedly, subject/subjectivity has played a key role in composition studies' evolution, permitting the field to develop a body of "research" about subjectivity and to claim an authority to govern over student subjects. In doing so, composition studies has created a disciplinary bureaucratic structure in which subject management and production has unfolded as the central function of the field. The primacy of the subject in composition studies is visible not only in its managerial emphasis, which I address in detail in the next chapter, but in the ubiquitous attention to subjectivity in its scholarship. For composition studies, writing not only takes a backseat to subject but is most often addressable only in light of/in the shadow of the subject. And, not unlike others relegated to the backseat, writing wants to know, "When are we going to *be* there?" That is, writing is most often addressed not as an object of study in and of itself but as a result of and purveyor of subjectivity and as servile to subjectivity. Without subject, we assume (perhaps incorrectly), writing cannot be produced, distributed, circulated, or consumed. In such a configuration, composition studies as a field generally has initiated (historically) inquiry into writing via inquiry into subject. What I hope to show in this chapter and in chapters 5 and 6 is, first, that the conceptions of subjectivity upon which composition studies has relied no longer accurately explain the location or function of subjectivity or agency within the networked, hypercirculatory, complex situation of writing in which we now find ourselves. Second, in later chapters, I argue that by adopting systems theories and complexity theories methodologies and insights, we might begin theorizing writing in more dynamic, complex ways that account for the current conditions of writing without the a priori condition of subjectivity.

Posthuman Subjectivity

As you gaze at the flickering signifiers scrolling down the computer screens, no matter what identifications you assign to the embodied entities that you cannot see, you have already become posthuman.
—N. Katherine Hayles, *How We Became Posthuman: Virtual Bodies in Cybernetics, Literature, and Informatics*

The task of posthumanism is to uncover those uncanny moments at which things start to drift, of reading humanism in a certain way, against itself and the grain. This clearly involves a rethinking of the meaning of the "post-."
—Neil Badmington, "Theorizing Posthumanism"

It is not as if we have a choice about the coming posthumanism; it is *already* upon us.
—Cary Wolfe, *Critical Environments: Postmodern Theory and the Pragmatics of the "Outside"*

Any decentering of subjectivity or the writing subject as composition studies' primary object of study needs to account for how theories of the posthuman and posthumanism inform postcomposition. In the remainder of this chapter, I examine the posthuman and posthumanism. I engage this work in order to elaborate more fully the need to liberate composition studies from the straitjacket of subjectivity and to further establish a basis from which I develop ecological/spatial/networked theories of writing throughout the remainder of this book. In this chapter, I begin by looking at the distinctions between popular and critical posthumanism, examining closely the posthumanisms of N. Katherine Hayles and Jill Didur. I then look to Mark Hansen's understanding of technesis as a way of better understanding posthumanism. Following this initial consideration of posthumanisms, I turn my attention to considering composition studies in light of posthumanisms, arguing for the need to rethink the idea of subjectivity as central to studying writing.

The difficulty in engaging the posthuman and posthumanism, though, grows from the fact that there is little agreement as to what those two terms mean. There are many posthumanisms. What's interesting in this disagreement is the very fact that there can be something called "the posthuman" or "posthumanism." It is in the inconsistency, disagreement, and uncertainty that I find potential. Postcomposition embraces the posthuman and posthumanism as a necessary way of (re)thinking subjectivity. I hope to articulate not merely a summary of some of the divergent approaches to posthumanism and the posthuman but a productive way of employing these discrepancies as a manner for thinking of subjectivity beyond the ways in which composition studies has. Given that work in posthuman thinking originates from a range of disciplinary perspectives—animal studies, cybernetics, informatics, genetics, philosophy, and literary studies, to name a few—there has yet to be any cogent agreement about a central notion of what posthumanism or the posthuman means. For instance, there is no agreement as to whether the posthuman is hypothetical, inevitable, or realized or whether in the posthuman there is potential or risk. Thus, I begin by distilling some principle ideas about the posthuman and posthumanism in order to develop an overarching understanding of how these concepts inform postcomposition.

The idea of the posthuman should first be recognized as distinct from posthumanism. Posthumanism can be thought of (reductively) as a philosophic reaction against classical and Enlightenment humanism. While most thinking in posthumanism does not reject the rationalism tied to humanism, posthumanism does critique the role of the autonomous thinker and casts human thought as imperfect and not the avenue through which the world is known or defined. Many posthumanisms work to realign humans not as superior to other species but as operating as any other species; in doing so, posthumanism denies humanity an ethical superiority above nature and, more important, sees humanity as not operating somehow above or outside encompassing systems: biological, ecological, technological, or other (see, for example, Donna J. Haraway's *When Species Meet*).

A good deal of posthumanist thinking evolves from the employment of technological conditions that alter the circumstance of being human. These conditions are imposed by or adapted from external technological sources.

Posthumanism is influenced by—if not triggered by—the changes imposed on the human by things like genetic manipulation, cybernetics, artificial intelligence, psychotropic pharmaceuticals, and other biotechnical research. Ultimately, posthumanism is defined by a kind of amorphous understanding of core human alteration brought about by some interaction with technology: biological, electric/digital, or chemical (pharmaceutical, for instance). As Cary Wolfe in his remarkable book *What Is Posthumanism?* explains, "Posthumanism names a historical moment in which the decentering of the human by its imbrication in the technical, medical, informatics, and economic networks is increasingly impossible to ignore" (xv). It should be noted, though, that some see the human's interaction with technology specifically as what defines the human as different from the nonhuman and is the primary characteristic of what it means to be human (see, for instance, Andy Clark's *Natural-Born Cyborgs: Minds, Technologies, and the Future of Human Intelligence*). Posthumanism, often addressed as the "posthuman condition," is a topic of consideration from a number of perspectives; its interdisciplinarity stands as one of its central characteristics. Notably, postmodern literary critic Ihab Hassan is often cited as the beginning point for discussions of posthumanism; his claim in "Prometheus as Performer: Toward a Posthumanist Culture" initiates the conversation: "We need first to understand that the human form—including human desire and all its external representations— may be changing radically, and thus may be coming to an end as humanism transforms itself into something that we must helplessly call posthuman" (205). What this change is/may be depends upon disciplinary perspective.

Within the disagreements as to what posthumanism is, there exists a split that has been characterized by Bart Simon as an unproductive division between a "popular and a more critical posthumanism" (2) and by Hayles as a "complacent posthumanism" and a more critical posthumanism. According to Simon, the popular approach to posthumanism is exemplified in Francis Fukuyama's 2002 book *Our Posthuman Future: Consequences of the Biotechnology Revolution*. Fukuyama, whose 1992 book *The End of History and the Last Man* provides David Smit with the foundational concept for *The End of Composition Studies*, argues in *Our Posthuman Future* that "the most significant threat posed by contemporary biotechnology is the possibility that it will alter human nature and thereby move us into a 'posthuman' stage of history" (7). For Fukuyama, this is important because "human nature exists, is a meaningful concept, and has provided a stable continuity to our experiences as a species" (7). Fukuyama's argument is, as Simon has characterized it, "an impassioned defense of liberal humanism against contemporary cultures of laissez-faire individualism and unregulated corporate technoscience" (1). Citing Christopher Dewdney's *Last Flesh: Life in the Transhuman Era*, Simon summarizes popular posthumanism: "[W]e are on the verge of the next stage in life's evolution, the stage where, by human agency, life takes control of itself and guides its own destiny. Never before has human life been able to change itself, to reach into its own genetic structure and rearrange its molecular basis; now it can" (qtd. in Simon 2). As Simon explains:

> This popular posthumanist (sometimes transhumanist)[1] discourse structures the research agendas of much of corporate biotechnology and informatics as well as serving as a legitimating narrative for new social entities (cyborgs, artificial intelligence, and virtual societies) composed of fundamentally fluid, flexible, and changeable identities. For popular posthumanism, the future is a space for the realization of individuality, the transcendence of biological limits, and the creation of a new social order. (2)

On the other hand, Didur's "Re-embodying Technoscientific Fantasies: Posthumanism, Genetically Modified Foods, and the Colonization of Life" explains a more critical posthumanism: "A more radical notion of posthumanism can serve as a basis for critiquing what is essentially a disembodied colonial attitude toward the theory/practice of biotech research today" (100). Didur's more critical, more radical posthumanism calls into question not only various humanisms but popular approaches to posthumanism as well. Like post-theory movements that demand more from theory, critical/radical posthumanism demands more from posthumanism.[2] Simon, for instance, critiques Fukuyama's *Our Posthuman Future* as being a popular humanist text, noting its important engagement with posthuman concerns, but lacking the critical engagement to provide any serious intervention. The kind of critical intervention into posthumanism that Simon and Didur initiate has been described by Catherine Waldby as "a general critical space in which the techno-cultural forces which both produce and undermine the stability of the categories of 'human' and 'nonhuman' can be investigated" (qtd. in Simon 3). Central to any work in posthumanism is the question of the human subject and, as Simon points out, "its traditional repercussions on questions of agency, identity, power, and resistance" (3). Just as postmodernism questioned the singular, identifiable, autonomous, rational subject forwarded by Enlightenment thinking, posthumanism has called into question the unstable, contingent, fluid postmodern subject.

To distinguish posthumanism from the posthuman, we might think of the posthuman as the object of concern for posthumanist thinking. The posthuman is beyond the human; the posthuman transcends the human. Some—like the World Transhumanist Society—view the posthuman as exceeding the capacity of humans to the extent that the posthuman is no longer recognized as human, the emphasis here on a concept of exceeding, becoming more than human. For some, posthumanism promotes the pro-active enhancement of the human experience through technological augmentation as a method of directing human evolution. Through technology, some posthumanisms argue, we can design the next phase of human existence. In many of these views (notably, those of the WTS, for instance), the posthuman is a hypothetical entity, something that might be ideally achieved. Such definitions of possibility, though, are problematic in their implication of "exceeding" as it implies improvement. To a lesser extent, we might understand "exceeding" as implying a spatial growth that is not linear, as in exceeding capacity, outgrowing, enlarging, to which we can attribute neither positive nor negative connotations without a specific context. Manipulation of the human toward exceeding as improvement is often criticized as lending to constructions like that of the *über*-human and wrought with implications of superiority. Other definitions, like Fukuyama's vision of control through information technologies and bioengineered life, cast the shift to posthumanism as apocalyptic, as a loss of humanity, or as antihuman. Others, like Neil Badmington, see posthumanism in the same light that Jean-François Lyotard cast postmodernism, as a measure of modernism, or in Badmington's argument, as a measure of humanism. The posthuman should be thought of as new circumstances imposed via technology—primarily electronic/digital, biological, and chemical/pharmaceutical—that transform the condition of being human to the extent that the posthuman either no longer retains all of the same characteristics as the human or assumes characteristics additional to those that might be considered human. "Transformation" may be read by some posthumanist texts, like Fukuyama's, as negative, potentially apocalyptic, something we must work to avoid in order to maintain core aspects of the human; to others it implies potential (see Pepperell, for instance), the possibility (or in some cases, the achievement) of humans' next evolutionary step. However, "the posthuman," Hayles has written, "should not be depicted as an apocalyptic break with the past. Rather, it exists in a relation of overlapping innovation and repetition" ("Afterword" 134). Such alterations may be identified in transformations rendered by technological interventions such as intentional and unintentional genetic engineering—for example, the long-term ingestion of genetically altered dairy products or the long-term exposure to chemical toxins—or pharmacological or psychotropic-pharmacological therapy. Likewise, information technology interventions such as networked space or wearable/portable devices that link users to information exchange systems render the human more akin to Donna J. Haraway's concept of cyborg, Bruno Latour's concept of the hybrid, or even, perhaps, Teilhard de Chardin's concept of noösphere. Central to comprehending posthuman subjectivity, critical posthumanism understands the posthuman to be able to perpetually shift identities. The posthuman, to borrow from Gilles Deleuze and Félix Guattari, is in a perpetual state of becoming. Composition studies has traditionally relied upon knowing the subject as fixed, a subject more commonly associated with Enlightenment thinking.

As I mentioned earlier in this chapter, attempts to embrace a postmodern concept of a fluctuating subject have been difficult for composition studies simply because no matter the openness to postmodern thinking about subjectivity, composition studies manages to reduce the postmodern shift of subject to a codifiable, recognizable subject that can be identified as somehow operating outside of writing—still *a subject*. The posthuman, on the other hand, should be seen not as outside of writing but as an integrated part of writing, of the whole, shifting like the postmodern subject, certainly, but able to flow and redefine as the surrounding environment demands it or imposes it. How the posthuman finds itself in such a condition is central to the work of posthumanism. Ultimately, while posthumanism's object of study is the posthuman, it might be more accurate to say that the *making of the posthuman* is the central posthumanist inquiry.

The technological augmentations that I have suggested as the primary catalyst in transforming human to posthuman seem at first to be changes accepted by or imposed onto the body. However, the posthuman experience surpasses the body, encompassing mental and philosophical shifts to the extent that the overall human experience is altered. Hayles's *How We Became Posthuman: Virtual Bodies in Cybernetics, Literature, and Informatics* traces the history of mind/body dualism and the issue of disembodiment as one of her primary investigations into the posthuman. Hayles's erudite critical posthumanism well exceeds much of the science-fictionesque conversations of the posthuman as an intentionally modified human mind/body designed to supersede the human. While many popular posthumanists argue for brain augmentations, pharmaceutical interventions to mask or eliminate mental constraints such as depression, or amplification through technological body enhancements like prosthetic devices incorporated into the human to create the cyborg, others see these same interventions as potentially extending not just the human experience but human life spans. Some extend such visions to the extent of immortality through pharmaceutical and biotechnological replacement or even the possibility of consciousness uploading, an idea that suggests human thought and consciousness can be measured and transferred to other housing bodies, like computer memories, allowing the individual the possibility of perpetual eternal upload, keeping the core consciousness "alive." These mutations are often cast as conscious decisions made by the human as a means of attaining the posthuman. Much of my argument regarding posthumanism and subjectivity revolves around the idea that the shift to the posthuman is not a matter of choice—though some may choose to transform more directly—but instead a phenomenon of the current conditions of networked societies, a concept I extend later in this chapter and in detail in chapters 5 and 6. We have accepted for some time that "race" is a construct and that it doesn't really exist as such in some biological, material way. "Human" is similarly constructed within particular historical, cultural, geographical, ecological, and networked locations. As those locations change, so "human" changes.

As I have noted, there is some difficulty in locating a unified approach to posthumanist inquiry. However, many writing about posthumanism, particularly those working in the humanities, tend to attribute the origins of posthumanist thinking to Ihab Hassan, whose claim in "Prometheus as Performer" as I have quoted it earlier is often noted as the first to directly suggest a posthumanism. Others, like Hayles and Byron Hawk, offer that Michel Foucault's *The Order of Things: An Archaeology of the Human Sciences*, which predates Hassan's article by about four years, first suggests posthumanism. Foucault explains that the very idea of "man" is a historical construction and that the era of man is soon to end.[3] Origins, though, as I have noted earlier, serve little purpose other than to tie down political positions. More important to the arguments set out here than origins are the critical interventions made in posthumanism, such as those forwarded by Hayles and others.

Hayles's *How We Became Posthuman* traces the history of cybernetics as a method for accessing the conditions that have allowed for the evolution of the posthuman. Hayles's assessments of the posthuman are the most nuanced and certainly some of the most frequently referenced. Significant to Hayles's work is the idea of embodiment and the question of whether identity resides within a body or within the information carried by the body. This question of identity provides an avenue of inquiry regarding the relationship between the carbon-based body and the silicon-based body: a question of cybernetics, of the cyborg. As Hayles explains: "When information loses its body, equating humans and computers is especially easy, for the materiality in which the thinking mind is instantiated appears incidental to its essential nature" (2). Hayles adopts the metaphor of "information" as a dominant concept, questioning the very idea that information can lose its body and move through systems without body. Information, as we will see in chapters 5 and 6, is a deeply problematic metaphor for writing studies; for now, however, it is useful to understand Hayles's position regarding information movement. Such an inquiry leads to a driving question regarding whether human consciousness can be thought of in terms of informational patterns that can be moved between bodies. This inquiry grew from Hayles's own reaction to a passage in Hans Moravec's *Mind Children: The Future of Robot and Human Intelligence* that claims one day it will be possible to download human consciousness into a computer. The body, whether carbon-based or silicon-based, then, no longer matters; Cartesian debate reigns on. The locus of human subjectivity, this position contends, resides not in the individual but in information that can be transferred between bodies. Hayles is bothered by such a formulation that devalues the body and works to understand how information became disembodied and to demonstrate that there is a dynamic relationship between information and the bodies that carry information. In making such arguments, she is critical of postmodernity's focus on discourse instead of on bodies and reacts against postmodernity's position that bodies are discursive constructs, an apparent acknowledgment of feminisms' interest in bodies, lived experience, and gendered subjectivities.

In *How We Became Posthuman*, Hayles asks three fundamental questions: How did information lose its body, or how did it become conceptualized as disconnected from material form? How has the cyborg been constructed technologically and culturally? And how has the liberal humanist subject been dismantled by cybernetic discourse, or how have we become posthuman? Hayles finds many ties between the answers to these questions, central to which is the connection of informational pathways between the organic body and "prosthetic extensions," assuming that information can flow between organic body and silicon body within a single system. Likewise, the concept of the feedback loop, a concept we shall see as central to systems theories and complexity theories, "implies that the boundaries of the autonomous subject are up for grabs, since feedback loops can flow not only *within* the subject but also *between* the subject and the environment" (2, emphasis in original).

A "common theme" of the posthuman, for Hayles, is "the union of the human with the intelligent machine" (*How* 2). The posthuman is characterized by four key assumptions:

First, the posthuman view privileges informational pattern over material instantiation, so that embodiment in a biological substrate is seen as an accident over history rather than an inevitability of life. Second, the posthuman view considers consciousness, regarded as the seat of human identity in the Western tradition long before Descartes thought he was a mind thinking, as an epiphenomenon, as an evolutionary upstart trying to claim that it is the whole show when in actuality it is only a minor sideshow. Third, the posthuman view thinks of the body as the original prosthesis we all learn to manipulate, so that extending or replacing the body with other prostheses becomes a continuation of a process that began before we were born. Fourth, and most important, by these and other means, the posthuman view configures human being so that it can be seamlessly articulated with intelligent machines. In the posthuman, there are no essential differences or absolute demarcations between bodily existence and computer simulation, cybernetic mechanism and biological organism, robot teleology and human goals. (2–3)

Hayles turns to C. B. McPherson's 1962 text *The Political Theory of Possessive Individualism: Hobbes to Locke* in order to explain the shift from the liberal humanist subject to the posthuman subject. Of the liberal humanist subject, McPherson writes, "Its possessive quality is found in its conception of the individual as essentially the proprietor of his own person or capacities, *owing nothing to society for them*. . . . The human essence *is freedom from the wills of others*, and freedom is a function of possession" (qtd. in Hayles, *How* 3, emphasis in Hayles). Hayles's highlighted phrases in the McPherson quote identify points of departure for examining the differences between the liberal humanist subject and the posthuman. "Owing nothing to society for them" is credited to arguments of Thomas Hobbes and John Locke about humans in a "state of nature" prior to the domination of market society. The idea of ownership of the self is thought to predate market domination and allows a relationship to be formed between the individual and the society; we might think of this as the ability to determine to sell one's self or labor for wages. "The liberal self," Hayles writes, "is produced by market relations and does not in fact predate them" (3). The inconsistency, Hayles explains by way of McPherson, "is resolved in the posthuman by doing away with the 'natural' self. The posthuman subject is an amalgam, a collection of heterogeneous components, a material-informational entity whose boundaries undergo continuous construction and reconstruction" (3). The idea that the subject maintains "agency, desire, or will" that can be distinguished from the "will of others" is "undercut in the posthuman, for the posthuman's collective heterogeneous quality implies a distributed cognition located in disparate parts that may be in only tenuous communication with one another" (3–4).

Where Hayles ends up is in a claim that human subjectivity does not face a future in a silicon bottle, that human embodiment prevents a complete melding between human and intelligent machine. She explains:

> Interpreted through metaphors resonant with cultural meanings, the body itself is a congealed metaphor, a physical structure whose constraints and possibilities have been formed by an evolutionary history that intelligent machines do not share. Humans may enter into symbiotic relationships with intelligent machines (already the case, for example, in computer-assisted surgery); they may be displaced by intelligent machines (already in effect, for example, at Japanese and American assembly plants that use robotic arms for labor); but there is a limit to how seamlessly humans can be articulated with intelligent machines, which remain distinctly different from humans in their embodiments. (*How* 284)

Yet, Hayles does not disavow the possibilities ensconced in a posthuman future. She concludes: "Although some current versions of the posthuman point toward the anti-human and the apocalyptic, we can craft others that will be conductive to the long-range survival of humans and other life-forms, biological and artificial, with whom we share the planet and ourselves" (291).

Drawing on Hayles's elaborate assessment of the posthuman, Jill Didur turns to comments made by Peter Sloterdijk comparing humanist ideals to genetic engineering as a method for establishing critical posthumanism and for unpacking Sloterdijk's claims as employing a rhetoric of improvement similar to that of genetic engineering corporation Monsanto. Sloterdijk maintains that "the advance of reason is not an emancipation from the body but a certain way of conditioning the body. Seen in this light, humanist education and genetic engineering—the selection or creation of genes that will fashion people who are more healthy, more intelligent, more attractive, perhaps more ethical—are closely related" (qtd. in Didur 99).

Of course, Sloterdijk's comments were not taken lightly by the German public media, given the suggestion that manipulation to the end of the *über-*human might be a possibility. From the popular posthumanist perspective, we might think of Sloterdijk as running in the opposite direction of Fukuyama, who asks, "What will happen to political rights once we are able to, in effect, breed some people with saddles on their backs and others with boots and spurs?," and then encourages global governmental regulation of biotechnologies (10). Sloterdijk, on the other hand, seems to cheer on the possibility that such "breeding" can occur. However, what Didur points out about Sloterdijk's equation is a similarity between his claims about genetic engineering as the end of humanism and the rhetorics used by biotech companies like Monsanto who "use similar rhetorical strategies to legitimate their research and patenting of genetically modified life forms" (100).[4] What Didur argues, then, is that both "Sloterdijk and Monsanto's discourse shuttles between a perception of identity as always already hybrid, or a chimera of nature and culture, while at the same time claiming to improve or even perfect nature in the name of humanity—effectively co-opting posthuman discourse and containing its critique of their universalizing, disembodied views" (100). Ultimately, Didur is working to promote a "more radical notion of posthumanism [that] can serve as a basis for critiquing what is essentially a disembodied colonial attitude toward the theory/practice of biotech research today" (100). Didur notes that the rhetorics of both Sloterdijk and Monsanto seem to want to present a perception of humanity and genetic modification (plant alteration, specifically) as essentially hybrid. Sloterdijk shows "man" as having always been bound to technology, his tools changing from stones to more contemporary "technologies"; geneticists (Didur cites Cornell rice research specialist Susan McCouch) show how all of the Earth's crops are genetically modified (101). For both Sloterdijk and Monsanto, then, their rhetorical goal is to show genetic modification as humans' way of perfecting nature and undermining any concept of division between human and nature. For Didur, though, critical posthumanism offers a way not of seeking origination and division between human and nature but of questioning whether such a division can even be identified.

While Didur's engagement with Sloterdijk, Monsanto, and genetic manipulation is itself interesting and extremely important, I find her method and ends telling, both in removing subjectivity as the cornerstone of study for composition studies and for developing a more critical approach to the "post"—in both posthumanism and postcomposition. As Didur makes explicit, Sloterdijk's and Monsanto's rhetorics are "key to agribusinesses' claim of ownership over the genetically modified organisms they produce" (102). By adapting a critical perspective that asks not of origin and ownership, critical posthumanism is able to reestablish the very kinds of questions and claims that could lead to such a position in the first place. This is the kind of critical perspective postcomposition seeks to engage. Yet, most telling is Didur's concluding recognition that critical posthumanism allows for a shifting, fluid approach to understanding debates like debates of genetic modification. Didur's final call for critical posthumanism encourages me toward a willingness to identify that key assumptions about central disciplinary issues (like subjectivity) can be rethought in beneficial ways or, more accurately, can be productively disrupted. What posthumanism provides first, then, is a vocabulary for such disruption and second, a literal, active disruption of subjectivity.

Given that much of that disruption is reliant upon an assumption of interaction between the human subject and the technological, it makes a good deal of sense to become hyper-alert to not merely the forms such interactions take but also the ramifications of such interactions. Mark Hansen's *Embodying Technesis: Technology beyond Writing* offers a sophisticated consideration of the technological relationship, positing an interaction that sees technology as a co-determinant in the evolution of the human and of all the world's systems. As Hansen explains, technology needs to be understood as an active part of the formation not only of human reality but of all reality. Hansen turns to Walter Benjamin as a means for moving beyond Deleuze and Guattari's account of technology, identifying that Benjamin's "view of technology as material force of natural history and his exploration of agency in the technological world on mimetic grounds" provide two key elements in understanding the relationship between human and technology: "(1) an account of the real that recognizes the *presocial* role of technology as agent of material complexification and (2) a correlative account of becoming (what Benjamin calls 'intervention') that foregrounds corporeal or physiological adaptation to the *alien* rhythms of the contemporary mechanosphere" (234, emphasis in original).[5] It is specifically Hansen's notion of adaptation that becomes crucial in understanding the posthuman, as it works to consider how technologies "complexify" human life. Hansen, then, evaluates "the role technology plays in twentieth-century theoretical discourse" in order to "prepare the ground for an expanded analysis of technological materiality, one capable of exploring specifically those materializations through which technologies mediate the material rhythms of embodied life" (4). Central to this project is the examination of the philosophical and rhetorical tradition of "putting-into-discourse of technology," or what Hansen identifies as "technesis" (4).

Technesis, Hansen argues, has been used reductively by thinkers as a method for "a progressive assimilation of technology to thought" (4). That is, technology, Hansen argues, has been seen as little more than a trope, not as a reality of existence. "From the groundbreaking explorations of Heidegger and Freud to the more localized interventions of Stephen Greenblatt and Donna Haraway, technology has been repeatedly invoked as a means of historicizing theoretical claims, of stamping them with the indelible mark of the empirical" (5). For Hansen, though, technology exists beyond the discursive, inextricably interwoven with human life and culture, more akin to traditional thinking regarding "nature," a force inseparable from life. As Hayles puts it, "For Hansen, technology is the primary determinant of the human lifeworld and has been so for thousands of years" ("Foreword" vi). What Hansen does, then, is disrupt theoretical thinking about technology, forcing a reconsideration of the relationship between discourse/linguistic interventions into culture and life and the traditionally neglected role of material technology. What Hansen also does is provide the posthumanist thinker with a more integrated vision of the technological/human amalgam beyond mere augmentation, a concept that emphasizes a central object/body that is transformed by the addition or alteration of parts rather than a concept that sees the central objects/body as being integrated to the extent that the parts render a new whole. When Picard is assimilated by the Borg, we still see Picard—his identifiableness continues. But integration suggests a way of identifying the whole rather than its constitutive parts. The bond between the human and material technology is recast as inseparable and the posthuman as both inevitable and achieved. Yes, resistance is futile; you will be/have been assimilated.

One of the failures of composition studies in recognizing the significance of the role of (information) technologies upon subjectivity is its continued adherence to ideas that writing technologies are somehow independent of subjectivity and that they serve as functioning tools for the production and distribution of writing, or in more sophisticated senses, the circulation of information. Posthumanist thinking, and Hansen in particular, though, expose imbrications of subject and technologies that insist upon not a reconsideration/rearticulation of the technologies employed by subjects—writing or otherwise—but a complete overhaul to the very ideas that (1) there can be identifiable separation between subject and technology and (2) the humanist idea of subject provides intellectual value to theorizing writing. Yet, few in composition studies have engaged technology in any form as inseparable from subjects. The technology is the subject; the subject is the technology. Given composition studies' focus on student writing-subjects and that those subjects are inseparable from technology—for composition students embroiled in the culture of corporate America, this is easily identifiable in the pervasiveness of wearable and integrated information technology devices—we can no longer address writing-subjects, student or other, —as subjects but instead must begin to consider the posthuman position (or at minimum transhuman). Such a shift, then, demands a realignment of focus not upon the individual as producer/originator of writing but upon the complex systems in which the posthuman is located, endlessly bound in the fluidity and shiftiness of writing. Metaphors like Lyotard's notion of nodes or Gregory Ulmer's idea of conductors may be beneficial in theorizing the position of subjects within larger systems and ecologies, but like all metaphors, they limit what we can know about the concepts they represent. And, as metaphors, those constructions stamp a form of authenticity onto the subject as somehow still identifiable within the complex systems of which they are part. Likewise, as I show in later chapters, concepts like nodes and conductors still rely upon identifiable agents within the system. One of the primary benefits to accepting posthumanism as a point of disruption to our understanding of subjects is specifically that it allows us to relinquish hold over nodes or conductors in favor of a more dynamic view of system, or the complexity of system; we can, à la Hansen, "complexify." Once we are able to dispense with the subject as central, composition studies is no longer composition studies; its future is one of postcomposition. Such a change also invokes a recognition that composition studies' past is not necessarily as we have told ourselves it was; our past is one not of writing but of subject.

Changing the Subject

As composition theorists, if we work in the realm of agents, subjects or consciousness, then our descriptions of writing will only ever present it as an instrument, as a means by which something else is arrived at. But if we give up the deep-seated and ultimate unfounded assumption that writing is a function and product of individuals interacting with the world, with culture, with tradition, or even with themselves, then we might begin to address the many implications of the proposition that writing is a phenomenon of constant (re)circulation, one that promises the representation of something else but never actually delivers. There is no theory of the subject that can contribute to this.
—Raúl Sánchez, *The Function of Theory in Composition Studies*

The subject for composition studies largely evolved as a concept from the early neo-romantics who created student-centered thinking. The subject of the early work in composition studies was understood to be the "self," and discourse regarding subjectivity in composition studies often conflates issues of self, subject, voice, and identity into rather generic, unproblematic formations. Subject, as we have come to understand, is a much more intricate issue. Interestingly, composition studies has retained a conservative Enlightenment humanist approach to considering the subject in singular, individual terms, yet current thinking about subjectivity clearly unfolds ideas that subjectivity in the new media era is produced as a collective, media-driven subjectivity, and posthumanist thinking acutely critiques any concept of the individual subject in light of numerous technologies, including informational and biological (more on this later). Likewise, systems theories and complexity theories question the very possibility of an autonomous subject. Whether or not there is any utility to such arguments (though I believe there is), it is important to take from such thinking the ability to consider how collective media, information technologies, and bio/cybernetic technologies influence subject formation as a method for considering the role composition studies and its disciplinary attachment to FYC employ to form a system for universalizing student subjects. Composition studies' attention to student subjects and its eagerness for normalized intellectual activity, FYC curriculum, and managerial oversight indicts composition studies as partner in larger political and institutional actions that actually deny subjectivity in favor of a normalized collective. And there can be no doubt that despite individual claims to the contrary—most often defended with claims of individual classroom practice as legitimate validation (or individual defensiveness)—and that as corporate universities, state legislative regulations, and disciplinary oversight become more the norm and more efficient at instituting control, composition studies becomes more adept at modifying student subjectivity, creating a greater homogenization of subjects. And, no matter how you slice it, administrative, institutional, curricular, and political normalizing can only be code for homogenization. One of the primary tasks postcomposition is to work away from such normalizing efforts in order to dodge composition studies' enchantment with subjectivity, primarily as resistant members of the discipline.

To begin such work, we must first acknowledge that the primacy of the student subject in composition studies results not from a genuine disciplinary interest in students as subjects, in students as writers, or even in subjects in general but grows from the simple fact that subjects are the primary capital of composition studies. And, in saying so, we can easily see how composition studies' conservatism grows from a desire to control that capital. It is, we must admit, much easier to identify and control this capital, particularly when the field retains the right of subjectification of the student under the guise of writing instruction, than it is to control something as amorphous and problematic as writing. Subjects are the economy of composition studies, and part of the field's encumbrance in this economy is its historic/bureaucratic adherence to economy rather than to (or at least not in conjunction with) ecology. In chapters 5 and 6, I will explain and develop a more expansive ecological approach to theorizing writing. For now, while acknowledging the similarities between economic and ecological methodologies and metaphors, I want to offer that these approaches are distinctly different and that composition studies' adherence to economic models have forced the field to value academic pursuits—those that deal in the capital of the institution, the students—over intellectual pursuits that often ignore the confine of capital in favor of the movement of speculation and possibility. Of course, I should also note that composition studies' adherence to economic models is less a composition studies problem per se than it is a condition of higher education in general. After all, it is difficult, if not impossible, for a discipline whose identity is bound to FYC (an academic cash cow) to do anything but adhere to economic models in the current economic and political climate in which higher education exists. In other words, though I criticize composition studies for entrenching itself in economic approaches over ecological approaches, it is probably unreasonable to suggest that the discipline has the power to actually make such decisions in the application of its work (teaching), even if it can in the abstraction of its work (theory), without the literal permission of the college, the university, and the state legislature.

My argument in this chapter is intended as a realignment that foregrounds the study of writing over the production of student subject through the teaching of writing. Inherently in this argument is a repositioning of subject as no longer central to writing theory. Rethinking the very idea of subject/subjectivity is crucial theoretical work, and as many theorists have already shown (Martin Heidegger, Friedrich Nietzsche, Louis Althusser, Jacques Derrida, Deleuze and Guattari, and Ulmer, for instance), subjectivity really can be dispensed with as the primary theoretical object. Reconsidering the subject as the primary object of study/management of composition studies and resisting the field's subjectification of the student, in particular, though, is a recasting not just of the writing-subject but of the very idea of subject and subjectivity. This is an actual rescuing of the subject by not allowing the perpetual manipulation and normalization of student subjects by the academy and instead freeing the subject into a constant process of becoming. Many will likely bristle at this turn, given composition studies' investment in the subject from a disciplinary standpoint. Without subjectivity, many may argue, we lose individuality, the opportunity for resistance, identity, and other opportunities for each of us—or more accurately, each of our students—to find position in the world exclusive to each. But such ideas are holdovers from romantic notions of Enlightenment thinking that the individual subject is unique, identifiable (even if only self-identifiable), and somehow of value. Even if we move beyond the romantic formation of subjectivity and adopt postmodern or feminist notions of subjectivity, which stress permeability and provisional identities instead of intrinsic consistency, the degree of flexibility in such formations of subjectivity neither account for the full degree of fluctuation of contingent subjectivity nor fully develop theories regarding the position of the subject within social networks. Each of these ideas, though—individuality, subject, resistance, and permeability, for instance—is a function of writing; they are not somehow extracted, removed from writing and able to appear outside the textual sphere. They are neither the reason for nor the result of writing but a function of writing. The removal of subject from the scene of writing confirms that it is not who writes that is important but that writing is there. The act of writing, for instance, is inherently an act of resistance; it does not require a subject; it does not need an identifiable outlet of transfer to the subject from the text. Disruption is inherent in the mechanism of writing (see Žižek; Badiou; Derrida); it is not the intent of the subject. Writing resists. Ultimately, though, the thing that probably matters least in understanding *writing* is understanding subjects. To be clear: this is not a claim that there are no subjects, that subjects do not matter, or that subjects do not affect what we know about writing. This is simply the claim that in order to develop more accurate ways of describing what writing is and what it does, the subject must be removed not just from the center of the stage but from the theater and perhaps the entire theater district. Such a maneuver asks for a change to composition studies' gestalt, but in doing so, such a change inevitably also changes the apparatus through which composition studies engages its objects of study, including subject. This shift, then, also provides an opportunity to reconfigure the very idea of subjectivity and the subject, both in relation to writing and beyond.

Of course, any claim that eliminates or even reconfigures subjectivity as the central object of study in composition studies or in relation to writing is susceptible to critique from feminist and other critical, theoretical, and activist perspectives. Given the persuasive arguments that many marginalized others have only relatively recently acquired subjectivity, recasting either the possibility or the value of subjectivity may be legitimately viewed by some as changing the game—moving the goal line—just as the underdog is gaining ground, and that to do so is detrimental to the interests of marginalized others (perhaps particularly when such arguments are made primarily by white male academics). Without dismissing such important critiques, it may be useful to acknowledge that, as Cary Wolfe notes in *Critical Environments*, it is not as though we have much choice about becoming posthuman; it is upon us. This is not an assertion; it is a condition. Feminist thinkers like Donna Haraway, as *Critical Environments* points out, have "argued as forcefully as anyone that our current moment is irredeemably posthumanist because of the boundary breakdowns between animal and human, organism and machine, and the physical and nonphysical" (44).[6] What we must keep in mind, too, is that we cannot assume that the biological alterations that can be considered part of the transformation to the posthuman also account for a recasting of constructs like gender. Since gender is a construct, we cannot link it to the "human"; it can and does operate just as forcefully, though perhaps in different ways, and with just as serious and material consequences, in the posthuman. The same can be said of other constructed markers like race. Any articulation of biological shifts in the posthuman should not be read as implying an equating of the posthuman with biology, and, thus, inadvertently race and gender with biology, therefore signaling that we can somehow dispense with such categories by simply saying the posthuman is unavoidable. To do so would diminish the importance of understanding how gender, race, and other critical categories operate within complex networks and systems, as well as in relation to/with the posthuman.

Composition studies' fascination with subjects reveals, perhaps, a will to stability, and as Sánchez and others have made clear, the networked hypercirculatory culture in which we now live not only resists stability but flat-out denies the possibility of stability. As Sánchez puts it, "The fiction of stability does not entirely explain writing's work in the world" (86). The embedded flaw of composition studies has been its ubiquitous attention to the subject in manners that romanticize the subject in ways that, as Sánchez explains, constrain "attempts to theorize the reproduction and circulation of writing" (86). As I noted in the previous chapter, postcomposition approaches to theorizing writing should now consider more directly spatial understandings of writing than does composition studies. Much of this spatial account can provide descriptions of writing in terms of circulation and network, facets of ecological, spatial thinking rather than economic thinking. In order to do so, the very ground of subjectivity must first be set aside, both the liberal humanist version of the independent subject-agent and the postmodern fragmentary subject. By foregrounding theories of writing in an idea that writing is produced by/originates in a subject, a writing-subject, any theory of writing is necessarily reduced to a secondary status behind a theory of the subject that produces writing. By seeing writing not as the product (or process) of a producing subject but as a never-ending (re)circulation in which larger producing/desiring machines generate and perpetuate writing throughout network, system, and environment, we are better able to attend to the issue of writing and circulation as primary to the theoretical work of postcomposition. Invocation of the subject as generator/producer/originator of writing inherently accounts for some notion of subject as individual and independent of the network/writing, a notion that becomes obsolete in the spatial, networked fluidity of writing circulation. Likewise, even if we are to fall back to a position that accepts postmodern, fragmented, multiple subjects or feminist provisional subjects as ways of talking about subjects in relation to writing, we are still talking about knowable subjects, and in doing so we are acknowledging that even in the fragmentation and fluctuation of the postmodern and/or feminist subject, there is still a deep-seated desire to identify the individual as encapsulating some identifiable, possibly unique, moment of subjectivity, whether immediately identifiable or not. To acknowledge the fragmentary subject or the unified subject is to embrace a myth of subjectivity that postmodernism works to demystify hand-in-hand with objectivity. To this end, composition studies remains a predominantly modernist endeavor (as are most forms of education) in its adherence to the primacy of subjects and subjectivity. Modernism serves composition studies well in that "the essence of Modernism," Clement Greenberg's "Modernist Painting" explains, "lies in the use of characteristic methods of a discipline to criticize the discipline itself, not in order to subvert it but in order to entrench it more firmly in its area of competence" (qtd. in Taylor 74). To borrow from Bruno Latour, "we have always been modern."

One way perhaps to shift away from a focus on subjects is to consider the role of agency in discussions of subjectivity and to recognize that agency is not an issue of the subject but rather an issue of the subject in ecological relationships. Just as writing is itself resistance, so, too, is writing agency. What is more interesting/useful in studying writing is not the agency of the subject or even of the writing-subject but the agency of writing itself, be it identifiable agency of specific texts, the recurring agency of writing in multiple, networked formations, or the intellectual agency of a concept, idea, or theory. Postcomposition works to account for subject agency not as independent of writing but as a function of writing. In turn, then, studies that theorize the ways in which writing and circulation convey agency become central to understanding the function of writing.

Jim Ridolfo and Dànielle Nicole DeVoss's essay "Composing for Recomposition: Rhetorical Velocity and Delivery" hints at thinking toward textual agency over subject agency. The essay relies on Ridolfo's concept of "rhetorical velocity," "a conscious rhetorical concern for distance, travel, speed, and time, pertaining specifically to theorizing instances of strategic appropriation by a third party." The article works to develop new ways of thinking about rhetorical concepts of delivery in a digital age, particularly in situations when writers anticipate "re-appropriation by third parties." Ridolfo and DeVoss pose two critical lines of inquiry. The first explores the need for composition studies (though they use the disciplinary marker "rhetoric and composition") to reconsider rhetorical theories of delivery the field has traditionally embraced given that traditional theories of delivery do not account for methods of delivery needed in writing via new media and digital technologies. Second, Ridolfo and DeVoss argue that because new media technologies not only allow for but encourage alteration in re-circulation and in what the authors identify as "remix" (a term borrowed from Larry Lessig's 2005 CCCC talk, which was borrowed from the music industry), new theories of delivery must account for an anticipation that content and form of writing will be appropriated by third-party users. Rhe-torical velocity, Ridolfo and DeVoss explain, is

> a strategic approach to composing for rhetorical delivery. It is both a way of considering delivery as rhetorical mode, aligned with an under-standing of how texts work as a component of a strategy. In the inventive thinking of composing, rhetorical velocity is the strategic theorizing for how a text might be recomposed (and *why* it might be recomposed) by third parties, and how this recomposing may be useful or not to the short- or long-term rhetorical objectives of the rhetorician.

Ridolfo and DeVoss go on to show that rhetorical velocity must also account for the speed at which "information composed to be recomposed travels—that is, it refers to the understanding and rapidity at which information is crafted, delivered, distributed, recomposed, redelivered, redistributed, etc., across physical and virtual networks and spaces."

Beyond Ridolfo and DeVoss's primary arguments, the concept of rhe-torical velocity participates in the crucial conversation regarding writing in a hyper-circulatory, networked space. Questions like Ridolfo and De-Voss's propel the postcomposition inquiry to develop new ways of thinking about writing beyond classroom situations and beyond student subjects. And though the rhetorical velocity essay does not directly address issues of agency, it subtly nudges toward a theory that embeds agency not in the writing subject but in writing itself. By combining concepts of information circulation and expectations of remix, Ridolfo and DeVoss anticipate a shift of focus from the writing-subject to the writing itself. Agency—what we have traditionally thought of as the power of subjectivity—moves free of the subject, gaining occupancy in space through circulation and through appropriation, remix, and recirculation. No longer does agency remain with individual agents; instead, it travels, shifts, and evolves through the circu-lation of writing. Agency gains power not in individual nodes or conduc-tors within the circulatory network but through its movement/velocity in network space, what Ridolfo has called "flows of information." (I take up "flow" and "information" in later chapters.) Agency can no longer be understood as province of individual subjects, what they do, or what they write. Instead, it is becoming increasingly more useful to understand agency as entangled with and as a function of writing and that writing is never attributable to individual subjects; instead, it is part of a more complex ecology within the network. Ridolfo and DeVoss, though, encumber rhetorical velocity within the same economic concepts and language that have limited what can be theorized about writing. Theorizing rhetorical velocity into a more ecologically based complex-system approach will better serve what rhetorical velocity can show about writing and writing systems.

There is no need to recount a history of subjectivity generally or specific to composition studies. Numerous texts have explained those intellectual histories, and recapping them would be superfluous (see Lester Faigley's *Fragments of Rationality*, for instance). Instead, in what remains of this chapter, I briefly look at two texts that have been influential in describing the role of the subject in composition studies as a matter of movement from composition studies' embrace of subjects and subjectivity to a postcomposition vision of the subject as minor consequence in the study of writing. I then consider the calls Sánchez makes at the end of *The Function of Theory in Composition Studies* to develop theories of writing not dependent upon theories of subjects.

Lester Faigley's landmark book *Fragments of Rationality: Postmodernity and the Subject of Composition* extends postmodern critique of both Enlightenment and romantic formations of subject into composition studies' assumptions about subjectivity. Working to clarify distinctions between concepts of subjectivity, Faigley shows how composition studies often conflates two primary ideas of subjectivity: that of a coherent self capable of knowing itself and its world (high modernism) and that of an individual capable of changing identities freely by way of what it consumes (postmodernism, or a really reductive version of postmodernism). Throughout *Fragments of Rationality*, Faigley maintains that many of the disciplinary arguments found in composition studies are the result of "disagreements over the subjectivities that teachers of writing want students to occupy" (17). Faigley's goal, then, is to examine the role of the subject throughout composition studies' history and how the discipline has articulated approaches to subjectivity as a means of defining the field's central inquiries as attempts to identify and manage student subjects. As Faigley puts it, writing teachers are "as much or more interested in *whom* they want their students to be as in *what* they want their students to write" (113, emphasis in original). Neither of these goals, of course, actually have anything to do with writing; one focuses on subject formation, the other on an appropriateness of content or thinking. Faigley argues that "even if assumptions about subjectivities that student writers should occupy are not as singular or as well understood as expressive realism . . . shared assumptions about subjectivities—the selves we want our students to be—still shape judgments of writing quality" (114). Yet, Faigley seems to waver between the modern and the postmodern subject, often leaning toward the postmodern but never quite embracing either position. Faigley accepts Lyotard's notion that subjects can be thought of like "nodes in networks of discourses" but offers little else to accept a full alliance with the postmodern. For Faigley, the subject is only "momentarily situated," able to cross social divisions and negotiate "among many competing discourses" (239).

Faigley, through a historical and disciplinary examination of the subject, argues that "the preservation of a truncated rational subject in writing pedagogy is not only a matter of relations between the educational system and the economic system but also involved in the disciplinary regime of composition studies" (133). Because *Fragments of Rationality* predates the new media, digital, and computer explosion of the turn of the twenty-first century, it cannot be critiqued for the oversimplified version of network it addresses in the final third of the book, relying predominantly on Lyotard's concept of node and network. Yet, in its address of networked classrooms, Faigley works to decenter student subjectivity, perhaps the first phase of recognizing that in networked environments, subjects cannot be the central figure of inquiry. Electronic discourse, Faigley argues, "explodes the belief in a stable unified self" (199). Turning to Baudrillard's notion of the "revenge of the subject," Faigley begins to extrapolate that "the space for the autonomous subject with a capacity for critical thought collapses" (213). For Faigley, then, composition studies has altered student subjects into objects. What Faigley tacitly anticipates is the need for new ways of theorizing subjectivity beyond the conflicting and constraining means adopted by composition studies. To be clear, Faigley calls for "new metaphors for the subject" as necessary for continuing to think about how writing is taught; however, he does not extend his consideration of subject beyond the teaching of writing directly upon the phenomena of writing. Nor does he call for substantial theoretical work to this end, only metaphoric description. Despite this typical entrapment in metaphors of disciplinary reductiveness, Faigley does begin to open the doors to disruption of the student subject as the center of composition studies' focus.

Fragments of Rationality is one of the most important interventions into the role of the subject in composition studies. However, despite its rigorous look at composition studies' approach to subject, the book also exposes the underlying difficulties in addressing subjectivity within composition studies: the reliance upon economic systems in order to understand subjectivity and, in turn, writing. Likewise, in relying upon economic metaphors and systems, Faigley clearly limits what is to be known within composition studies about subjectivity to a notion of student subjects.

Predating *Fragments of Rationality* by three years, Susan Miller's groundbreaking book *Rescuing the Subject: A Critical Introduction to Rhetoric and the Writer* provides the first substantial address of subjectivity in composition studies via a historical survey of rhetoric and its relationship with writing. Within a historical examination of writing and rhetoric, Miller poses two crucial hypotheses for composition studies. The first is that histories of writing demonstrate that there was an inevitable move to a distinct writing-subject—the writer. For composition studies, the writing-subject was embraced in the form of the student writer. Student writers, a construct unique to composition studies and to American education, Miller posits, are and should be the central object of study for composition studies as student writers possess the same characteristics as all writers. Thus, examination of student writers provides insight into the processes of all writers and, by way of writers, into the phenomena of writing. Miller specifically names the (student) writer and the processes through which those writing-subjects write as the central object of study of composition studies. But, central to Miller's purpose in naming the subject as composition studies' object of study is also to argue that subjects are "mere metaphor," offering no significant perspective on the world; yet, Miller is not willing to fully relinquish the unified speaker, instead, just as Faigley would later do, conceiving of a subject that hovers somewhere between embracing and rejecting the unified subject. Miller implies the possibility of the postmodern subject, but that implication is not realized.

Second, by linking writing to rhetoric, Miller reveals a history of rhetoric that proceeds from rhetorics that work in accompaniment with oral traditions to rhetorics that are more applicable to traditions of writing. This historical shift, which echoes Walter J. Ong's description of shifts from orality to literacy, helps establish a disciplinary need for melding rhetoric and composition into a unified—or, at minimum, a tightly attuned—center of inquiry.

Miller's primary claims about the relationship between rhetoric and writing and her claims about the writing-subject as composition studies' central object of study serve as crucial historical markers in and of themselves in the field. Recognition of the differences between oral-based rhetorics and writing-based rhetorics provided composition studies with validation for tying writing and rhetoric together in academic atmospheres of the middle to late 1980s. Likewise, definitive acknowledgment of a need to embrace the student writer as the primary object of study signified a key moment in composition studies' ongoing quest for disciplinary identity, validating not only the field's attention to student writers but providing an indirect claim over writing via subject's production of writing. Walking hand-in-hand with the decade-earlier process movement's provision of something identifiable to teach in writing classrooms, Miller provided the rationalization that composition studies also had a research object beyond the writing classroom: the inhabitants of those classrooms. But, like Faigley, Miller could not anticipate the dramatic shift in what writing has become in the twenty-plus years since the publication of *Rescuing the Subject*. Miller's claims provide an accurate and important historical look at rhetoric and writing-subjects, but those moments have passed. Current hyper-circulatory, networked approaches to understand writing demand not only that Miller's history of rhetoric and writing be extended to identify that new modes of rhetoric must now be understood as being tied to digital, electronic writing systems but also that those same rhetorics must now evolve independently of rhetorics that were retrofitted to writing from oral traditions. Gregory Ulmer has extended the transition from orality to literacy (reading and writing) to include electronic/digital-based technologies, identifying the next shift in this history to "electracy," which, according to Ulmer, is an emerging condition of writing that "is to digital media what literacy is to print," in which writers perpetually invent electracy (*Internet* 7). Historical examinations like Miller's would now turn toward the electrate. Likewise, composition studies should no longer accept the student writing-subject as the central object of study. Instead, composition studies can acknowledge that by focusing on writing-subjects, little will be revealed about writing in its current formations.

Sánchez's *The Function of Theory in Composition Studies* is the first scholarly work to extend the idea that writing can and should be studied without binding that study to subjects. Using Miller as a departure point for assessment of the subject in composition studies and the role of rhetoric in developing more useful understandings of writing, Sánchez proposes that "if we can account for writing without recourse to the subject, we will come closer to describing its proliferation and circulation in an increasingly networked world than we currently are" (86). Sánchez is quick to grant Miller clemency for her willingness to fictionalize writing's stability because as "writing pours forth from countless computers and travels to multiple places around the world instantly, simultaneously, and continuously, Miller's postmodern proposition seems less certain" (86). The fiction of stability,

Sánchez argues, no longer applies. Sánchez's final chapter, "Writing without Subjects," critiques composition studies' mystification and romanticizing of the subject as an encumbrance that constrains "attempts to theorize the reproduction and circulation of writing" (86).

According to Sánchez, composition studies' long-held attachment to and elevation of rhetorical theory and rhetorical theory's kinship with hermeneutics have prevented any theoretical advancement of notions of agency or subject beyond a "highly individualized and prediscursive notion of the subject" (87). Sánchez works, then, to evaluate the sticky alignment of traditional rhetorical theory with postmodern theory. The result of this analysis is a question regarding the perpetual rehabilitation of the subject's presence as the *one* who must speak or write in order for something to be spoken or written. Neither rhetorical theory nor its intersections with postmodern theory, Sánchez posits, is "equipped even today to address writing beyond the measure of the individual" (90). "What remains," Sánchez continues, "is to explain that the cultural work that *is* writing is more complex, more pervasive, and therefore more worthy of sustained intellectual inquiry than the content contained *in* writing by individual subjects" (94, emphasis in original). Sánchez anticipates the criticism that it might be argued that composition studies take into account the social nature of language and situate the writing subject within "complex networks of cultural, political, ideological, and hegemonic forces" (95). Accurately, then, he explains that the result of composition studies' social turn has been the investment of traditional writing subjects *into* such systems or networks, not altering in any way the presence or authority of the subject and not providing any substantial theorization of the subject separate from or different from traditional conceptions of the subject. Continued authorization of and attention to the subject, Sánchez contends, might be "fraught with peril and, in the end, quite possibly beside the point" (95).

Sánchez concludes with a call for a new paradigm that focuses composition theory inquiry specifically upon writing, not upon subjects. Sánchez proposes a crucial question for composition studies: "At the level of the individual body, how does the socially and culturally embedded (f)act of writing occur and what can be said about it?" (97–98). In the remainder of this chapter and the rest of this book, I take up Sánchez's question and call but in a way, perhaps, that he did not imagine, moving the attention even further from individual subjects toward more complex understandings of the ecological systems of writing circulation.

Very few works in composition studies have turned to theories of the posthuman or posthumanity as means for theorizing writing or even the writing-subject. The exception is Byron Hawk's Winterowd Award–winning *A Counter-History of Composition: Toward Methodologies of Complexity*, which turns to posthumanism in its attempt to rethink the role of vitalism in composition studies' history via a range of methods, including complexity theory. I will return to complexity theory in chapters 5 and 6, but for now I want to look at Hawk's posthumanist turn, which he employs as a means for establishing what he calls "complex vitalism" (158). Noting a distinction between theories of human action that "operate from an opposition between human intention as active and material context as static and passive, thus privileging human action," and a humanist model in which human action functions as part of the feedback loop, Hawk proposes a posthumanist model that "sees humans as functioning parts of life, and any theory of action or change must take this larger, more complex situatedness into account" (158). Hawk ties this posthumanist model to Deleuze and Guattari's desire to see any body "organic or inorganic, not as a whole but as a constellation of parts that participate in multiple systems" (158). Turning to the opening section of *Anti-Oedipus: Capitalism and Schizophrenia* called "The Desiring-Machines," Hawk brings Deleuze and Guattari's notion of machines into the posthumanist perspectives as a means of showing the interaction not just between human and machine but between the machines themselves, machines that are neither objects to be used by subjects nor objects that suppress subjects. Instead, each machine is connected and is part. "Everything is Machine," Deleuze and Guattari explain (2). The human (though they use the word "man"), they continue, "does not live as nature, but as a process of production. There is no such thing as either man or nature now, only a process that produces one within the other and couples machines together. Producing-machines, desiring-machines everywhere, schizophrenic machines, all of species of life: the self and the non-self, outside and inside, no longer have any meaning whatsoever" (2). This is the basis for Deleuze and Guattari's posthumanism (though they don't employ the term) and, tied with Hayles's address of cognitive distribution and feedback loops, is the place from which Hawk establishes a posthumanist theory for composition studies. Through Deleuze and Guattari's posthumanism, Hawk is able to reposition the subject not as individual but as part of the whole: "The subject is not a person, a whole, but a part of the whole that is made up of parts: it is part of the machine and also itself divided into cuts from the continuous material flow and parts of the detached signifying chain" (160). This kind of relationship between subjects and whole systems/networks is also taken up by others attending to complexity theories in composition studies, such as Edith Wyschogrod in "Networking the Unpredictable: The

Lure of Complexity," in which she cites Jean-Pierre Dupuy's "subjectless processes in which 'the subject is not a ghost in the cerebral machine but the machine itself'" (871).

Hawk's objective in turning to posthumanism is to develop more fully a theory of complexity and as part of this task to develop a posthuman pedagogy for composition studies. Yet, embedded in his objective is a sophisticated theory of the subject that radically disrupts composition studies' traditional consideration of—and, I would argue, encumbrance with—the subject. He writes, "The subject, then, becomes a side effect of the pedagogical-machine that cannot be completely determined" (*Counter-History* 255). For Hawk, subjects are more akin to Ulmer's notion of the conductor; Hawk explains: "As conductors we are active initiators of movement and organization, passive conduits that allow discourses and forces to pass through and reconnect to other circuits and function in new machines, and participants in constellations that are co-responsible for our conduct. We are our accidents and our connections as much as our choices" (155). As noted earlier, I find the metaphor of conductor problematic in its desire to retain some form of identification of subject embedded within the system; yet, despite this criticism, Hawk's posthumanism embarks on a Foucauldian recast of the subject, not as antihuman, but as a collapse of seeing the subject as an individual and rather as an intricate complexity inseparable from technology and language.

If the posthuman is characterized as the human rewritten by technological influence—biological, pharmaceutical, informational, digital, chemical—and if humans have always been enmeshed with their technologies, as Hansen and Clark suggest, then we can say that humans have always been cyborg, hybrid, or posthuman. The degree to which humans become posthuman comes into question depending upon the level of technology and the scale of integration. This begs the question as to whether the technological interaction can be thought of as inherently part of the human or inherently what makes the human always already posthuman. This is also a question of embodiment, as Hayles has rightly addressed. The argument of degree of technological interaction and complexity of the technology perhaps answers such a question: for instance, does the use of a moldboard plow make one any less cyborg than does the use of fiber optics at the moment of use? But such arguments seem pointless. What seems more applicable is the degree to which the imposition of the technological upon the human allows for arguments that lend to a conclusion that the posthuman condition is more universally ubiquitous than we have been willing to admit thus far. While we can easily argue that the posthuman condition is more readily applicable to privileged bodies that control the capital to acquire technological enhancement (wearable information devices, Internet, plastic surgery, psychotropic pharmaceuticals such as Prozac, Ritalin, and the like), it is more telling to examine the imposition of the posthuman condition onto bodies that do not choose enhancement. Given the ubiquity of genetically manipulated crops (Didur cites a Monsanto geneticist, for example, arguing that all crops on the planet are genetically altered), toxins released or intentionally placed into environments worldwide, global waste disposal, and so on, it is reasonable to say that in some way or another, humans are all impacted by genetic manipulation technologies. If we examine the materials economy system, we can argue that humans are all affected by corporate forces in some form or another, be those via biotechnologies or digital technologies, all of which are bound to the function of the materials economy. Moving from the economic view, however, to the ecological view, we can begin to see how the materials economic system has far-reaching effect, even upon bodies not directly tied to or participant in such economic systems. Given these conditions, it could be said that to some degree or another, humans are already posthuman. Or, to be more direct, we can say that it does not matter whether one considers oneself to be posthuman or not because we live in a posthuman world. In all instances, degrees of posthuman augmentation are controlled by capital: in some, this is the ability to obtain and implement augmentation; in others, augmentations are imposed on inhabitants of economically dependent regions, like the Global South.

If we are to accept a broad definition of the posthuman without becoming embroiled in disciplinary questions as to what technologies most accurately or aggressively inform posthumanism and what technologies can be brought to bear on the human to form the posthuman, then we can acknowledge that technological augmentation/alteration to any degree results in some measure of the posthuman. From this perspective, then, I argue that continued liberal humanist or postmodernist thinking about subjects and subjectivity no longer serves in understanding the posthuman. Technological encroachment has rendered a new subject that is more fully integrated into complex systems and not readily identifiable or analyzable beyond those systems. Subjectivity can be dispensed in favor of more ecological understandings of the complex systems in which posthumans function.

Postcomposition is particularly interested in the role of information technologies, not only the pervasiveness of information technologies and wearable information technologies—which seem to make evident a cyborg culture—but also in the complex systemic reaction to information technologies. We might think of systemic reaction as an ecological effect, the way that a complex system responds to/reacts with fluctuation within a system, an idea I develop more extensively in chapter 6. Marilyn Cooper's "The Ecology of Writing" famously describes writing's effect on a discourse group as metaphorically similar to movement upon a spider's web, the vibration affecting more than the immediate point of contact. Cooper's metaphor is useful as a beginning point in describing systemic reaction; however, alterations and accommodations must be made to the metaphor, as I detail in chapter 5. The web is not independent from the agent that makes the web. We must not think of vibration as being initiated by some knowable external agent acting upon the web. All agents are part of the web to the extent that there are no agents, only web. Likewise, we can no longer think of the web as web; the metaphor limits the extent of the complexity of thinking about the *system*—a metaphor that is problematic in its own rights but that encompasses a sense of intricacy beyond the fine, flat linearity of a web—numerous connected lines. The posthumanist, complex web/system not only resists metaphoric description limited by physical representation (like a web) but emerges at a level of shifting complexity that refuses metaphor. There is a chaotic dynamic of the system that extends beyond metaphoric capture.

Systemic reaction to technology (or anything, for that matter) can be thought of as emerging from three points of interaction. First is the intellectual reaction. Intellectual reaction encompasses the theory/thinking from which technology emerges. In this way, technology should not be thought of in a material sense, or even as *techne*, which implies thinking with the *intent* of application. Nor is this view of technology relegated to Foucauldian episteme. Instead, technology can be cast as hovering between the two while extending across the two. Technology, then, occupies a more complex intellectual position within a system than as potential for application; ideas themselves are seen as a kind of technology. That said, though, the intellectual reaction is certainly also triggered by *techne*, by the thinking that has potential to lead to the production of material devices most often identified as the technologies, not necessarily the embodiment of the technologies. *Techne*, in this way, may emerge by design with an active intent of rendering material manifestation of technology, or it may become known retroactively (much in the way Richard Rorty's abnormal discourse can be identified only in hindsight) if it does not result in material expression, remaining solely as an intellectual formation. Technology can be thought of as encompassing more than the material manifestation of the technology but as an intellectual position both a priori and posteriori the material. The intellectual reaction extends across everything from inventive emergence, to the idea of the technology's use, to the ideas that lead to the development of the materials used in making the physical expression of the technology, to the ideas that lead to the economic approach to disperse the technology, to how users think about integrating and employing the technology, to the thinking that disrupts or alters the thinking about how the technology is *intended* to be used—and, certainly, any thinking that is altered by the technology. In other words, the intellectual reaction's catalyst is thought or, more specifically, posthuman thought, which is not attributable to any agent origin.

The second point of systemic reaction might be identified as the cooperate/material reaction that is triggered by the extraction of resources to make expressions of the technology, the production of any material demonstration of the technology, the distribution/circulation of the technology intellectually or materially, the consumption of the technology and the material representations of the technology, and the disposal of the technology and its material mechanisms. While this point of systemic reaction is presented in economic terms, with its metaphors borrowed from the materials economy system model, its reactive effects are ecological.[7]

Third is the energy reaction, or what we might think of as the power of integration reaction. This reaction evolves from the agency the technology attains and its ability to sustain, reinscribe, and spread its agency—its rhetorical velocity. The energy reaction is political; it is not inseparable from the intellectual or the corporate. The energy reaction results not from the ubiquity of a technology but from its invisibility, its ability to naturalize itself as not-technology. The predominant characteristic of technology's ability to form the cyborg, the hybrid, the posthuman is its invisibility, not its ubiquity. The energy reaction might be thought of as a *power* reaction; however, the metaphor of power carries entirely too much baggage to be of any real use in describing the posthuman world.

In the closing paragraph of *How We Became Posthuman*, Hayles offers a précis of posthuman subjectivity: "The chaotic, unpredictable nature of complex dynamics implies that subjectivity is emergent rather than given, distributed rather than located solely in consciousness, emerging from and integrated into a chaotic world rather than occupying a position of mastery and control removed from it" (291). We have always been posthuman, Hayles argues, noting that the "seriated history of cybernetics—emerging from networks at once materially real, socially regulated, and discursively constructed—suggests . . . that we have always been posthuman" (291). Hayles's argument is one of cybernetic technology, of artificial intelligence, of information technologies, intellectual enterprises that necessarily rely upon the information metaphor as central to their projects. The posthuman, however, can be thought of as more encompassing, as resulting from engagement with all forms of technologies, including not only cybernetic technologies or digital/electronic technologies but biotechnologies, nanotechnologies, psychotropic-pharmacological technologies, and others as well. Bioshifts are as human-altering as cybershifts; Rachel Carson made that clear as early as 1962. Given the historical context of technological ubiquity, there is an identifiable distinction between the Enlightenment subject and the posthuman subject. But to say "we have always been posthuman" is to simplify. To say that all technologies render us posthuman is to simplify. Posthuman differences between the intellectual move beyond the human—that is, a theoretical shift in understanding what it means to be human; as Hayles calls it, "a general intellectual sense that displaces one definition of 'human' with another" (283)—versus literal changes to the physical, philosophical, and mental human being to the extreme of "human displacement as the dominant life on the planet by intelligent machines" (283) disrupt such simplification and demand a more complex vision of the posthuman condition. Whether the age of the human is or is not drawing to a close is less significant than what the possibility of the posthuman suggests about subjectivity. As Hayles puts it:

> The posthuman does not really mean the end of humanity. It signals instead the end of a certain conception that may have applied, at best, to that fraction of humanity who still had wealth, power, and leisure to conceptualize themselves as autonomous beings exercising their will through individual agency and choice. What is lethal is not the posthuman as such but the grafting of the posthuman onto a liberal humanist view of the self. (286)

Arguably, this is how composition studies engaged postmodern subjectivity: by grafting onto an identifiable subject in order to retain the comfort and security of recognizable subjects without falling too far into the contingency of postmodernism, a contingency that is too often understood as nihilistic. Arguably, too, Hayles's assessment of conceptions of humanity echo composition studies' student-based understanding of subject. Composition studies, like most of the humanities, embraced a version of subjectivity that recognizes a stable, coherent self. This vision of the subject, as Hayles notes, is empowered to "witness and testify to a stable, coherent reality."[8] This metaphysics of presence, Hayles argues, "front-loaded meaning into the system" (285). Meaning in this model is guaranteed because the stability of the origin of meaning—the subject—is not questioned. In this way, meaning and the subject are guaranteed. "When the self is envisioned as grounded in presence, identified with originary guarantees and teleological trajectories, associated with solid foundations and logical coherence," Hayles explains, "the posthuman is likely to be seen as antihuman because it envisions the conscious mind as a small subsystem running its program of self-construction and self-assurance while remaining ignorant of the actual dynamics of complex systems" (286).

Borrowing again from Hayles, we can now recognize that there is a distinct difference between what the posthuman *will* be and what it *can* be (288). If those of us interested in understanding writing continue to think of the subject as an autonomous subject, what we can know about writing is constrained by a myth of stability and origin, a myth that no longer explains writing in current systems. Myths, of course, explain our fears and give easy, archetypal answers to questions that require more. Reliance upon the myth of the subject demands a fear of ideas like the posthuman, but an acceptance of their possibility suggests potential in what can be.

4. Beyond the Administration of Subjects

> What worries me is that composition's center of gravity may slip imperceptibly toward management of teaching and away from teaching itself.
> —Doug Hesse, foreword to *The End of Composition Studies*, by David W. Smit

> The problem is that theorists are largely unaware that composition studies exists. They do know about Freshman English, however.
> —Sharon Crowley, *Composition in the University*

> Simply to collapse the work of administration into the work of theory does everybody a disservice.
> —Lynn Worsham, "Deconstructing Composition"

In his preface to Barbara L'Eplattenier and Lisa Mastrangelo's 2004 WPA Best Book Award–winning *Historical Studies of Writing Program Administration: Individuals, Communities, and the Formation of a Discipline*, Edward M. White offers a greatly abbreviated history of writing program administration, a history that is explicated and amplified throughout in the essays that follow. White alerts readers to an ambiguous history, a history with indistinct origins, a history muddled in a tradition recognizable only by amassing distinctions in an indistinct past. White charts the beginnings of writing program administration not to 1970—according to him, the year of the formation of the Council of Writing Program Administrators (a date that the book's editors list as 1976 in their introductory essay "Why Administrative Histories?"; see p. xvii)—nor even to 1946, as Edward Corbett does in his 1993 "A History of Writing Program Administration." Instead, White explains that writing program administrative work "needed to be done as writing programs developed at least 200 years ago" (xiii). But the ambiguity of this origin is never clarified (not that it should be), nor is the history of the *idea of* writing programs examined in the preface or the essays that follow. Many of the essays in L'Eplattenier and Mastrangelo's collection work to identify early moments of administrative struggle and success (notably, Randall Popken's essay about Edwin Hopkins that documents writing program administration struggles at the University of Kansas beginning in 1889) in order to coalesce individual program histories into a larger narrative of writing programs and writing program administration in general. More so, the essays in the L'Eplattenier and Mastrangelo collection, like much of the historical research written about writing program administration, work toward a more encompassing goal: the verification and validation of administrative work as central to the development and identity of composition studies as a discipline. White, along with the editors of and contributors to *Historical Studies of Writing Program Administration*, seeks a form of historical validation, but that quest leaves a number of unanswered questions, the foremost of which can be summed up by asking, "When did 'writing program' enter into the professional lexicon?" The answer (or answers) to such a question reveals less about either the archival research needed to trace the appearance of the term or about the beginnings of writing program administration than it does about the rhetorical function of how the term/idea of writing program rendered writing academic, something to be administered over, and its users to be managed.

Arguably, a good deal of the institutional power that composition studies has attained—perhaps most successfully over the last twenty-five years—has been due to its willingness to function in an administrative capacity, to act as a manager of subjects—that is, to administer writing programs. The distinction I wish to make here is that while writing program administration may be muddled a bit in its origin (though I'm not interested in identifying or relying on such origins), the invocation of *writing program* authorized and formalized an academic administrative control not (only) over writing but over subjects, those who were identified as "needing" instruction in writing, providing writing-instructors-turned-administrators with something tangible to manage and a distinct capital within the American academy. Likewise, as a sort of secondary result of implementing the idea of the writing program, the administrative imperative embraced by composition studies made programmatic what could be named as writing, the function of writing, writing instruction, and writing inquiry. "Programmatic," of course, implies a sense of structured parameter or sequential mechanized control. That is, writing program administration made writing academic.[1]

Historically, we know that much of composition studies' embrace of the administrative imperative was tied directly to the field's bonds to the first-year writing course. As Susan McLeod's *Writing Program Administration* succinctly puts it, "Writing program administration has from the beginning been tied to freshman (or first-year) composition" (23). This history, as many have documented, is bound directly to the history of the evolution of English departments in the American academy, to the rift between literature and composition studies, and to the historical role/position of rhetoric in English departments and the university. But what has not been addressed by historians of English departments, first-year composition, or, specifically, writing program administration/administrators is the question of what happens/happened to writing (and writers) the moment it is/was made programmatic, or, perhaps more important, what happens to writing subjects or the idea of subjectivity when administrative principles dictate the management of a particular population of subjects. Certainly, Sharon Crowley's *Composition in the University* articulates a relationship between FYC and mechanized subject formation/manipulation into a larger military industrial ideology, but little critical work has considered the ways in which the establishment of writing programs and writing program administration has rewritten the very idea of subjectivity for composition studies. I should note, too, that, as both Lynn Worsham and John Trimbur have astutely pointed out about writing instruction, composition studies' administrative imperative is fueled as much by student expectation as it is by disciplinary need or upper-administrative influence (see Worsham, "Writing," and Trimbur, "Changing").

While it would appear that this lack of critical consideration necessitates a need for such work, in fact my argument in this chapter moves in a different direction, one distinctly away from writing program administration. Given the arguments presented in the previous chapter regarding outmoded concepts of subject and writing-subject and the ubiquity of the posthuman condition, I argue here that in order for phenomena of writing to be better theorized and for the work of theorizing writing to be better situated in contemporary intellectual work, postcomposition must abdicate its administrative imperative. By linking the very identity of composition studies to writing program administration, any study of writing is interminably haunted by academic prescription, economic and management thinking, and subject-driven approaches. If we are to disavow the subject as a theoretical matter, as a matter of attuning theoretical work postcomposition toward writing rather than subject, then so too should composition studies drastically reconsider its attachment to academic positions that focus upon subjects and the management of subject.

In what follows, I offer some thoughts regarding the pervasiveness of writing program administration in the composition studies gestalt and the need to move beyond the administration of subjects, writing-subjects, and writing. These critiques are intended not as denial of the importance of writing program administration in composition studies' history but as a (violent/abrupt) move away from that history in favor of a contingent future not fettered by administrative constraints. Much of this critique, too, employs a language of space and place, a distinction clarified in chapter 2. I bring this language into play here to emphasize a distinction between spatial thinking and chronological/historical thinking about the positions of administration in the academic and intellectual efforts of writing research.

(Re)Placing Writing Program Administration

What, then, fills the program space?
—Jeanne Gunner, "Ideology, Theory, and
the Genre of Writing Programs"

A material connection between the theories we embrace and institutional practices, values, and power eludes us.
—Jeanne Gunner, "Ideology, Theory, and
the Genre of Writing Programs"

Administration is wealth, consolidated and put at the service of command.
—Antonio Negri, "Constituent Republic"

The question of the place of writing program administration, of the contingent frontiers and occupied territories of the WPA and the wpa, is an insistent question.[2] It is a question, as I noted earlier, with history, but this history is of less interest than is the place of this question. In its desire to find the security of place, the WPA has foregone the freedom of space in favor of a guarded conservatism to protect its place. The WPA not only has renounced critical perspectives of its work in favor of the safety of perceived legitimacy and place but also has succumbed to a false security bound up in a mythology of administrative power that fails to question the very safety of its place and denies the potential critical, theoretical, and political work than can be done beyond the borders of WPA-place. It is specifically in the WPA agenda that we find the locus of composition studies' resistance to theory, its unrelinquishing grasp on subjectivity, and the economic/managerial impetus that drives disciplinary doxa. This is an argument opposed to the hegemony of the WPA and an articulated worry that the omnipresence of the WPA and its managerial focus will continue to quiet theory's voice in composition studies. It is an argument that questions the manner in which the work of the WPA fails to be critical of its own positioning beyond ways that stand to reinforce its hegemonic, managerial/economic agendas. It is a question about the direction in which the WPA moves (or fails to move).

Writing program administrators seek out hegemony for safety. In the local place of the wpa, hegemony becomes the very mechanism of control manifest in managerial presence: curriculum, policy, orientation, practicum. The cultural capital of the wpa is conveyed, control is implemented, and safety ensues—so long as there is not questioning or critique of the wpa master narrative. On a more global scale, the WPA seeks a similar safety in hegemony, veiled as disciplinary unity or identity: this is what *We* do. As Lester Faigley explains in *Fragments of Rationality*, "The use of *we* in these discourses reproduces the primary tension between a diverse and contingent present and the promise of a unified future. The *we* assumes the right of *I* to speak for the *you* and the *they*" (218, emphasis in original). Likewise, the search for collective identity, as Manuel Castells has shown, often becomes the only source of meaning, as individuals and organizations "organize their meaning not around what they do but on the basis of what they are, or believe they are" (*Rise* 3). Identification with a collective identity often breeds conservatism about that identity, particularly when the collective perceives (or creates the perception of) a threatening force or chaos determined to undermine the collective identity. And though the We of composition studies, as Marc Bousquet points out in "Composition as Management Science," is problematic in determining exactly to whom the We refers (499), what We do is often manifest in the validation of the local through the global: Do our curricula, our methodologies, our approaches fit within the rubric, in the boundaries of WPA dictates (think: WPA Outcomes Statement for First-Year Composition, the Portland Resolution, and other WPA resolutions/statements)? Have I, the local wpa, forged a place here in this space in the image of the motherland? Would They approve? And, of course, if I, the local wpa, seek that validation, They will come, inspect, and offer documentation of my legitimacy, my right to claim membership in the collective by having demonstrated an acceptable local version of the national vision (think: WPA Consultant-Evaluator Service). And, as recent conversations have shown, there is a blatant—though uncritical—conversation about such homogenization: the question of whether We are all training graduate students the same way, making sure *they* all have the same foundational understandings of what composition studies is, of what administration is, before they can be validated as We. I'm thinking here of work like Theresa Enos and Stuart Brown's 2005 CCCC presentation "Exploring and Enhancing Relationships between MA and PhD Programs in Rhetoric and Composition Programs," which was offered as a study of consistencies in textbook selection and curricular approaches to MA and PhD programs nationwide but which seemingly argued for a need for more consistency between disparate programs at various institutions. This process was professed as in the best interest of the discipline, as an act of confirming disciplinarity by way of common objects of study. This kind of disciplinary consistency simultaneously serves the field and limits the field. Composition studies is a complicated endeavor that is at once both composition studies and postcomposition, simultaneously. While the WPA and the very idea of writing program administration have served composition studies historically, *We* may no longer be best served by that focus. And just as conditions like modernism don't give over to their posts in easy conversion, so, too, are the transitions away from an administrative focus likely to be lengthy and messy. Composition studies is still served by the administrative imperative, but in terms of developing more useful theories of writing and (re)grounding the field in intellectual work, writing program administration should also be considered in its limiting capacities. In other words, postcomposition may acknowledge the positive aspects of wpa work but asks that *We* consider the harder choice of not continuing what we have been doing and instead make some drastic changes.

The move toward disciplinary consistency can be read as a process of reinscription of the WPA master narrative, and as I mention in the previous chapter, such forms of disciplinary maintenance are understood as methods of homogenization and subjectification. The WPA's colonization is masked in altruism, masked in the rhetoric not only of We but of what We do—an active, participatory forwarding of the mission. In saying this, however, I want to be clear that I am not attempting to create a false dichotomy between the local and the global, between the wpa and the WPA, as though the local should defend against the hegemony of the global. Too often the difference between the local and the global is cast as the local maintaining individuality, heterogeneity, and difference, while the global works toward homogenization. The local, we assume, preexists the global. However, what needs to be addressed is what Michael Hardt and Antonio Negri refer to in *Empire* as the "production of locality" (45), the manner in which the global machine produces the identities of the local in order to suggest difference. The wpa should be understood as produced by the WPA and dependent upon the WPA for identity. In no way can the local wpa operate outside of the context of the WPA. The wpa and the WPA are inseparable parts of the larger complex administrative system.

The notion of what-we-do, though, breeds a kind of nationalism, a need for fidelity driven by an ongoing inquiry that asks, "What do We do?" (a question to be understood first as "What do *We* do?" and second as "What *do* We do?"). The potential answers to this kind of question are of less importance than the acceptance of the notion that there is a "We" and that we all do similar things. The comfort of place seems to have bred a nationalism of administrators, brought together under the banner of We, and created a territoriality that is defended and propagated by fear, by fear of what could happen without the motherland at one's shoulder and by fear of what has been painted historically as an unadministrated chaos. The WPA itself was born out of a fear of the place to which composition studies was exiled rather than given title and claim. That history is well known and rides under the banner of oppression, its narrative gaining power with famous labels such as Susan Miller's "sad women in the basement" (*Textual Carnivals* 121), "woman's work" ("Feminization" 45), or the handmaiden to English ("Feminization" 42). In response to this historical placement of composition studies (and I don't mean to suggest that Miller is alone here, as it is nearly every "history" of composition studies that places the discipline in this context), the WPA rose under the not-quite-articulated professional banner of "never again," the rhetoric of an oppressed population given power not over its oppressors but within its ranks; not a population liberated but one that lives among its oppressors with consistent reminders of the potential of *again*. Historical memory, coupled with a rhetoric that aggrandizes the actual power of place held by the WPA, gives rise—and validation—to the necessity of a profes- sional We, of a place where We can stand and defend among comrades.

Of course, this notion of professional camaraderie of the We is part of composition studies' larger quest for identity, the desire to situate and ground what it is We do in the temporal, in the historical situation of com- position studies and the WPA as its administrative voice. The WPA's mis- sion is overtly about control and maintenance of power, of the power over writing programs and writing pedagogies, but its veiled mission is one of identity. Identifying one's self as a wpa is to embrace a particular precon- ceived identity, an identity with a neatly packaged history (canon). But, identity, as Leon Wieseltier's *Against Identity* explains, is "a euphemism for conformity" (4). To embrace the identity of a wpa is to validate the identity- making of the WPA. "It is never long before identity is reduced to loyalty" (Wieseltier 9). The loyalty of identity is a driving force in the construction and propagation of a WPA place; it gives rise to the safety of place. Identity is always social; it is always public. The place and imagined safety of the WPA is given breadth in identity. For the WPA, the placing of hegemonic identity is crucial as it is the centerpiece to the WPA ur-narrative. Identity, Wieseltier writes, "is too eager to commemorate itself. It is nourished by its nightmare, by the possibility of its extinction" (15). This possibility propels the WPA; it is a possibility confirmed through its narrative history and confirmed in the testimonials of those who have met resistance to their identities, their authority challenged locally and refuge and comfort sought in the safety of the WPA place among comrades with similar testimonials. In fact, the narrative of persecution is central to the WPA narrative; it is, perhaps, one of the most prevalent forms of "research" conducted under the WPA banner. "This happened here; don't let it happen to you, brothers and sisters." This is the lore of the WPA; it is one of the functions of WPA dogma and that which breeds camaraderie. We have all suffered together, so we must stand together, have breakfast together. Identity imposes discipline. In this case, it even attempts to define the discipline.

But there is great disconnect between the identity of comrade wpas and the WPA organization. The disconnect between WPA dictates and wpa actions can best be described as the collective fantasy Fredric Jameson's *The Political Unconscious: Narrative as a Socially Symbolic Act* addresses in its discussions of master narratives (34). There tends to be an open acceptance of—or more to the point, a resistance to criticism of—WPA discussion because of the fantasy-driven desire for collective agreement. The collective produces safety in that the master narratives promulgated through the collective depict a simulacra of agreement, of coordination, of order—even when We disagree. Hence, in mimicking and adhering to that master narrative, the wpa population seeks to align itself with the fantasy of the WPA narrative as a method of ensuring its own safety in that any venture into territories where a wpa might have to act is defended by a master narrative that identifies the response of the party, what to say, what not to say.

The difficulty here, though, lies in the fact that in wanting to adhere to any sort of master narrative and embrace the collective fantasy of that narrative, the WPA fails for the simple reason that it attempts to apply the master narrative across situations, primarily dissimilar situations. The WPA master narrative cannot fit the various missions of different contexts, different schools, nor should a singular homogeneous approach to administration be advocated (to this end, too, the recent conversations about "certifying" or "licensing" wpas to ensure that the properly trained people are occupying such positions nationally seem dangerous, potentially calling for a different degree of certification and approval: a new kind of gatekeeping). For instance, the WPA master narrative encounters great difficulty speaking directly to Research One institutions in the same breath as it does to Two-Year institutions. The demands of those institutions vary too greatly for any one collective to be able to address those needs. Ultimately, there can be no We of the WPA in such instances, and failure to have a collective We is itself a conflict for the WPA master narrative.

This is precisely the moment of spatial freedom: the moment when the We recognizes the fantasy of We and becomes open to critique of the places We occupy. To say that the WPA cannot speak to all wpas is evident and embraced under a standard of difference in order not to disrupt. It is OK to administer differently, as long as we are all doing it. The role of the WPA, then, is not a role of mediation between meanings but one of meaning-making, an attempt to create a master narrative of meaning under which administrators nationally operate with little or no open critique of what it means to administer, or of why administration has become such a central (and powerful) position within the ranks of composition studies, or of what implications and ramifications those positions hold over the work that can be done and validated in composition studies. In fact, writing program administration has become so central to the "work" of composition studies that some inside and outside (notice the including and excluding metaphor) the field (fields suggest order, boundaries, safety, protection) cannot and do not separate administration from composition studies; they are the same. In this way, just as I have identified the inseparability of the wpa and the WPA, so too are composition studies and the WPA indivisible parts of a singular whole. There can be no composition studies without the WPA in the same way that there can be no WPA or wpa without composition studies. It is for this reason that postcomposition must disassociate from the administrative imperative. Failure to consistently critique and rework the function and operation of a disciplinary oversight entity such as the WPA can only support a hegemonic structure that not only stands to corral writing program administration into limited places within the American academy but seriously stands to neutralize the potential of writing research in general. The question of "what We do" keeps us from doing work outside of the master narrative in order to assure/ensure the We.

Validation and Authentication

Authenticity is a measure of provenance, and provenance has nothing to do with substance.

—Leon Wieseltier, *Against Identity*

To say "here" homogenizes all sorts of richly diverse places.

—Terry Eagleton, *After Theory*

The immediate critique of the postcomposition criticism of the WPA drive toward uniformity and collectivity might come in the form of need: a need not for homogenization as I have cast it but for standardization, as the argument in favor of wpa certification has claimed. That critique would likely point out that I have adopted a negative connotation of "homogenization," whereas "standardization" lends itself to the professional credence so desperately needed within the confusion of composition studies' search for disciplinary identity (see chapter 1). The question, of course, of what We do is not a question solely for the WPA but is one grounded in the larger body that the WPA serves (or, more accurately, purports to serve, as such administrative bodies actually serve the larger institution more than the discipline): that of composition studies in general. The field of composition studies is obsessed with its own history, with its own identity, and how that identity is manifest historically. As I began to explain in chapter 2 regarding composition studies' attachment to temporality, talking about what composition studies is/does is so much a prevalent part of what composition studies does/is that having such conversations *is* what composition studies does.[3] Asking as to composition studies' identity is (part of) composition studies' identity. Composition studies spends a good deal of energy and time attempting to situate itself historically. Of course, the desire to claim history is an attempt at validation; things with histories must be (or at least must have been). An ever-accumulating past signifies a solidity of present and the potential for future. Even the recent passing of first-generation compositionists (James Berlin, Jim Corder, Edward Corbett, James L. Kinneavy, Wendy Bishop, Robert J. Connors, Alan W. France, John C. Lovas, Maxine Hairston, W. Ross Winterowd) helps confirm composition studies' place temporally as it accumulates historical figures; their deaths allow composition studies to identify its own pantheon, to claim a canon. History will likely not rob those who died as compositionists of their composition studies identity, thereby securing historical markers for composition studies. Context for composition studies is historical. As Romy Clark and Roz Ivanic explain in *The Politics of Writing*, "The past is revered as cultural heritage, as if it somehow confers glory on the whole [field]" (39–40). But the past, we also know, is a deeply problematic concept. As Gilles Deleuze makes clear in *Bergsonism*, "The past, on the other hand, has ceased to act or to be useful. But it has not ceased to be" (55).

A recent national conversation among wpas that ran under the heading of "wpa genealogy" took this notion of cultural heritage to an extreme. Starting as a casual conversation about mentors and wpa training prior to the development of formal graduate training programs, the thread attempted to identify a "genealogy" of administrative training. The conversation smacked of elitism, of lineage, of royalty, of dynasty. More to the point, the conversation was an attempt to validate through bloodline: register your pedigree today. By the end of the four-day thread, there were calls for "research" and publication that traced these lineages. Mudbloods were to be expelled. Publication of such descents would give credence not only to the genealogies themselves but to the very act of tracing bloodlines as a valuable piece of WPA "research." This desire to seek identity in the traceable lineage of "golden" compositionists is precisely the kind of conversation that hampers any sort of move beyond composition studies' limit-situation by refusing to align the work of administration with potential in favor of aligning with historical narrative, looking aft instead of fore. Yet this attempt to validate through ancestry lacked any real critical attention to the homogenizing effect of the conversation (granted, I do not mean to argue that the informal site where the conversation was held is the site where such critical work is to always be done, so perhaps my criticism is a bit unfair). Throughout the thread, I was reminded of Nathaniel Hawthorne's story "Main Street," when the omniscient narrator says, "Let us thank God for having given us such ancestors; and let each successive generation thank him, not less fervently, for being one step further from them in the march of ages" (1039). I'd like to think that the thread could have evoked conversation regarding, say, Friedrich Nietzsche's genealogy (and Deleuze's reading of Nietzsche) as an attempt to historically situate forebears in such a way as to separate oneself from them. But such is not the work of a community seeking historical validation. Yet, this brief episode in the collective history stands as exemplary of the overall agenda of the WPA (and countless wpas who have found comfort in the WPA place) to seek out and codify the identities of its population and to self-validate those identities. Such a strategy, as I have indicated, grows from a fear of loss of territory, a loss of control, and a need for validation to provide comfort for that loss.

The genealogy thread also provides insight into the larger function of the WPA in terms of its own ideological self-validation. Being able to historically locate one's place in the WPA lineage is also a recognition that the WPA master narrative self-replicates; it breeds a desire for such lineage as indicator of sameness. I do what I do because my father and my father before him did. Such a maneuver leaves little room for dissent or, more important, for critical work or for any work that extends what we know about writing. The system replicates ideologies that have traditionally been less critical, more defensive of the WPA place. Second-, third-, and now fourth-generation wpas reproduce administrative approaches and "research" that first-generation wpas set in motion. Organizational leadership—those who do the work of the WPA—rarely change, if not in individuals then in method and agenda. The WPA voice is normalized, and in that normalization there is little desire from within to do the critical work that reveals the seams of the historical narrative. The WPA becomes blinded by and to its own discourse and defensive against those who present discordant views, particularly from those who cannot produce evidence of membership, of lineage, of the historical location the WPA craves. Such a defensive position becomes reductive in authorizing who can speak and determining who are warded off as enemies of the state. It is a politic of recycling.

The drive to historically locate what We do is certainly a form of self-validation, and it works hand-in-hand with a push toward standardization in order to more easily confer what we do upon a population under the commonality of discipline or, more accurately, the discipline of commonality. One can easily argue that standardization is a crucial step in discipline formation, in validation of a field's boundaries, of the place that a given field occupies. Standardization operates as a mechanism specifically of boundary formation. This is what We do; everything else falls outside our governance. Standardization makes validation easier, but standardization is always a reduction, not an elevation.

Work toward standardization is crucial to the WPA mission. As Shirley K. Rose and Irwin Weiser put it, in the process of professionalization, "writing program administrators are becoming more interested in defining the nature of their work for others and setting standards for its evaluation" (5). Such a concept of standardization, though, carries with it undercurrents of policing mechanisms. Turning to, say, Jean-François Lyotard's definition of "legitimation," we see that to legitimize is to give authorization to one who can make statements within a given discourse (*Postmodern* 8). While it may be argued that understanding legitimization as such gives credence to standardization as a method for ensuring consistency within a discourse, the argument may also be seen not as affirming but as exclusionary in the sense of promoting a territoriality based in conformity and voiced as authenticity. Validation, as it is manifest in conversations such as the genealogy thread and elsewhere, reveals a desire for authentication, for confirmation of being real. I am a *real* wpa. Authenticity, though, as Wieseltier puts it, "is a reactionary ideal. Speaking strictly, it is an anti-ideal. It says: what has been is what must be. It is the idolatry of origins" (56).

In the genealogy conversation, then, we can easily identify a grasping for authentication. However, what is more telling regarding the WPA and validation is the media through which the conversation was presented. Legitimation is dependent first upon internal process; communication drives that process. Such processes of legitimation, Hardt and Negri explain, operate by way of a "subject that produces its own image of authority" (33). In this way, legitimation "rests on nothing outside itself and is reproposed ceaselessly by developing its own languages of self-validation" (33). The WPA serves this communicative function. Hardt and Negri again: "If communication is one of the hegemonic sectors of production and acts over the entire biopolitical field, then we must consider communication and the biopolitical context coexistent" (33).

To be clear here, I am not disavowing the need for disciplinary status nor for standardization within the boundaries of that discipline. Rather, I issue a cautionary criticism that con/fronts (bolstered up against the frontal position) that legitimation as formed through processes of standardization. To paraphrase Lyotard, a discipline that has not legitimated itself is not a true discipline (*Postmodern* 38). That discipline can validate itself only through a discourse that has been approved following that very discourse. Validation through predisciplinary discourses (again, to borrow from Lyotard) demotes the discipline rather than elevates it. Elevation occurs through self-validating discourse only. However, there cannot be emancipation at the same moment of validation. There cannot be emancipation within a place that requires for its own self-identification a never-ending self-legitimation. Emancipation requires a relinquishing or at minimum a crossing of boundaries. Hence, contingent frontiers encourage not only emancipation but perpetual moves into the beyond and not a reliance on validation. Emancipation, for the wpa, means an active shedding of the chains of oppression cast by the WPA/composition studies historical narrative, an opportunity to redefine what it is We do in a very different place, in a place defined not by the service/pedagogical identity historically foisted upon wpas by university administrations but determined by the wpas/WPA themselves as an act of doing rather than as a confirmation of *We*. Emancipation for the wpa must be an active (re)placing of the wpa position in a critical space. Emancipation for composition studies must be an active move away from administration of subject. We must recognize legitimation as a spatial argument, an argument about how spaces are occupied, ordered, and named. That is, legitimation is about safety of place, both of which the multitude believes to be necessary: (we think) we need the WPA now because of what now offers us, self-validation. As Jeanne Gunner's "Ideology, Theory, and the Genre of Writing Programs" explains, part of the safety that ideological structures impose is a control mechanism accepting or rejecting particular theoretical positions as they do or do not serve the purpose of the structure: "theories that come into being within, or are imported into, established writing programs are already discursively constrained: they will comply with or be contained by the larger ideological strictures and purposes of the program" (8)—or, more to the point, the WPA specifically.

The Administrative Empire

The multitude called Empire into being.
—Michael Hardt and Antonio Negri, *Empire*

Writing program administrators have come to identify the wpa position as a position of power and have defined the wpa place as holding the possibility of power, albeit of questionable and questioned power. Such a depiction is necessary in order to allow the power of the wpa to operate safely within the WPA narrative. Wpas, given the right context, can more than influence the shape of writing programs, of writing curriculum, and, in turn, of the lives of students and those over whom they immediately administer. Wpas are given the "power" to design curricula; to devise, implement, and run training programs for teachers; to design syllabi; to select textbooks; to determine teaching schedules. In other words, the wpa is often given singular control over the production of a given program's cultural capital. Whether recognized or not, this is a significant power in that it is often individual wpas who disseminate the cultural capital not just of a given program but of composition studies in general through mechanisms such as orientations, in-service workshops, practica, and curricula—all mechanisms that are often controlled by individual wpas by default. These instruments reach both future members of the composition studies or WPA community and nearly all graduate students (and part-time or adjunct faculty) who teach writing around the country. These mechanisms, then, stand to influence the population new to composition studies specifically and most of those who seek employment in English departments, who, then, in turn form opinions of what it means to be a wpa or to be of composition studies and ultimately what constitutes the work of composition studies and what can be validated as legitimate research within the field. By way of "standardization," the WPA plays a powerful role in determining how these individual mechanisms are employed and in turn how the cultural capital of composition studies in general, and the WPA more specifically, is promulgated, including what constitutes and what does not constitute research in composition studies. Such is often the operating function of a body seeking a position of control.

It would be rather simple to say that the WPA seeks to become an Empire, to be the ruling power over a group of "independent" administrators, and that its banner of standardization can be read as a banner of centralized rule. But such a definition and accusation limits the manner in which the WPA Empire should be addressed, particularly regarding the importance of the WPA Empire. There are benefits in recognizing two things about the position of writing program administrators. First, the wpa is more often than not given his or her power because others with (more/real) power in the institution don't want to have to commit time and resources to such work. In other words, the wpa might be considered the king of the geeks: in charge of the one population of which no one else wants to be in charge.[4] Hence, the wpa position is a position of false power, one of servitude to the institution. Certainly, the counter-argument can be made that the wpa position is given over to the professionals of composition studies since writing program administration falls specifically under the aegis of composition studies. Yet, such an argument fails to recognize and own up to composition studies' own historical narrative. The professionalization of wpa positions evolved as a result of the poor conditions in which wpas found themselves. The wpa position did not develop because professionals in the field of composition studies needed outlets for their work but as a manner of validating that research in writing program administration does, in fact, count as "work." As I have repeatedly noted, such work has done little to teach us anything about writing and, perhaps, little to teach us anything about teaching writing; it has taught us about the administration of subjects. Perhaps more important, too, the acceptance of such "power" binds composition studies to a position of management, to academic functions rather than to intellectual pursuits. There can be little argument that the majority of the work that gets done in composition studies is tied directly to the administrative imperative by way of ties to FYC, student subjects, or pedagogy, and that imperative has evolved into the primary defining characteristic of composition studies, particularly to the perception of those outside of the field.

This leads to the second point: the power of an administrator always operates in service to the power of the manager; administrators stand as representatives of higher authorities. Nowhere can this be seen more clearly than in the testimonials of wpas who have articulated their frustrations that despite their roles as administrators, as professionals schooled and validated in composition studies, upper administrators have acted upon their own motivations in ways that undermine wpa power and narrative or alter programs without consultation with or consent of wpas or even the WPA. Thus, the wpa occupies (at least) two simultaneous positions: the position of power over one population and the subservient position to the higher power, to the institution (as does any midlevel management position). Thus, one's power can extend only as far as exercising that power supports the mission of the institution. For instance, a wpa who supports composition studies' abolitionist movement does not necessarily have the immediate or direct power to eliminate the FYC requirement if doing so would be counter to the institutional system. Hence, the wpa's power is strictly administrative in that the wpa administers not over a population but under an institution.

Identifying the WPA as a true Empire—in the traditional sense of the word—seems a bit far-fetched; however, examining the WPA from the critical gaze of the ideas of empire and statehood is crucial to better understanding the function of a hegemonic entity, particularly since it seems that two of the overriding issues that face individual wpas are money and workers (bodies), or what Machiavelli might call "arms," while the WPA operates primarily regarding workers. The WPA can claim hegemonic power, control over this citizenry, administering governing discourse in order to align and control its arms to produce capital wealth that is then disseminated through its workers. At one level, this dissemination of cultural capital from the WPA through the wpa to curricula and production seems refreshingly resistant, a small revolutionary force operating under the radar of individual institutions. At first glance, it seems that the WPA recognizes the subservient position of the wpa and provides the discourse for the wpa to best use his or her position to forward the WPA mission. But, that glance is often uncritical, failing to see the seams in the WPA discourse and the danger in propagating a unified cultural capital, institution to institution. Such a critique also reveals the WPA's encumbrance by economics.

Empires often form in part by using a rhetoric of safety, espousing protection of individual difference under imperial rule. Unification and standardization are imperial tools for consolidating rule. Disparate locals fighting individual institutional battles are willing to offer votes of confidence to a ruling system if that system stands as an ally (underhanded though it was, this was specifically how Palpatine was able to gain control over the Senate and achieve a vote of nonconfidence in the Republic, leading eventually to the formation of the Empire). Hence, the immediate benefit of empire is the manner in which the homogenizing force is able to counter previous oppressions of individual entities. In this sense, standardization and homogenization become better systems than those previously in place. The history of composition studies' oppression is countered in the building of Empire, a fantasized community named and defended, safe and protected. But, we must recognize, too, that the WPA Empire is an imagined place; it is named and given identity, but it cannot be codified in any cartographic method that shows its borders as definable or defendable. This distinction between the place of the WPA community and the imagined place of the WPA Empire is crucial in that we must understand entities such as the WPA as always working toward a condition of empire but never truly achieving such a place. It is within the space of the yet-to-be empire that the critical work must be done to resist the potential of empire while strengthening the WPA community's ability to name its own places. But this, of course, is old news. This is how power works, how we have known power works. What composition studies might benefit from, though, is a reminder that because this is how power works, there is a need for work that works against this kind of power, that disrupts the system. Losing something like the power of the WPA/wpa might seem detrimental, but what is gained is something much more powerful: the ability to do different, more likely better, kinds of work free of the writing program administrative shadow.

Turning to Michael Hardt and Antonio Negri's acclaimed book *Empire* and their follow-up to that book, *Multitude*, we can begin to examine the WPA Empire from a critical position that considers the manner in which the wpa population calls into existence a WPA Empire and the benefits and drawbacks of such an empire. First, according to Hardt and Negri, the "multitude called Empire into being" (43). Suffering under the oppressive conditions foisted upon composition studies and writing program administration for the past many decades (over two hundred years by Edward White's account), wpas seek the safety of an empire as a defense. Many see this alignment as not only useful but necessary, and perhaps it is. The Empire provides haven. Standardization gives vocabulary to this safety, providing a rhetoric through which the wpa camaraderie can be managed and professional status validated. However, as Hardt and Negri point out, while the Empire may have played a significant role in altering the oppressions levied upon the various populations, we must acknowledge that despite the emancipation from the older regimes, the power of the Empire stands to employ a more devastating system of control. That is to say, while under the rule of the Empire, conditions may at first appear to have improved, there is great potential for new conditions to emerge that place the population in worse circumstances than the original situation. In the instance of the WPA, we easily see the formation of Empire as the herald of professional emancipation from a history of oppression, but in doing so, we must also question whether the limit-situation boundaries that the new Empire imposes are going to be "better" for the place of writing program administration in the long run, and in turn for composition studies more generally, and for intellectual inquiry into the phenomena of writing specifically. Just because a new history is being written for composition studies under the watch of the WPA does not mean that it will be beneficial. In fact, much of my argument here is that this new history is writing composition studies into a limited academic position relegated to little more than managerial work and removed from furthering the pursuit of theorizing writing. We can easily anticipate a stagnation of the wpa research potential—not to mention work to understand writing outside of the wpa agenda—forced through the new limits of "professional standardization," and we can easily identify the limitations being imposed upon composition studies work in general through the rhetoric of program administration research and the often unspoken anti-intellectual, anti-theoretical atmosphere in composition studies that I have attributed in part to the administrative imperative. Note, for example, Richard E. Miller's argument in "Let's Do the Numbers" that composition studies graduate programs should focus primarily on training administrators and that composition studies itself should be grounded in its service role (more on this in a moment). Consider, too, the prevailing distrust and rejection of theory work in composition studies as I have explained in chapter 1 and of writing program administration in particular. By engaging in conversations that do not move beyond the safety of a WPA place but instead recycle familiar territorial discourse, the WPA is able to maintain a stricter definition of its boundaries.

What worries me here is not the lack of theory per se in administration research, since the work of administration is not the work of theory and my claim is not that the WPA should do theory work, but that the influence of the WPA on the rest of the field affects how theory is received. Besides, as I have cited Lynn Worsham, theory and administration impede each other. Similarly, I am not concerned about the overwhelming embrace of the WPA as a saving organization but with the rapid reduction of the variety of work produced and accepted by administrators affiliated with the WPA and, in turn, what is validated as the larger area of study in composition studies. That is, the potential answers to questions of what We do are rapidly being truncated into a limited number of possibilities, few of which provide any insight into the phenomena of writing. The borders of the wpa place are being hemmed in, contingent frontiers neutralized, and the possibility for composition studies' Becoming reigned in.

I do want to be clear here, too, in following Hardt and Negri's assessment of Empire: I am not suggesting a return to the way things were pre-WPA; I hold no nostalgia for the good old days of composition studies and of writing program administration. The call to Empire is a step forward in ridding our discipline of its previous placement in power and system. Empire, according to Hardt and Negri, "increases the potential for liberation" (44), but liberation is never open-ended; populations are liberated into new occupations. Liberty and emancipation, that is, are merely resituations, replacements in relation to the same system. My concern is the need to develop ways of considering the ecologies of the complex systems themselves, not the placement of the empire within them and the simulacra of freedom and safety that the WPA Empire offers as potential. We know that no local wpa can exist outside of the formation of the WPA Empire, that all wpas feed the WPA Empire. Any local work toward emancipation is always work in support of the Empire's homogenization. Emancipation is never possible within a rhetoric of standardization.

Ongoing work toward emancipation for the wpa is critical because, first, it resists stagnation. Stagnation is specifically what individual wpas and composition studies, in general, cannot afford. Composition studies is, to borrow from Jacques Derrida, reaching its own exhaustion. Stagnation ensures that the historical placement of composition studies and writing program administration remains ensconced in an identity bound to FYC courses, the administration of those courses, and the economic management of subjects. Likewise, the standardization and validation implied in the WPA Empire have much more important effects than simply control over the WPA population and the limits of what can and cannot be WPA research. The WPA push to standardization, toward Empire, also implies a standardization of wpas and, in turn, of the populations they ultimately administer over: subjects. Standardization within the WPA Empire is work in support of a universal student subject, a standard student. Hence, postcomposition rejects the managerial and imperial objective of writing program administration because writing program administration, first, insists upon loyalty to outmoded visions of individual subjects and, second, works to homogenize those subjects as a matter of capital control. In a posthuman world, such conservative fidelity drastically inhibits what can be theorized about phenomena of writing and confines composition studies to academic, low-level managerial positions.

Critical Mass(es)

Prefer what is positive and multiple: difference over uniformity, flows over unities, mobile arrangements over systems. Believe that what is productive is not sedentary but nomadic.
> —Michel Foucault, preface to *Anti-Oedipus*,
> by Gilles Deleuze and Félix Guattari

Thinking is trying to think the unthinkable: thinking the thinkable is not worth the effort.
> —Hélène Cixous, *Three Steps on the Ladder of Writing*

In order to countersign the WPA imperial push, postcomposition insists on a future of critical mass, one in which the cultural capital of WPA approaches

is perpetually questioned and the role of the local wpa is set aside as a primary function of disciplinary work. I do not mean to set up a local/global
dichotomy between the wpa and the WPA because, as I have explained,
the two are inseparable. As Sean Hand explains in his introduction to Deleuze's *Foucault*, "the individual is the product of power. What is needed is
to 'de-individualize' by means of multiplication and displacement, diverse
combinations. The group must not be the organic bond uniting hierarchized
individuals, but a constant generator of de-individualization" (vii). Following
Hand, postcomposition proposes an agenda not only of de-individualizing,
of working to con/front identity/subjectivity and questions of who We are
and what We do, but of deterritorialization, a type of un-administering of the
administrators, in which wpas work toward a more critical position, a decen-
tered position, a shifting position, a position that specifically questions its
own positionality, its own place.[5] Such deterritorializing, de-individualizing,
de-identifying positions are strategies that disavow the safety of the WPA
Imperial Place in favor of the freedom of (institutional) spaces, one where
wpas work against (again, I do not mean in opposition to but buttressed up
against) WPA capital. The de-identified wpa is a move toward the posthuman wpa. Such work could be considered a "return" of wpa potential powers
in order to continually reform the principles that drive any given writing
program. The idea here is simple, one gleaned from Antonio Negri, that
administrative principles should not be inherited from the past but rather
should be continually recast as something entirely new. Such restructuring,
reformation of administration, works not simply to recast the same emperor
in new clothes again and again (as Negri cites Marx, it's "all the same old shit"
[qtd. in Negri, "Constituent" 219]) but to allow for total reconceptualizations
as to what writing program administration might be and, ultimately, binds
neither individual wpas nor, more to the point, composition studies to an
identity driven by the WPA Empire, administrative/academic work, or economic management. The potential, of course, is that critical work might be
realized in new frames, not merely work that attempts to readjust well-worn
models yet again into contexts where they stand to fail or, at best, that mimics
historical narratives in an attempt to perpetuate rhetorics of standardization
and work toward continual reaffirmation of the state of the WPA. Administrators must emerge from the (same old) shit to ask if there is not another
way to think about how we administer, why composition studies itself has
become trapped by an administrative dictate, and, ultimately, how to disavow
that dictate. If the systems that wpas serve write composition(ists) into a
position from which composition(ists) must administer, does the fear of non-
administration, of relinquishing that position, relinquishing the safety of the

place of administration, hobble the WPA and composition studies into place, inscribed in an illusion of safety and a blindness of the contingent frontiers of composition studies' space? Postcomposition openly resists adherence to such places in favor of exploration of the complex spaces of writing.

Recent conversations about "Comp Droids" and "Boss Composition-ists" contribute specifically to the place(ing) of composition studies and writing program administration into occupations molded by cookie-cutter homogenization and standardization in some rather dangerous ways. Such conversations are deeply *composition studies* and rapidly (if not already) (re)forming the essence of how we and others understand that term. For instance, the argument made in Richard Miller's "'Let's Do the Numbers': Comp Droids and the Prophets of Doom" to recast graduate education in composition studies as graduate studies in administration may serve the WPA Imperial drive but is short-sighted, fails to see the possibilities of ad-vanced work in composition studies beyond its minimal links with admin-istrative positions, and offers little, if any, attention to learning more about writing beyond classroom management functions or as phenomena in and of its own right. For Miller, administration is power, and the interdisciplinary administrative curriculum the article suggests moves composition studies not away from its millstone of FYC but into the realm of taking on more administrative burdens. Such a move recasts composition studies not as an intellectual endeavor, one with the potential for important theoretical and critical work, but specifically as a professional, administrative, academic endeavor, one endlessly tied not only to FYC but to an inflexible position and place in the academy. Miller's argument regarding the reformation of graduate work in composition studies, in conjunction with the familiar argument about not restricting composition instruction to compositionists, is a concession to the power of institutional systems that have historically bound composition studies to a place of servitude. Miller's claim that it "is a mistake to abandon the ethic of service that defines the field" (103), that composition studies should focus its attention on training (and here I mean all that the word evokes; see Fulkerson, "Foreword") administrators as the primary means for best ensuring the future place of composition studies, is a problematic, conciliatory argument that bows to the very power structures that have historically enslaved composition studies. It is a state-ment of concession, a signature of surrender. In no way does this argument move composition studies beyond its limit-situation; rather, it embraces that boundary in an attempt to find safety in the place of servitude. Emancipa-tion and the possibilities of spatial freedom are surrendered in favor of the institutional safety of a well-defined and ordered place.

By introducing models of graduate education that center upon administration, composition studies is (short-)leashed to that center, its identity bound. Such a focus would be disastrous for composition studies, even more so than its current situation in which administration and subject management have become the central focus of the field. This does not mean, however, that composition studies should abandon administration or refuse to offer courses and professional work in administration—particularly if composition studies is unable to overcome the neurosis of the pedagogical imperative and accepts its academic leash, crawling like a (beaten) dog back to the safety of the house its master has built. Acknowledging administration as a primary object of study places great limits on research that are already difficult to overcome. If we aim to decenter the administration Empire, graduate programs cannot move toward standardization and focus on administration. Similarly, administrators must recognize the need for wildly new approaches to talking about and enacting administrative theories. I am not suggesting new models of writing program administration merely for the sake of newness—revolution for revolution's sake. Nor am I suggesting that the shifts in administrative approaches be so drastic that new wpas are drafted from ranks beyond composition studies, or that new administrative approaches are gleaned from other well-worn models like business administration or education administration. Wpas, I agree, must be steeped in the conversations of composition studies; however, my concern grows from a rapid homogenization of those conversations veiled in a rhetoric of standardization and in service of a territorial defensiveness that prevents critical questioning or critical restructuring of administrative approaches in favor of consistency and party-line rhetoric. In this context, violence becomes an option—perhaps the only option.

I take the term "violence," here, broadly to encompass concepts of disruption. Working from Deleuze and Foucault, I don't mean violence as a negative, destructive act; rather, violence operates to change the object upon which it is enacted. That is, violence does not work toward destruction in the negative but instead creates possibilities through disruption or, at minimum, through Foucault's notion of thinking "differently." Earlier I noted my wish that the conversation about wpa genealogies had taken into account Nietzsche's understanding of genealogy and Deleuze's critique of that position. Deleuze's attention to Nietzsche works to identify how the violence enacted against idols is not a destructive act but an act of productivity that amounts to a move beyond the entrenched system and traditional thoughts, theories, and perceptions. Complex systems, we know, work to exclude or assimilate. Systems exclude and assimilate through processes of standardization emphasized and enacted by way of regulation and reitera-tion. Standardization insists that the totality of signification occur within its own boundaries—boundaries built and reinforced in the shadow of obliga-tory and unavoidable repetition. Exclusionary signification becomes the ground on which a homogenized reality names its place. Critical work—in particular, theory—pushes to exceed the limits imposed by such places, to see beyond the illusion of safety those places profess. For Deleuze (see specifically *Cinema 2*), it is precisely the enactment of violence against the systemic that provides the opportunity to disturb hegemonic formations. For postcomposition's spatial and ecological approaches, this means atten-tion to the complexity of system in order to resist systemic homogenization. Thus, the wpa postcomposition must not only question the power, methods, and institutional function of the wpa but also work to disrupt those very powers, methods, and roles. The critical wpa has reached the point of the wpa phenomena to enact drastic alteration and to sustain the critical mass needed to spark chain reactive changes, not only locally but within the wpa/ WPA community, participating in critical concentrations of new ways of thinking of administration for composition studies and disavowal of the administrative imperative postcomposition. The critical wpa is not merely one who questions, who is discerning, who evaluates, judges, and responds (that is, is critical), but one willing to fill the critical need for disruption.

Post-Labor

[W]riting is an academic enterprise—and composition studies is a service profession—that seeks to meet the needs of the university and corporate capitalism for minimally literate and maximumly docile and useful subjects.

—Lynn Worsham, "Coming to Terms: Theory, Writing, Politics"

It is not clear that "lower management" as a group has ever figured in any substantial transformation of society or its institutions, or that lower management represents a particularly strong standpoint for individuals "advocating" change to upper management. Indeed, despite the occa-sional exception, the opposite would seem to be the case. Lower manage-ment is particularly vulnerable, highly individuated, and easily replaced.

—Marc Bousquet, "Composition as Management Science: Toward a University without a WPA"

"I would prefer not to."

—Herman Melville, "Bartleby, the Scrivener: A Story of Wall-Street"

Managerial/economic disruption for postcomposition initiates in (at least) three likely spaces: first, the resistance to the administrative imperative, particularly as the central identifying factor of composition studies; second, in radical approaches to what we might call the contingent labor problem; and third, in the shift of research and scholarship away from areas pertaining to the first two spaces. By now, this first and third space of disruption should be evident, and despite the deeply ingrained disciplinary history and protective conservatism into which such disruptions will inevitably run, these are central to postcomposition's agenda in making the phenomena of writing the central theoretical object of study. Unfortunately, the second site of disruption, the problem of contingent labor, will likely be read as a polemic, an argument not grounded in the reality of the "situation" in which composition studies finds itself. However, it is specifically regarding composition studies' tradition of approaching contingent labor that must be radically disrupted as those traditions act as the proverbial ties that bind composition studies to its service identity and restrict the kinds of scholarships that are valued.

Before elaborating upon disruption to the contingent labor position, though, I want to take a moment to anticipate some reaction and criticism. I preface my argument by first turning briefly to a criticism regarding administrative and managerial positions in the American academic institution forwarded in Marc Bousquet's insightful "Composition as Management Science: Toward a University without a WPA." In one of the opening epigraphs to the essay, Bousquet cites James Porter and his colleagues' 2000 *CCC* article that won the 2001 Braddock Award, "Institutional Critique: A Rhetorical Methodology for Change," which makes the claim that because institutions are human-made, "we" can change them. Bousquet takes to task Porter and his colleagues' supposition that "change presupposes a managerial insider prepared to make the sorts of arguments by which universities are 'likely to be swayed,' to 'ask for' resources using 'effective rhetorical strategies' and to work to build 'disciplinary status' that can be 'parlayed into institutional capital'" (494). Bousquet goes on to explain that such a supposition maintains a tradition of thinking in composition studies that because of an assumed expertise in "making arguments," the insider manager will be able to persuade "those with power" inside the institution of the necessity for those changes. Bousquet calls this the "management theory of agency," which employs the "rhetoric of pleasing the prince" (494). Like Bousquet, I remain overwhelmingly unconvinced that such tactics are useful—or as Bousquet says, necessary—in attempts to incite institutional change.

Bousquet proposes a counterapproach to the management theory of agency named the "labor theory of agency" (494), to which I will return in a moment.[6] For now, I want to adopt Bousquet's lack of confidence in "insider" institutional arguments for the wpa for the simple fact that, as I explained earlier in this chapter, wpas are not true insiders; they are (for the most part) low-level administrators serving (at) the will of management, often acquiescing to that will under what Jeanne Gunner in "Among the Composition People: The WPA as English Department Agent" calls a conviction of "benevolence" (159). Because of this, any change that can be initiated by way of management agency will always be limited and regulated by institutional management to first serve the institution, and this is often complacently supported and enforced by the administrator. Participation in this method always relegates change in writing program administrative approaches to bonds of institutional/academic need/desire. While this is not inherently negative in total, it should be noted that such bonds innately limit what constitutes the work of composition studies and always relegates that work to direct ties with writing programs, first-year courses, administration, and student subjects. Institutionally, then, composition studies can be understood only as an academic discipline; an anti-intellectual pall cast over the discipline from the outside has been generally accepted and encouraged from within, primarily because "We" have accepted that management agency actually grants authority. Not only is management agency false agency but its purchase has been reinscribed in WPA lore as the avenue of not intellectual freedom but academic security, a security We have eagerly accepted, duping ourselves to believe that it is the same thing as intellectual integrity. It is not.

In addition, it is likely that some will bristle at the second position regarding contingent labor as somehow outside the realm of reality, a position that disregards the situations of real people with real economic issues, real lives that are affected by their abilities to earn livings as composition instructors. We might think of this as the "facts of life" critique, a position that is satisfied with saying that that's "just how things are." I do not wish my position regarding this type of labor to sound as though I am heartless or that this proposition is suggested in a vacuum free from sympathy. Instead, I intend it to sound frightening, ruthless, and severe for the simple fact that this form of disruption is likely to be just that. And, as I have said, violence in this context is necessary.

The position, then, is simple: postcomposition should remove itself from questions of contingent labor, questions that have relegated composition studies' primary identity and most of its anxieties to questions of labor and labor management. This position includes the difficult posture of no longer supporting contingent labor as a viable option for work in writing studies. While composition studies may be ethically bound to continue seeking solutions for the uncomfortable situation of contingent labor in writing instruction by improving the conditions of those contingent laborers, postcomposition disavows these conversations because they are not beneficial to furthering any understanding of the phenomena of writing or the position of writing studies in the academy. Postcomposition adopts a position that arguments about contingent labor have been influenced by a focus on subjects rather than upon the systems and ecologies of those systems in which subjects believe they require agency. The quarrels about contingent labor have evolved because of an assumed rhetoric of victimization that has done little other than to maintain the narrative of oppression upon which the WPA Empire and, in turn, composition studies have relied as their primary institutional argumentative tool. Individuals who accept long-term contingent labor positions have made ethical decisions of self-sustainability over the systemic objectives of the discipline. Those who accept positions that contribute to the problem of contingent labor in writing instruction while understanding how their choices contribute to the larger debate regarding the conditions of contingent labor should do so knowing they have made bad ethical choices in regard to the more encompassing disciplinary and institutional conversation. Those in positions of managerial power—wpas, specifically—who knowingly and willingly develop, support, and maintain writing programs that rely upon contingent labor do so to the disservice of composition studies. Composition studies, in its support of such programs, despite its recognition that such programs are detrimental to the intellectual and pedagogical ideals of the discipline, has openly accepted its role of service component, has accepted complacency as its primary academic philosophy. It is here, in the occupation of writing instructor and the management of those positions, where the disruptive surge must begin in order to separate writing studies from the engulfing institutional control of management and labor.

Arguments about contingent labor can occur only as long as the discipline accepts the subject as the central figure of knowledge making. Resistance is couched, then, in the subject rather than in the system. Jean Baudrillard's *Simulacra and Simulation* identifies this as the "liberating claim of subjecthood" (85). In this model, when individual subjects identify a moment of contestation against a system, the system transfers responsibility of the situation onto the subject. In such situations, there are, Baudrillard contends, three possible responses of resistance. The first is rebellion, but rebellion fails as it is co-opted by the system, since the rebellion is always already based upon and within the system. The second is hyper-conformity, which reveals a subject's total dependence upon the system and his or her willingness to subscribe passively to the system (this, seemingly, has been the general approach taken by composition studies). The third is "non-reception," which is better understood as nonparticipation (see also Hardin, "Writing Theory and Writing the Classroom"). Total disengagement from the system, of course, is impossible, but nonparticipation, refusal to accept the institution's prerogative, is the ground from which the contingent labor issue should be radically challenged. Yes, seemingly Baudrillard's suggestion of nonconformity runs counter to the postcomposition positions of disavowal of the subject and attention to complex ecologies of systems in that Baudrillard is clearly working toward a "resurrection of the subject of history" and resistance to the system (86); however, adaption of the non-reception method of resistance provides a functional answer to the question of contingent labor postcomposition. When wpas are presented with institutional situations that exacerbate the problem of contingent labor, when individuals find themselves dependent upon contingent labor positions, the response postcomposition is simply to adopt the position of Melville's Bartleby.

Of course, such an argument, as I mentioned, will likely garner a good deal of resistance itself. After all, composition studies has built its place in the academy based upon the perceived demand for large contingents of working bodies and the need to manage those bodies. In fact, composition studies has established itself as a juggernaut in the American university by convincing the institution that there is a need for a required course in writing, a need for large staffs of instructors to teach the required courses, and a need for a validated administrator to oversee those instructors. While the job market in English studies and other humanities areas has been dreadful for candidates with PhDs for more than fifteen years, the job market for composition studies faculty has maintained a comfortable stability by first developing an institutional need for a writing program administrator at any institution where writing is taught and then convincing the institution that such administrative work is too important and too burdensome for just one person. Without the very idea of writing programs (read: specifically required first-year composition courses), in fact, there would be little if any institutional demand for writing specialists. That history and the narrative itself are what drive and perpetuate the perceived demand for a large contingent labor force.

Likewise, composition studies has adopted a collective mind-set in which arguments that work to eliminate contingent labor rather than work to secure better conditions for contingent labor are seen as, for lack of a better phrase, "not nice." Certainly, many in composition studies recognize the problems of contingent labor but accept those problems as the condition of the times simply because taking any sort of substantial stand against using or relying upon contingent labor would force them to take stands against those individuals who have accepted the contingent labor positions or the role of development and administration of programs that thrive on the contingent labor factor. Those individuals are, of course, people we know, care about, and respect, people with real families, real economic needs, and real feelings—but they are people who have made ethically poor choices in light of the discipline, and saying so, well, it's just not nice. But violence rarely is.

Which brings us, at least for the moment, back to Bousquet's "Composition as Management Science," which surveys the "degree to which the managerial subjectivity predominates in composition studies, distorting the field's understanding of 'materialism' and 'critique' to the point that it consistently attempts to offer 'solutions' to its 'labor problem' without accounting for the historical reality of organized academic labor" (494). For Bousquet, composition studies has failed in its address of the labor struggle for a number of reasons, including, as I mentioned earlier in this chapter, confusion over whom the We might be in composition studies. Taking a materialist stance, Bousquet asks the important question, "How can composition's 'success' be separated from this story of failure for academic labor more generally?" (500). He continues:

> Clearly, the emergence of rhetoric and composition into some form of (marginal) respectability and (institutional-bureaucratic) validity has a great deal to do with its usefulness to upper management in its legitimating the practice of deploying a revolving labor force of graduate employees and other contingent teachers to teach writing. The discipline's enormous usefulness to academic capitalism—in delivering cheap teaching, training a supervisory class for the cheap teachers, and producing a group of intellectuals who theorize and legitimate this scene of managed labor—has to be given at least as much credit in this expansion as the heroic efforts that Porter and his coauthors call the WPA's "strong track record for enacting change." (500)

It is because of this honesty that Bousquet is able to see why Joseph Harris's "Meet the New Boss, Same as the Old Boss" and Richard Miller's "The Arts of Complicity" embrace the safety of complacence and urge composition studies to cater to and support such academic managerialism.

Yet, Bousquet is not content with such a position of compliance. Instead, he identifies a number of larger disciplinary conditions that lend themselves toward composition studies' perceived need for compliance, of which the need to be recognized as a legitimate part of the institution is central, a need that has been institutionalized as an intrinsic part of composition studies' identity. In Bousquet's words, though, composition studies "will never feel like 'one of the gang' of disciplines until its labor patterns are more like those in other fields" (502).[7] He continues: "To put it in blunt terms, so long as composition's discourse remains a management science—or alternatively, until history, engineering, and philosophy are management sciences to the same extent—it is likely to fail to enjoy the status it seeks: the status of a discipline among peers" (502–3).

Bousquet goes on to show how much of the complacence with the position of composition studies and the perpetuating of the labor issue it faces grow from an atmosphere of acceptance that assumes that given that conditions *are* as the reality We face, the best approach is to work within those realities in order to "get ahead" (504). Miller's *As If Learning Mattered: Reforming Higher Education* refers to this as "conceding the reality of academic working conditions" (qtd. in Bousquet 504). Such a position, Bousquet explains, though, not only entraps composition studies in institutional stagnation but drastically hampers what can be theorized about agency and change and, I would add, more important than theorizing about agency, theorizing writing. Bousquet goes on to rightfully critique various works that support such positions, arguing that "rhetoric and composition's enthusiasm for this kind of appointment should be, at the very least, up for debate" (505).

So as not to fall into a prolonged summary of Bousquet's "Composition as Management Science" (which is difficult to avoid as the article presents a number of important points regarding such issues and is one of the most well thought-out works addressing composition studies' labor issues), I want to note a key argument of the essay: that the few changes afforded composition studies and its managerial arm—the addition of graduate programs for certification and validation, increased budgets for writing centers or increased course offerings, and so on—have all been granted because they support the economic mission of the institution. But any form of real change regarding either the labor conditions (specifically of the contingent labor force) or the intellectual capital of the field has not occurred due to managerial influence. In fact, I argue, it is specifically because of composition studies' obsession with the administrative imperative and its complacence with the position the institution grants because of that imperative that composition studies will continue to render itself of little intellectual value to the university at large. It is in these sites of labor dispute and the acceptance of administrative consideration as a viable research object where disruption postcomposition initiates. To quote Bousquet again and to align myself with him: "In my view, composition's best chance to contribute to a better world and to achieve disciplinary status depends on learning to write as colleagues among colleagues—a condition predicated on working toward a university without a WPA" (518, my emphasis).[8]

Toward the end of *Simulacra and Simulation* in a segment called "The Spiraling Cadaver," Baudrillard argues that "the university is in ruins" (149) and places knowledge in opposition to power, giving power the upper hand over knowledge. "Power (or what takes its place)," he explains, "no longer believes in the university"; the university serving only as a "zone for the shelter and surveillance of a whole class of a certain age" has become a "rotting referential" (150). We can confidently—though perhaps disappointedly—say the same of first-year writing, of writing programs. But like Baudrillard, we can also argue that "by rotting, the university can still do a lot of damage," but "it is necessary to transform this rotting into a violent process" (150), a process that does not save certain objects as holdover from the old in order to build the new, as if the ideals of the rotted can serve the new situation. Instead, this is the (symbolic) violence of total deterritorialization, the relinquishing of the safety of place, the "liquidation of culture and of knowledge" (151). Postcomposition's move beyond the subject, beyond the administration of subjects, and beyond the issue of contingent labor is not, à la Baudrillard, an attempt to save composition studies but a brandishing of its cadaver.

5. Ecocomposition Postcomposition

> Ecology must stop being associated with the image of a small nature-
> loving minority or with qualified specialists.
>
> —Félix Guattari, *The Three Ecologies*

Writing is an ecological phenomenon. It is spatial, relational, and complex and thus requires complex theories (and a complex of theories) in order to attempt to understand its intricacies, functions, and possibilities. Forward-ing this notion that writing is ecological, a small number of composition scholars began to import ecological methodologies into composition studies just after the millennial shift. The culminating efforts of those writing about ecology-and-writing has been dubbed "ecocomposition," a term meant to signify the intersection between ecology and composition studies.[1] While the term "ecocomposition" did not make its debut until the mid-1990s, eco-logical methodologies began to appear in composition studies scholarship as early as the 1970s.

Working from the premises I have established thus far regarding the shift of focus postcomposition from subject to writing, from time to space, and from academic to intellectual work, I want to offer another disruptive move, this one geared toward a realignment of the ecocomposition agenda as it has developed over the last ten years or so.[2] To begin, I want to look at the definitions of ecocomposition that have become most prevalent. I am not, however, going to provide a history of ecocomposition, as that his-tory has already been detailed in the 2002 *College English* article "Breaking Ground in Ecocomposition: Exploring Relationships between Discourse and Environment," which I coauthored with Christian R. Weisser and in which this first definition appeared (it was also repeated in our book *Natural Discourse: Toward Ecocomposition*)[3]:

> Ecocomposition is the study of the relationships between environments (and by that we mean natural, constructed, and even imagined places) and discourse (speaking, writing, and thinking). Ecocomposition draws primarily from disciplines that study discourse (chiefly composition, but also including literary studies, communication, cultural studies,

linguistics, and philosophy) and merges the perspectives of them with works in disciplines that examine environments (these include ecology, environmental studies, sociobiology, and other "hard" sciences). As a result, ecocomposition attempts to provide a more holistic, encompassing framework for studies of the relationships between discourse and environment. (572)

The second comes from the Wikipedia entry for ecocomposition:

Ecocomposition is a way of looking at literacy using concepts from ecology. It is a postprocess theory of writing instruction that tries to account for factors beyond hierarchically defined goals within social settings; however, it doesn't dismiss these goals. Rather, it incorporates them within an ecological view that extends the range of factors affecting the writing process beyond the social to include aspects such as "place" and "nature." Its main motto, then, is "Writing Takes Place." ("Ecocomposition")

On the surface, each of these seems important, but I want to argue that these definitions do not really talk about writing, do not establish an ecology of writing. They talk about discourse and literacy, and, as Raúl Sánchez has now made clear, in composition theory, "discourse" (and by extension, I'd add "literacy") is often addressed in place of writing and often argued to have "more explanatory power than writing. Discourse, in particular, with its Foucauldian resonance, is intended to cover a broader range of culturally embedded signifying functions. Its scope is thought to exceed writing" (*Function* 9). This substitution is understandable, Sánchez explains, because so many in composition studies sought to "connect our field's interests to the cultural practices that comprise an increasingly complex, interconnected, and written world" (9). "And so," the argument continues, "in an effort to broaden the range, applicability, and potential influence of composition studies, they have changed the object of study on the assumption that the category of *writing* alone cannot describe the theoretical and cultural situations they see before them" (9, emphasis in original). But like Sánchez, I believe that writing can and does do this work, and I see less need to shift the object of study of ecocomposition and postcomposition to issues of discourse than to develop ecological approaches to writing qua writing, without becoming hampered by the ambiguities of discourse.

Likewise, these definitions address writing processes and writing instruction, not writing (I hope by now I have made these differences distinct). Even in claims that ecocomposition is a type of postprocess theory, we must now acknowledge that postprocess theories, because they serve as reaction against and critique of the process paradigm, can never be more than theories of the teaching of writing, not about writing itself. As the Wikipedia definition so clearly puts it, "It is a postprocess theory of writing instruction" ("Ecocomposition"). Similarly, as I address later, postprocess theory is fettered by rhetorics of the social epistemic. Moreover, though unstated, these definitions, by way of the invocation of terms like "place," "environment," and "nature," have not validated inquiry regarding the relational characteristics of writing systems or writing as complex system but instead have tentatively validated the examination of problematic concepts like "nature" or "environment" from—more often than not—a kind of cultural studies position that examines the relationship between subject or identity, and, say, nature. As the Wikipedia entry beyond the definition explains, ecocomposition's "main concern has been the relationship between the writing process and natural places," and "ecocomposition asks what effects a place has (or different places have) on the writing process. In what ways is our identity influenced by place, and what bearing does this have on our writing?" ("Ecocomposition"). That is, these definitions have simply given way to claims that concepts like place or nature or environment should be included alongside the critical categories of race, class, culture, and gender as primary categories for examining factors that influence subject formation. These approaches have given rise to an increased use of environmentalist texts—often in the form of nature writing—in composition classrooms as artifacts for analysis. In fact, no work in ecocomposition of which I am aware (including my own previous work) provides any insight to the functions of writing as an ecological system outside of ways of engaging environmentalist politics in terms of the teaching of writing (the notable exceptions here are the pre-ecocomposition work of Marilyn Cooper and Richard M. Coe, which I address in the next section of this chapter). Instead, ecocomposition has been an attempt to reinvigorate subject formation of student subjects (most often first-year writing students) with environmental political positions, positions designed to spark "thinking" about the environmental or ecological "crisis." This work, of course, is at all times political and melds nicely with composition studies' agenda of subject improvement. By turning to concepts like nature, ecocomposition is never more than another maneuver toward subject formation, toward political improvement and subjectification. In this way, ecocomposition is not an approach to thinking about writing but a misnamed approach for giving students something to write about, a political content addressed as the thing that fills writing with meaning.

Much scholarship in ecocomposition has addressed the ways in which environment and location work to help form identity, as Weisser's "Ecocomposition and the Greening of Identity" contends. This has been the primary work of ecocomposition to date. Fortunately, a very small number of compositionists have recently embraced ecological methodologies for understanding writing that move away from the ecocomposition project. In this chapter, I work toward developing an ecological postcomposition approach to writing theories by way of reconsidering the writings of three scholars whose work was central to the evolution of ecocomposition but that might be reread to adjust the ecocomposition project to a more beneficial postcomposition project. Following this reconsideration, I examine the work of two compositionists who have turned to ecological methodologies outside of ecocomposition and three approaches to ecologic/systems thinking that inform ecocomposition postcomposition: methodologies of complex ecology, posthumanist systems theory, and ecosophy.

The Failure of Ecocomposition

Ecocomposition has (already) failed as an intellectual enterprise. It has failed to produce any substantial theory regarding the ecological facets of writing or even the relationships between writing and any ecological or environmental "crisis." Its failure grows from four primary spaces. First, it falls prey to composition studies' pedagogical imperative even before any substantial ecological theories of writing have been forwarded. That is, ecocomposition has never established any ecological methodology for understanding writing—or even the teaching of writing—while instantly rendering itself a strictly academic effort. Ecocomposition, one might suggest, is expressly the kind of undefined chaotic study that Stephen M. North warned against in *The Making of Knowledge in Composition*. This is not a call for the standardization of ecocomposition approaches but a critique acknowledging that ecocomposition hasn't really paid much attention to the ecology of writing.

Second, and perhaps more significant, ecocomposition has failed (thus far) as an intellectual endeavor because of its embrace of floating signifiers like "nature" and "environment" as its primary objects of study rather than writing, encouraging instead conversations about nature/culture relations and the like. If composition studies was quick to set aside writing as its object of study in favor of discourse in order to be more connected to cultural practices, as Sánchez argues, and to appeal to a broader sense of "what we do," then ecocomposition has mirrored this pattern, attaching itself to the more culturally popular agendas of "greening" and other environmentally appropriate investigations. But this also boils down to matters of ease. Like my earlier critique regarding the difficulty of the work of theory as opposed to the ease of working with institutionally provided and validated subjects, ecocomposition has rejected the difficult work of devising ecological theories that provide insight into the phenomena of writing. Certainly, it is admirable to take up eco-friendly work, particularly as green campuses become all the rage and grants for developing courses about sustainability and other eco-friendly subjects offer ecocompositionists the opportunity for institutional validation and support, but this work does little for writing studies. I do not mean to suggest that this work should be abandoned, either as the work of ecocomposition, composition studies more generally, or any other academic endeavor. Instead, I wish to argue beyond this work, the work of ecocomposition postcomposition, removed from subjectivity, from the problematic of things like nature.[4]

Third, the ecology of ecocomposition has always been an anthropocentric ecology, focusing on the human agent's relationship with environment, both the agent's influence on the environment and the environment's affect on the agent. Influence, in this ecology, is most often a discursive influence, one tied more directly with concepts of social interaction than with ecological relationships.

Fourth, we must also recognize that one of the failures of ecocomposition grows from the simple fact that so few people have taken up the ecological imperative as a direction of research. The increase in publications and conference presentations about ecocomposition-related subjects that Christian Weisser and I noted in our "Breaking Ground in Ecocomposition" article was premature, as there have been relatively no publications about ecocomposition and limited conference panels since we made that claim so few years ago. The ecocomposition dialogue as a scholarly conversation has gone all but dormant. These four limits not only have encumbered what ecocomposition can provide regarding writing but also have prevented ecocomposition from developing any substantial theory of the complexity of writing and writing systems.

Fortunately, some compositionists have begun turning to ecology to theorize writing via avenues other than ecocomposition. Jenny Edbauer's "Unframing Models of Public Distribution: From Rhetorical Situation to Rhetorical Ecology" works to disrupt the entrenched—and perhaps sacrosanct—model of the rhetorical situation proposed by Lloyd Bitzer and embraced by composition studies as the foundational paradigm for understanding communicative interaction. Edbauer destabilizes the rhetorical situation by proposing that situations operate in more ecologically complex networks of "lived practical consciousness or structures of feelings" (7), then proposes a theory of "rhetorical ecology" to account for the complexity of network. Likewise, Collin Gifford Brooke's award-winning *Lingua Fracta:*

Towards a Rhetoric of New Media contends that because of our familiarity with understanding rhetoric by way of print culture, we have overlooked the technical dimensions of rhetoric. Brooke adopts a radical approach to reconceiving new media rhetorics by way of "ecologies of practice." Dànielle Nicole DeVoss, Heidi A. McKee, and Richard (Dickie) Selfe's collection *Technological Ecologies and Sustainability* examines the complex ecologies of interaction between humans and computers in computerized writing environments. While Edbauer's and Brooke's works forward ecological theories of rhetoric (not writing), they are the closest research to the kind I envision ecological work providing writing studies. DeVoss, McKee, and Selfe unfortunately trap their ecological frames—insightful as they are—within the vocabulary of composition studies' pedagogical imperative.

Byron Hawk's *A Counter-History of Composition*, like others (the Wikipedia definition, for example), ties ecocomposition to the move postprocess, explaining that "Breaking Ground in Ecocomposition" puts "forward the concept of ecocomposition in an attempt to push post-process further toward the concept of ecology than the critical categories of race, class, and gender" (222). By way of ecocomposition, Hawk contends that ecology becomes a crucial avenue for composition studies: "The use of the concept of ecology moves discussions of writing, rhetoric, and invention beyond the standard inventional heuristics and social categories toward models that integrate environments into writing and invention processes" (223). But Hawk rightly critiques the limits ecocomposition imposed on itself, arguing specifically about the ecocomposition of "Breaking Ground in Ecocomposition" that "while Dobrin and Weisser's work is clearly on the right track, they do seem to be held back from pushing the concept of ecology to its limits by continuing to rely on forms of social-epistemic rhetoric and social construction," largely because, Hawk contends, "there is no other completely articulated and accepted paradigm beyond expressivism and social-epistemic rhetoric in which to place their work" (223). The critique continues:

> Consequently, their pedagogy still leans heavily on public action through discourse, on discourse determining and changing material contexts, and on ecocomposition's "links to Paulo Freire's dialogic methodology." ... This emphasis on discourse and dialectics is a blinder to ecological complexity, which is post-dialectical. Dialectics still appear in their work because rhetoric and composition is a field that privileges language and the social and molar levels of explanation and operation. Each of these has its affective place in the overall economy, but ecopedagogues may continue to run into the same trouble as those espousing older

forms of critical pedagogy. . . . In the end, when they over privilege language or social construction they can actually over simplify the ecology rather than account for its complexity. (223–24)

This criticism is perhaps the most important and insightful made of ecocomposition to date, and it is with Hawk's points in mind that I move to disrupt ecocomposition from its social-epistemic and, often, expressivist groundings in order to push ecological methodologies into the potential spaces that Hawk suggests can best serve our understanding of writing. However, it must be noted that Hawk's critique also seems to imply that there necessarily must be an in-place, accepted rhetoric from which, in which, and through which writing theory must emerge. Such a claim might be debatable. Certainly, it is critical to consider how composition studies has regulated disciplinary rhetorical possibilities (what is and can be thought of as composition studies), limiting the numbers and approaches of accepted paradigms to those that best serve the pedagogical imperative and managerial impetus. It is, though, another thing to say that there necessarily *must be* other rhetorics made evident in order for new/other paradigms to emerge. Such a claim is problematic. While this chapter operates under a similar assumption, proposing ecology as one possibility toward such a rhetoric—or grammar—in which to formulate new theories of writing beyond the trappings of the entrenched rhetorics, we must also not overlook the possibility that assuming that there must be a rhetoric from which to operate masks a potentially empty shift between rhetorics. What may be more desirable is to produce writing theories free of rhetorical paradigm constraints that require naming, instead either allowing new rhetorics to emerge from autonomous theories or, perhaps, even setting aside the very idea that there are or need to be rhetorical paradigms from which things—like theories—emerge or reside.

With this acknowledgment in mind, though, this chapter argues that in order for ecocomposition to move toward a complex ecology of writing postcomposition, one moving beyond issues of language, dialectic, and social epistemic, an ecological rhetoric/paradigm seems to best serve this agenda. Of course, such a move inherently serves to disrupt composition studies from its limitations of expressivism and social-epistemic and to open the doors for other approaches, such as spatial, posthumanist, and ecological. In many ways, composition studies may be witnessing a move in such directions already, particularly given the recent prominence of work in both complexity theories and network theories (both of which I will address in the next chapter) and the trickle of ecological-based theories just beginning to emerge; however, as is often the case in composition studies, even the exciting new theories making their ways into the field do so tempered with pre-inscribed limits of subject, management, and pedagogy. The richness of Hawk's work, for instance, is trapped by composition studies' pedagogical discourse; its posthumanism is an attempt at a posthuman pedagogy in which *pedagogy* is predetermined to be a *composition studies* pedagogy. For example, Hawk explains: "In order to enact the 'post-cognitive, postprocess, post-expressivist' shift that ecocomposition hopes to usher in . . . pedagogues will need to put more emphasis on the material and effective ecologies that exist in and link to their classrooms and start inventing methods and heuristics out of those complex ecologies" (224). To revise these early claims about ecocomposition, I would add that in order for ecocomposition to provide theory of writing of any importance, it must move beyond postcognitive, postprocess, and postexpressive, but also beyond postpedagogy, postsubjectivity, postmanagement, and of course, postcomposition. It must also be noted that Hawk's attraction to ecocomposition and ecological methodologies grows from ecocomposition's agenda to develop a complex vitalist paradigm tied to theories of system and in this way should not be critiqued for operating within the predesigned boundaries of the composition studies pedagogy neurosis; instead, we should look to Hawk's work to further push ecocomposition postcomposition.

Hawk's work, the Wikipedia definition, and my early work with Weisser all tie ecocomposition to postprocess theories. Prior to the advent of "postprocess," there was little that could be said in composition studies about writing or writing theory beyond what the process model provided, and critique of that model was (and still is) often met with disciplinary resistance. Postprocess, of course, has been methodologically problematic, and locking down any specific characteristic of what exactly postprocess is has been more than illusive.[5] Instead, "postprocess" is probably best read as indicating multiple disruptive moments in composition studies' own will to stability, disruptions that identify potential avenues of departure from the pedagogically driven motivations of the process movement—agendas that I hope to have shown as tied to subject formation, subject management, and disciplinary advancement. At its core, postprocess serves as an institutional critique and an attempt to show that writing theory can sever itself from the sacrosanct subject as the central imperative of writing studies. In this way, postcomposition and ecocomposition emerge from and with postprocess agendas, working to expose the institutional situation that provided composition studies with the authority to naturalize not just the process paradigm but what constituted writing in the university and what writing subjects should be. In doing so, postprocess provides the first resistance in composition studies for pedagogical application, insisting instead on models that account for theoretical contexts outside of the pedagogical imperative; we might think of this as a call to ecological thinking. This shift, while not a shift distinctly away from pedagogy, but one that includes other approaches besides or in addition to pedagogy, might be thought of as the initiation of postpedagogical approaches to writing theory, ways of thinking about writing that are not inherently tied to either the classroom or traditional/ entrenched composition studies methodologies in any codifiable way. If we play with this notion a bit, we can see that postprocess served as a disruption to the established understanding of writing as always already forming relationships with particular agents (subjects) and established institutional contexts (classrooms, composition studies), suggesting instead that writing is, indeed, relational but that those relations have not been established as concretely as process models espoused or as composition studies would have us believe. That is, postprocess has not yet considered the complexity of the relations it works to expose.

The introduction to Thomas Kent's edited collection *Post-Process Theory: Beyond the Writing-Process Paradigm* points out that among the various approaches to postprocess thinking, all of the contributors to the collection share three common assumptions about writing: writing is public, writing is interpretive, and writing is social (1). But as Hawk explains, this assessment of postprocess's central assumptions is limited by its attachment to social constructionist concepts and grounded in hermeneutic traditions. Hawk's "Reconnecting Post-Process: Toward a Theory of Posthuman Networks" in the collection *Beyond Post-Process* argues that "if rhetoric and composition truly wants to break out of traditional notions of the subject and process, as post-process seems to desire, these three grounding principles have to be reconfigured" (75). For Hawk, this occurs when postprocess is recast in light of posthuman models of network that "ultimately argue that the subject of writing is the network that inscribes the subject as the subject scribes the network" (75). It is toward this type of ecology, one that looks to the whole of the agent/system relation, privileging neither above the other, that ecocomposition postcomposition works. In order to do so, however, moving outside of the language/metaphor of social constructionism, postcomposition requires developing posthuman, ecological alternatives that reconsider the subject/agent as parts irreducible from the complexity of the whole system.

At its core, ecocomposition postcomposition is postprocess; it is also postpedagogy, postnature, and postsocial epistemic. It works to provide complex theories about writing instead of developing ways to encourage students to talk about or even write about particular types of "issues." In the posthuman world, nature/culture, nature/technology, and technology/culture binaries are no longer useful; instead technology, nature, and culture are seen as component parts of the same whole, each functioning in harmony at times and in conflict at others, and still at other times even functioning *as* the other. One of the failures of ecocomposition in its adherence to the empty signifier "nature" has been a failure to engage technology in any substantial means other than perhaps to identify an amorphous, unnamed technology as a factor responsible for ecological or environmental "crises." Ecocomposition postcomposition initiates a posthuman approach to nature and technology, identifying them as more than interconnected within complex systems, by way of being parts of the same wholes.

Looking Back to Move Beyond

It is just that within the past few decades the world has changed so much that our traditional perceptions, logic, and rhetoric are no longer as well adapted as they once were.
—Richard M. Coe, "Eco-Logic for the Composition Classroom"

[I]t is still a struggle to see relationships as primary, rather than focusing on—especially on—the human actors relating to human and nonhuman others, and even harder to see writing as part of a whole, interrelated, ceaselessly changing environment rather than as a social system through which humans act on and make conscious choices about the nonsocial other system, the natural environment.
—Marilyn Cooper, "Foreword: The Truth Is Out There"

Before moving ahead with work toward complex ecological theories of writing, it will be useful to look at some key works that framed the possibilities for ecocomposition to evolve and reconsider their ramifications. I look back to these works not to dismiss them but to identify previously overlooked facets that support my agendas for ecocomposition postcomposition. As I have noted, though, some of this work was embraced for having provided opportunities to integrate environmentalist rhetorics into composition classrooms more than for what they provide regarding understanding writing per se. Yet, work by three key thinkers needs to be reexamined in order to redirect the theoretical work ecocomposition can potentially engage without disregarding the groundwork that has been laid. I begin here, then, by reexamining Marilyn Cooper's "The Ecology of Writing" (1986);

Richard M. Coe's "Eco-Logic for the Composition Classroom" (1975), "Rhetoric 2001" (1974), and "'Rhetoric 2001' in 2001" (2001); and James Thomas Zebroski's "Toward a Theory of Theory for Composition Studies" (1998). While Cooper and Coe are often recognized as early contributors to the development of ecocomposition and Zebroski is overlooked in this capacity, a more detailed consideration of all of their works provides direction toward more significant ecological theories of writing and helps to redirect ecocomposition away from academic, pedagogical trappings and toward more intellectually productive work.

Though it postdates Coe's work by more than a decade, Cooper's "The Ecology of Writing" is most often cited as the preeminent work in initiating ecocomposition, though Cooper neither employs the term nor alludes to the possibility of the kinds of work that have unfolded under the ecocomposition agenda. "The Ecology of Writing" is only retroactively ecocomposition. Cooper critiques composition studies' process movement. For the 1986 composition studies' audience, writing theory was pedagogical theory, the two indistinguishable, and Cooper addresses the process movement as such, invoking the term "writing theory" to account for cognitive process models, theories that we can now understand not as theories about the phenomena of writing but as theories of how subjects write or as theories of how subjects think about writing. Given the immediacy of their pedagogical applications, all of these are more accurately understood as pedagogical theories than as writing theories. The distinction here should now be clear and recognized as important: much of what composition studies identifies as "writing theories" are actually theories about teaching subjects how to write; these are markedly different kinds of theories. Cooper argues against composition studies' pedagogical theories (turning to James Berlin's taxonomy as a way of identifying those theories) as reliant upon a concept of the individual writer writing, instead proposing that writing is, indeed, a social act. Along with Kenneth Bruffee's 1981 article "Collaborative Learning" and James A. Reither's "Writing and Knowing: Toward Redefining the Writing Process," which summarizes the ideas of Gary Larson, Lee Odell, Patricia Bizzell, and John Gage, "The Ecology of Writing" really stands as a primary signaling moment that the cognitive process model was to be dethroned by the social epistemic vision of writing and writing pedagogy.

Cooper proposes an ecological model of writing "whose fundamental tenet is that writing is an activity through which a person is continually engaged with a variety of socially constituted systems" (367). Unfortunately, in making this important claim, Cooper is reductive in her use of the term "ecology," limiting its meaning to "the science of natural environments"

(367). Yet, what Cooper provides is a dynamic opportunity to engage writing as a complex system. Granted, Cooper's model requires a little adjusting:

> An ecology of writing encompasses much more than individual writer and her immediate context. An ecologist explores how writers interact to form systems: all the characteristics of any individual writer or piece of writing both determine and are determined by the characteristics of all the other writers and writing in the systems. An important characteristic of ecological systems is that they are inherently dynamic; though their structures and contents can be specified at a given moment, in real time they are constantly changing, limited only by the parameters that are themselves subject to change over the longer spans of time. (368)

This model is influenced a good deal by its own reaction against the cognitive process model and composition studies' pedagogical imperative. Its central figure of investigation is first and foremost a consideration of the individual writer, the writing-subject. Yet, this model also hints at the role of complex system and fluctuation. Though the article could not anticipate the hyper-circulatory condition of writing systems of the late twentieth and early twenty-first centuries, it does suggest a need to encompass writer, writing, and system within a single gaze. If we grant Cooper the restriction of subject as a result of historical position and adapt her reaction against stability of system, what we find is that she begins to forward a different kind of systems theory, not leading toward a social epistemic model but toward a posthuman, hyper-circulatory concept of system in which agents become indistinguishable from the system itself—no matter if we embrace Cooper's idea that they both "determine and are determined by" characteristics of each or choose to accept the system as the predominant feature of the ecology, the agent indistinguishable from the system. If we nudge Cooper's proposition a bit, we can easily move from her claim that "the ecological model postulates dynamic interlocking systems which structure the social activity of writing" (368) to a more direct understanding that ecological methods (a term I prefer here to the limits and agendas of "model") postulate dynamic interlocking systems, which are themselves the structure of and structured by writing.

But it is here that ecocomposition postcomposition breaks with Cooper's ecological model, as "The Ecology of Writing" falls prey to the will of stability, identifying that "systems are concrete" and that all writers are involved in systems in which they can "specify the domain of ideas activated and supplemented" (369). But, systems are not always stable, and, as I hope to explain later in this chapter and in more detail in the next, metaphors like "ideas" work to signify that something (often couched as "information," "meaning," or "knowledge") operates separate from writing and can be identified as either the content of or as "something else" outside of writing, a concept Sánchez has effectively debunked in light of contemporary writing theory. Similarly, ecology for Cooper is as much an economic model as it is an ecological model. Ecology is employed as a method for charting writers' activities in the same ways that one can chart "investment patterns for consumer spending patterns from hiring patterns in a nation's economy" (369). Such a comparison entraps ecological consideration not only in light of economic metaphors but in an unspoken agenda of management, which, as I have noted, is one of the primary distinctions postcomposition (and ecocomposition postcomposition) makes between economic and ecologic models.

Finally, Cooper proposes a now-famous metaphor for thinking about writing: the web, "in which anything that affects one strand of the web vibrates throughout the whole" (370). The web metaphor alludes to the purported words of Chief Seattle often invoked in environmentalist discourse: "All things are connected." This metaphor, while adopted by many working in ecocomposition, fails to provide any substantial understanding of writing for three key reasons. First, as Christian Weisser and I originally critiqued the metaphor in *Natural Discourse: Toward Ecocomposition* and as I explain further in "A Problem with Writing (about) 'Alternative' Discourse," webs assimilate disruption; they localize vibration, subsuming energies. Through a more complex understanding of writing as disruption and writing as system, we can begin to dismantle the web as not addressing the role of assimilation and disruption to any substantial end. Second, as I have explained, the web model cannot account for the fluctuating complexity of systems as we now encounter them. This is not to suggest we need more dynamic metaphors to supersede the web metaphor but instead to suggest we move away from the will to metaphor as a primary mode of theorizing writing or even as a phase of theory making as Louis Althusser suggests it is (see chapter 2). Writing resists metaphor as a means of explanation both in its complexity and in its instability, or more accurately in its variation. And, third, the web suggests an identifiable separation between the system (web) and those things (agents) that make or affect the system. Postcomposition argues for a more infused approach to the whole-part relationship, not wanting to separate parts of the system from the system in ways that allow either to be reducible to examination free from the other (the land is Arthur; Arthur is the land). They are the same. Likewise, many who employ the web metaphor often overlook or disregard the fact that, according to Nedra Reynolds, "the metaphor of a web also evokes entrapment" (*Geographies* 35), a point more clearly explained by Mark C. Taylor's *The Moment of Complexity: Emerging Network Culture*: "Webs link and relate, entangling everyone in multiple, mutating, and mutually defining connections in which nobody is really in control" (23).

"The Ecology of Writing," of course, was not always embraced for its ecological approach. Laurence Hayden Lyall blasted Cooper's ecological approach for trying to make writing studies "scientific" (358), attacking her for suggesting an ecological model where none was needed (presumably because Kenneth Burke has already provided us all we need to know). On the other hand, "The Ecology of Writing" was embraced as providing key insights into Erika Lindemann's inquiry "What is the principal focus of English 101?" in establishing an approach for writing as system (295). Lindemann's "Three Views of English 101" turns to Cooper in order to develop a position of writing as system. Writing "is a way of living in social groups, of interacting with others and having them interact with us. Though we write to make meaning and discover the self, we also write to make a difference in the world," Lindemann explains (296). "The ecological model," she continues, "usefully complicates the learning and teaching of writing because it reminds us of the social context in which all writers work" (296). In this type of interpretation, and in Cooper's own language, we see how (and perhaps why) early ecological models become linked with social epistemic rhetoric. But, as Hawk clarifies, there have been no other rhetorics within which to frame such inquiries for composition studies; the same can be said of the trappings of the pedagogical obligation. Like most, Lindemann's adoption of the ecological model is grounded in the pedagogical imperative and in wanting to see writing in light of social contexts, a rather limited form of social ecology. While I can critique neither Lindemann nor Cooper for grounding their work in the pedagogical imperative, given the disciplinary zeitgeist from which they wrote, it is specifically these employments of ecological models that ecocomposition/postcomposition now moves away from, developing, as I hope to show, more complex notions of ecological methods through which to theorize writing and establish a new ecological rhetoric of writing that moves beyond the disciplinary limits of the rhetorics of the social epistemic, expressivism, and pedagogy.

Interestingly, though, once retroactively assimilated into the ecocomposition camp, Cooper expressed ambivalence about ecocomposition in her 2001 foreword to Weisser and Dobrin's collection *Ecocomposition: Theoretical and Pedagogical Approaches*. Cooper articulates this ambivalence as a sympathy for the need for a more systems-based approach to writing than ecocomposition forwards but also a nervousness about the reduction of ecocomposition to simply the teaching of nature writing—a worry that has, as I have discussed, been all but ignored in ecocomposition. Cooper's foreword to the *Ecocomposition* collection works to support the systems approach to writing over issues of nature versus culture for the simple fact that "it is through an ecological understanding of writing that the field of composition studies aligns itself with the dominant paradigm shift of the last century" (xi). Cooper goes on to explain the need for a detailed systems approach to understanding writing, an approach composition studies has resisted. She also works to adjust and update some of the claims she makes in "The Ecology of Writing," explaining that had she read at the time Martin Heidegger or Hubert L. Dryfus or Bill Green's book on Antarctic lakes, she might have "written more about changing patterns in the systems of writing and less about the structures and contents of the system" (xiv). Likewise, Cooper identifies that the metaphor of ecology for a way of thinking about writing must be more than—or not a—metaphor: "The systems that constitute writing and writers are not just like ecological systems but are precisely ecological systems, and . . . there are no boundaries between writing and the other interlocked, cycling systems of our world" (xiv). It is hard, she explains "to see writing as a whole, interrelated, ceaselessly changing environment rather than as a social system through which humans act on and make conscious choices" (xiv). It is here that the complexity of writing's ecology begins to unfold, in the difficult shift to seeing writing as a more dynamic, encompassing system inseparable from, well, everything.

Predating "The Ecology of Writing" by more than a decade, Richard Coe's ecological considerations have been greatly under-considered in ecocomposition research, and while they, like Cooper's work, are historically limited by the contextual discourse of their time (notably the complete dedication to the pedagogical imperative and the reliance on pedagogical conversations as the only location in which to forward ecological—or any—theory in mid-1970s composition studies), Coe's work offers enormous potential for developing ecological understandings of writing, the foremost of which is the need to look at wholes rather than parts. Coe's "Eco-Logic for the Composition Classroom" critiques composition pedagogy for seeking rhetorical approaches that work to break wholes into manageable parts. The problem Coe notes is that such methods work only when wholes can be attributed as the sum of all of their parts but are inefficient for addressing more complex phenomena—such as writing, one might extrapolate. Coe explains that rhetorical traditions reflect the dominant logics of Western science, logics that are contradictory to eco-logic, a logic that scrutinizes wholes over the reduction of wholes to parts, which could be ordered, named, and managed. What Coe calls for, then, is a systems approach to writing that accounts for whole systems rather than subsystems. Though Coe's eco-logic gets bogged down in an overblown concept of the contextual (something Cooper smartly avoids), eco-logic operates at a significant level of complexity that does not reduce the idea of system to something convenient, or even manageable (in both senses of that word). The distinction Coe makes, for instance, between rules and principles suggests a form of systemic flexibility or fluctuation.

While we might read "Eco-Logic for the Composition Classroom" today as simply proposing a detailed notion of rhetorical situations, its argument regarding rhetoric as unable to attend to the complexities of writing also provides an opportunity to question the disciplinary relationship between composition studies and rhetoric, a relationship that has been problematic, manifest in the very question of whether the field is to be called rhetoric and composition, composition studies, writing studies, or something else. First, we need to ask, à la Coe, if rhetoric can provide any substantial insight regarding phenomena of writing, particularly in the current hyper-circulatory situation of writing, or if we have inhibited (what we know about) writing by retrofitting it to traditional rhetorical models. Second, though this is unstated and irrelevant to Coe's context and agenda, "Eco-Logic for the Composition Classroom" suggests an important disciplinary question regarding the historical convenience of hitching the composition studies wagon to rhetoric. Rhetoric, we know, had an established relationship with English departments and the university in general (granted, at times this was a rocky relationship) and with educational philosophies even more generally since classical Greek schools. But if we accept the ramifications of Coe's argument, then we must also ask whether this attachment of composition to rhetoric didn't serve the disciplinary validation and bureaucratic advancement of the arrival of composition studies. That is, while the historical narrative most often treats the marriage of composition studies to rhetoric as an epistemological or philosophical arrangement, we should also consider the relationship as a (perhaps savvy) bureaucratic or political maneuver.

Such an observation aside, however, "Eco-Logic for the Composition Classroom" is, in essence, a summary of a more fully developed sense of eco-logic that Coe first forwards in his 1974 *Freshman English News* article "Rhetoric 2001," an article that not only proposes an ecological approach to thinking (about writing) but might be read as containing posthumanist tendencies, or perhaps reactions against posthumanism, depending upon how it is read. In 2001, Coe revitalized the "Rhetoric 2001" argument in a follow-up piece called "'Rhetoric 2001' in 2001," published in *Composition Studies*, the current manifestation of *Freshman English News*. In it, Coe contends that more fully developed concepts from the original article are as important at the beginning of the twenty-first century as they had been twenty-five years earlier. I want to focus here, though, on the first "Rhetoric 2001" article as serving the development of ecocomposition, primarily because the second article makes specific links to the ecocomposition effort (albeit differently, as Coe notes) and really should be considered an inherent part of the ecocomposition canon, despite its expansion upon the earlier article. "Rhetoric 2001," like other works that have been tied to the ecocomposition movement, begins by invoking an "ecological crisis" that unless arrested will lead to catastrophe. "Only a change in certain outmoded attitudes and thought-patterns," Coe explains, "can prevent disaster" (1). That is to say, Coe lays the blame of ecological crisis not only at the feet of technological advancement and population increase but also squarely in the hands of thinking and communication. English studies, the argument goes, has the ability to convey the scientific data that needs to be shared in order to adjust attitudes and halt the ecological crisis. I do not intend here to address the role of ecological crisis or the role of the humanities in conjunction with science in affecting cultural change. Instead, I want to focus on the ecological/systems model Coe proposes.

Coe turns to systems theory to explain the difference between the transfer of energy and the transfer of information. He contends that information transfer is much more complicated than energy transfer and that information transfer occurs in open systems, which are difficult to predict, while energy transfer suggests movement in a closed system and is more readily predictable. According to Coe, then, "information systems operate on an entirely different logical order than energy systems and by a distinct set of rules. If this is true, it follows that applying (conscious or unconscious) energy analogies to an information dominated system is a type of logical fallacy" (3). While the metaphor of information is problematic here, Coe's position is important to consider for ecocomposition, but to do so we should first set aside the metaphor of information, as "information" implies that there is something—or as Sánchez identifies, "*something else*, something that is not itself related fundamentally to writing or language"—that writing carries (4, emphasis in original). Assuming that information—and other metaphoric signifiers like "meaning," "concept," or "knowledge"—is conveyed via writing relegates writing to a particular kind of technology whose primary function is as a mechanism of transfer and, as Sánchez makes clear, suggests that composition studies attends not to studying the phenomena of writing but to the politics of representation. We should "take representation neither as writing's signature function, nor as an ontological given (as literary studies do), but as a structural component within a general system of discursive circulation and dissemination. From this perspective, the function of com-position studies, and of composition theory in particular, is to describe and explain all features of that general system" (4). If we disrupt the metaphoric attachment to information and shift the focus from information/meaning to writing and concentrate on developing ecological understandings of writing instead of on the things that we (incorrectly) assume writing to convey, we can begin to consider writing from an ecological perspective that accounts for writing as an open system. Second, we can embrace the interdisciplinary agendas of systems theories and complexity theories in conjunction with ecological methodologies and move away from ecology as a strictly scientific methodological approach, developing more complex ecological understand-ings of writing as a dynamic open system, one not bound to stale metaphors of energy transfer (more on systems theory later in this chapter).

What we can extrapolate from Coe and Cooper beyond their evident arguments is, first, a recognition of systemic thinking about writing, of whole over part and an idea of instability or open systems, an idea of fluc-tuation system, more dynamic in complexity than fluctuation theories tied to early systems theory, approaches that have not been addressed in any substantial way in ecocomposition. Systems theories and fluctuation theo-ries, then, become central to a complex ecological theory of writing; thus, a rudimentary overview of both is warranted before continuing with my look at Coe, Cooper, and Zebroski.

Most systems theories began in biology to solve the problem of ex-plaining complex ecological systems. Systems theory methodologies were then adapted and evolved as methods for explaining human-made systems, primarily technical systems toward the end of debugging those systems (systems engineering). In the late 1970s, systems theories applied to "natural" systems began to address "fluctuation" to account for anomalous fluctua-tions within a system that rendered the system more complicated or more muddled than scripted human-made systems might be. Initially, fluctuation theory developed in statistical physics to account for anomalous condensa-tions in gaseous materials, which are known as "fluctuations." However, fluctuation theory grew to account for system fluctuation, which looked beyond fluctuation within a system to the entire system as a fluctuation. Though the terms carry the baggage of these scientific approaches, I want to appropriate the idea of fluctuation system but expand the idea, accounting not for either fluctuation within a system or a system that is a fluctuation but for systems that fluctuate their very constitution, either momentarily (perhaps not even identifiably) or endlessly, as is the case for writing. The fluctuation system is an unstable system, a system that resists stability to the point that it attains its momentum from its instability. In this sense, instability should be read as leading to or anticipating not collapse but growth and velocity. Writing cannot be interpolated as either a human-made system or a natural system, as both "man-made" and "natural" are themselves functions of writing. Many may want to argue here that writing is necessarily a human-made mechanism and thus a human-made system. However, writing has been naturalized in such a way that the very ideas of human-made or natural can no longer be identified separately from the phenomena of writing itself, and writing is rendered as both and neither. As fluctuating system, both natural and human-made while always already neither human-made nor natural, writing as system supersedes its parts.

While Cooper's and Coe's works have been adapted to ecocomposition, though in limited and often limiting ways, ecocomposition has not—or at least not that I have noticed—considered the important work of James Thomas Zebroski. In "Toward a Theory of Theory for Composition Studies," Zebroski develops his own form of ecological approaches to writing and anticipates ecology as providing theoretical possibilities for composition studies. I want to confess here that had I discovered Zebroski's ecological theories prior to my earlier work in ecocomposition, that work would have looked drastically different. Zebroski's "Toward a Theory of Theory for Composition Studies" argues that composition studies can no longer afford to rely on the simple importation of critical theory from other disciplines like literary criticism but instead should work to develop its own theories, theories that "arise from the grassroots of composition" (32). He explains:

> We need to resist the land rush in certain quarters of composition to appropriate postmodern Theory and convert composition as quickly as possible to what in literary studies is already outdated. How can we construct concepts that will allow us to make use of the insights of postmodern Theory, but that still preserve a space of us to learn about and teach writing? This requires a theory of theory in composition. Such a theory of theory emerges from a philosophy of internal relations. (32)

While I do not embrace Zebroski's resistance to the import of Theory into composition studies (as my own reliance on theory throughout this book makes evident), his argument reveals an important need for a "philosophy of internal relations" that can be understood as a systems or networked approach to theoretical development.[6] As Zebroski explains, "A philosophy of internal relations approaches concepts ecologically . . . that is, a concept is seen as coming out of an environment, a social formation with histories, and the concept retains traces of that ecology and, in fact, is still a part of that ecology when we appropriate it" (34).[7] By way of Bertell Ollman, Zebroski develops an ecological theory of Relations/relations designed to show how concepts are linked with "other social components to form a particular structure" (35).

While Zebroski's relational structure offers much for ecocomposition postcomposition, we should restructure his argument slightly, moving the expression of the relations from being understood as social formation to being seen as functions of writing. Casting the manifestation of the relationship as social formation attempts to situate the concept (or knowledge, information, idea, or whatever "something else" metaphor you choose to apply) as able to transfer from the whole of writing into an autonomous structure that can be made independent of writing. Such a movement suggests that there are identifiable spaces in which information, concepts, ideas, meaning, or knowledge can exceed the transfer mechanism of writing and liberate themselves from the whole. This is not the case. Instead, writing itself by way of system fluctuation renders new spaces in which the appearance of information, concepts, meaning, knowledge, and so on obtain velocity within the system so as to occupy spaces within it for brief moments of what we perceive to be separation, though those moments are nothing more than (or perhaps critically important to) the perceptions we rely on to lay claim to things like information, ideas, meaning, or knowledge. Instead, we might think of those moments as pauses in the system, delays in the fluctuation, which we can perceive and identify only retroactively and for the sake of a need to perceive and name them metaphorically as identifiable. It is here in the fluctuating relationships that the ecology of writing holds the potential for radical disruption, for it is here that the contingencies of space reveal the complexities of writing systems.

A Complex Ecology Approach

The Age of Ecology has arrived.
—Bernard C. Patten, "Why 'Complex' Ecology?"

The ecology of ecocomposition has only flirted with the "systemness" of writing and the complexity of writing systems.[8] Ecocomposition's ecology, for the most part, has been flat, limited to an ecology bound by metaphors of web, some consideration of the "placeness" of writing, and an overexerted attention to nature writing and environmental politics instead of any serious attention to the ecologies of writing as system. Perhaps this is the case because ecocomposition embraced a definition of ecology that focused particularly upon the relationships between organisms and their environments as a manner of expanding social epistemic agendas. It is for this reason that ecocomposition postcomposition turns to complex ecology and systems ecology as a more productive avenue for ecological theories of writing due to their focus on wholes rather than parts. Ecocomposition, like the science of ecology, requires a more complex notion of ecological methodologies in order to account for the complexity of writing as system, particularly as the current hyper-circulatory condition of writing now demands more complex theories than composition studies has previously provided, theories that can evolve within a context of new rhetorics—like ecological or posthuman rhetorics—without being bound to ensconced rhetorics of social constructionism, expressivism, or the pedagogical imperative. Like the complex ecology of scientific ecology, ecocomposition's complex ecology does not lend itself to immediate application. Instead, it works to push at the theoretical boundaries of the ecology embraced by ecocomposition. In this way, we might think of the intervention of complex ecology in the postcomposition manifestation of ecocomposition as post-ecology, echoing post-theory's demand for more from theory, though I am minimally reluctant to dub it as such, given the scientific baggage the word "ecology" inevitably carries and the qualms that might come with the posting of yet another methodology.

The science of complex ecology is most often credited to the work of George van Dyne, the first director of the Natural Resource Ecology Laboratory at Colorado State University (1970–73), who argued for interdisciplinary methods of ecology and promoted some of the first systems-based approaches to ecology. Complex ecology evolved as a kind of critique of traditional ecological methods that, van Dyne and others argued, could not provide answers about the incalculable complexity of the world's ecologies. Complex ecology, Bernard C. Patten points out, though, is a transitional ecology designed to move ecology "from an empirical descriptive science to a powerful systems science of wholes," but its current phase is "an alchemic phase. . . . the movement is just beginning" (xiv). A similar thing might be said of ecocomposition. Interestingly (and as one might expect of a science), complex ecology operates at two levels: microscopic (addressing issues like thermodynamics, quantum mechanics, information theory, and cybernetics, the latter two holding great import for posthuman ecocomposition) and macroscopic (addressing issues like model aggregation and modeling applications). For a number of reasons, including the desire to not make "scientific" the ecology of ecocomposition postcomposition beyond perhaps a grammatological science, I am not going to distinguish between micro and macro approaches in establishing complex ecological theories of writing, though there may be potential for doing so in future theoretical work.

Ecology, as it was adopted by ecocomposition, was understood to be the study of relationships between organisms and their environments, and within such study it is considered legitimate to concentrate on specific organisms (in the case of composition studies and ecocomposition, student subjects) or on the environments in which those organisms thrive (in the case of composition studies and ecocomposition, by way of issues like culture, race, class, gender, and so on). System ecology, which is closely tied to complex ecology, was first expressed by E. P. Odum in a 1964 issue of *BioScience* as addressing the "structure and function of levels of organization beyond the individual and species" (14). What is interesting about this approach isn't that it serves to overturn the "old" ecology but that it works in conjunction with it to provide a more holistic view of systems, bringing together multidisciplinary approaches that inform the larger picture. Granted, much of systems ecology is founded in the application of mathematics to understanding ecosystems; its broader approach of attention to systems becomes useful for ecocomposition postcomposition, particularly in its claim that systems approaches require different theoretical and analytical tools than have sufficed in standard ecological methods. I take this as an indication that if ecocomposition postcomposition is to provide any insight into the functions of writing as complex system, such investigations cannot rely upon the methodologies already in place in either ecocomposition or composition studies.

The technological/media boom of the late twentieth and early twenty-first centuries has revealed writing to be complex in ways that composition theories have not accounted for, nor are they likely to account for without radical shifts in the methods by which composition theories are made and in the rhetorics in which those theories are forwarded. Complex ecological approaches begin to account for the complexities of writing, complexities that we must admit are so diverse and divergent that we may never be able to fully account for all of the facets and functions of writing, particularly as writing endlessly fluctuates as a system, making it difficult, if not impossible, to ever identify an unchanging moment about which concrete theories might evolve. Consequently, we can assume that the theoretical methods used to engage writing in the past no longer provide the expansive needs of writing theory. Like the science of complex ecology, which ventures off the beaten track of traditional scientific methods, ecocomposition postcomposition should provide new approaches to examining systems of writing that are not bound by the narrative of "what we already know," particularly in those instances when what we already know is tempered by research and theory tied to administrative and pedagogical imperatives, linked directly to subject formation, and ingrained with social construction and expressivist rhetorics.

The limits of classroom writing do not provide substantial accounts of writing as a system; instead, more complex, holistic approaches should begin to account for the whole of writing by way of the whole-part relationship without elevating the individual parts to a status that renders the system of secondary value, as has been the case with the focus on subject at the expense of system. Can't see the forest for the trees, we might say. Instead, postcomposition's attachment to complex ecology contends that there is a need to address the complex relationships between parts in order to develop more holistic concepts of writing while understanding that we will never be able to fully understand all of the complexities and fluctuations of the system. Likewise, no one theory can begin to work toward understanding such complexities; as complex ecologist Sven E. Jørgensen explains, "complex systems need a complex of theories to expose all their many facets" (xix).[9]

As complex system, writing should also be understood as a fluctuating system, one not moved toward stability. Likewise, writing is not an independent system but a system integrated within, across, and interspersed with—what I will show in the next chapter to be a kind of *saturation*—larger networks of systems, notably networked societies, a concept I will address in greater detail in the next chapter. Like writing, the systems that writing encounters—or, more accurately, the systems with which writing shares relationships—are themselves also often fluctuating systems, adding to the complexity of writing by contributing to writing's velocity (away from stasis and, in turn, away from stability) while dependent upon interconnectivity to provide structure within never-ending fluctuation. Writing, because of its expansive interconnectedness with countless systems—some not easily identifiable—forms a ubiquitous network, the functions of which inform, disrupt, and propel systems with which it shares place and interconnects. In this way, primarily, we begin to see that the whole of writing can never be explained by way of its parts but instead through the properties of its interconnectedness. Like my claims regarding the fact that whether one considers oneself posthuman or not, all humans now occupy a posthuman world, so too might we argue that given the velocity at which writing circulates, all facets of network societies are saturated by systems of writing, even those societies that do not directly engage writing but are, nonetheless, affected by writing's ubiquity. That is, contra to claims Nedra Reynolds makes in *Geographies of Writing* regarding the pervasiveness of electronic media, or "the Web," that "the whole world is *not* in the Web" (35, emphasis in original), in fact, the whole world—or, more specifically, writing—*is* in the Web because the Web/writing is (in) the whole world, whether an individual or society is consciously aware of it or not.

Writing systems, though, are not limitless. Like all systems, in order to be attributed as system, they have boundaries, albeit those boundaries may be amorphous and contingent. Within the boundaries of a system, factors—like context, for instance—provide structures of control. Factors like time and space become the locations in which controlling factors operate. Controlling factors may or may not be independent of one another, but their function of control operates in relation to the system and its boundaries. Controlling factors are multidimensional, themselves interwoven with numerous fluctuating networks, their influence affected by their connections and carried between and among networks and systems. Changes to controlling factors—triggered through connection—result in systemic fluctuations that exceed in complexity beyond the ability to be explained via metaphors of web. Instead, we should think of the interconnectivity of writing systems and countless networks as engaged in a never-ending exchange of velocity transfer running along endless paths of interconnectivity, moving between and among all of the networks, simultaneously at times, independently at others. Velocities of various fluctuations within a fluctuating system are dependent factors, constrained by the spaces of the systems and networks through which they travel. However, these velocities and fluctuations are not to be read as movement of information, ideas, meaning, or the like (or even Foucauldian utterances) but instead are the very accumulations of writing that we *perceive* to be the carrier of meaning, ideas, or information. Writing, then, should not be perceived as a ganglion-like entity through which information flows but rather a complex (fluid) system of interconnected relations, a function of which is to provide an appearance of representation.

In other words, in order for us to name writing as system, within the vacillation and inconsistencies of a fluctuation, equilibrium is achieved by way of numerous ordered or predictable interrelations, or what we might identify as order within fluctuation. Systems, like writing, require some level of internal consistent repetition in order to maintain systematicity. This kind of order within fluctuation might be thought of in the same vein as the passing and prior theories Thomas Kent and other postprocess theorists, by way of Donald Davidson, have suggested as central to paralogic hermeneutics. Of course, relying on paralogy does not move us any further from the social epistemic or the hermeneutic tradition that Hawk argues ecocomposition and postprocess theories must abandon, but the basic tenet that a system will retain aspects of those fluctuations that it has found to be functional, effective, and perhaps efficient over time in order to extend its movement in other directions seems a useful way of thinking about how writing theories might evolve regarding fluctuating systems. This is not to say that those moments of order are not dynamic, flexible, or malleable; in fact, I contend that it is specifically variations in velocity occurring throughout the system that allow for a fluctuating system to retain cohesion. Some fluctuations adjust where needed, not constantly, and certainly not randomly. Fluctuation is dynamic, ordered, yet complex. Ordered relations, then, are a requirement of the system in order to maintain equilibrium and promote fluctuation, ends that seem, at first, counterproductive but that, in fact, serve the longevity of the system. Over spatial occupations (and time), these dependent elements are expressed in recessing patterns, each pattern changing or replaced as the system requires.

Systemic change, in this way, borrowing again from complex ecology, might be thought of as either cyclical or directional. Directional change can be thought of as the progression of a system in order for the relations with other systems and networks to be of use. We can think of this as, say, the *techne* beyond *techne*, the advancement of technologies not yet rendered in material form in anticipation of specific application. Language and technology serve as visible networks tied to writing systems in which directional change is (we assume) observable. Directional changes are triggered directly through relations with other networks and systems. Directional change, however, should not be considered necessarily as progress in the sense of forward direction or inherent improvement or growth, as directional change may require regress at times. Directional change contributes greatly to a system's complexity and may be gradual and/or continuous. Cyclical change should be thought of as autogenic and more difficult to identify. All fluctuations of the system are informed by directional and cyclical changes to the system and affect the relations to and with other systems and networks. Rates of change and rates of fluctuation vary within the system. It is here, specifically, that we can again see the web metaphor as no longer serving the complexity of system, as the vibrations theorized in the metaphoric web must be seen as moving/changing not only the web but also the connections the web makes with other webs with which it necessarily connects.

A Posthumanist Systems Theory Approach

In the current social and critical moment, perhaps no project is more overdue than the articulation of a posthumanist theoretical framework for a politics and ethics not grounded in the Enlightenment ideal of "Man."
—Cary Wolfe, *Critical Environments: Postmodern Theory and the Pragmatics of the "Outside"*

A number of times, now, I have employed the term "systems theory," providing only a rudimentary gloss of the historical evolution of scientific systems theory. However, the intriguing work of Cary Wolfe's *Critical Environments: Postmodern Theory and the Pragmatics of the "Outside"* resituates scientific and social scientific systems theory alongside pragmatism and poststructuralism as a method for exploring the "theoretical, political, and ethical dimensions of how some of the major theorists within 'postmodernism' have confronted the problem of thinking the 'outside' of theory" (xxiii). Wolfe's systems theory approach provides three crucial components to the ecocomposition postcomposition project. First, it anoints systems theory in the realm of postmodern/poststructural theories, granting it authority to operate outside of the constraints of scientific rhetorics, rendering it perhaps the most critically important theoretical perspective that informs postcomposition. Second, it provides an energizing method for addressing complex systems. Third, it accomplishes the first two components via an unabashed posthumanist theoretical agenda, an approach desperately needed to reinvigorate ecocomposition.

By way of Bruno Latour, Theodor Ardorno, and Michel Foucault, Wolfe contends that it is not enough "to hold on to the concept of the human and then simply embed it dialectically in networks of symbolic, discursive, and material production, for doing so would simply reenact the retreat-and-return of the subject-as-origin" (*Critical Environments* 42–43). Instead, Wolfe argues that there is a need to rethink the "notion of the human *tout court*," as disciplines other than those involving critical, cultural, and social theories have begun to do, because "it has become abundantly clear that the humanist habit of making even the *possibility* of subjectivity coterminous with the species barrier is deeply problematic" (43, emphasis in original). By way of critique of feminist philosophy of science (manifest in the works of Sandra Harding and Donna Haraway) as needing a disengagement from "objectivist epistemological pretentions that undercut its political and ethical commitment," Wolfe proposes systems theory as the compelling avenue toward more dynamic theoretical inquiry (51). Systems theory, he claims, unlike feminist philosophy of science, "does not cling to debilitating representationalist notions" (53). This is of crucial interest to ecocomposition postcomposition because it provides a way to move outside of the trap of representationalism, a problem for composition studies as Sánchez has shown, as writing is traditionally understood to be a technology of representation through which meaning, information, ideas, and the like are transmitted. Likewise, Wolfe shows that, "unlike Enlightenment humanism in general," systems theory's "formal descriptions of complex, recursive systems are not grounded in figures of 'Man' and in the dichotomy of human and non human" (53). Instead, in light of a posthumanist context, Wolfe proposes that the single greatest virtue of systems theory is that it has (citing Dietrich Schwanitz) "progressively undermined the royal prerogative of the human subject to assume the exclusive and privileged title of self-referentiality (in the sense of recursive knowledge about knowledge)" (53). For Wolfe, and I would argue for ecocomposition and postcomposition, "the promise and power of systems theory reside not only in its posthumanism . . . but also in its ability to offer a much more rigorous and coherent way to theorize" complex systems (53). This power comes from "its ability to mobilize the same theoretical apparatus across domains and phenomena traditionally thought to be pragmatically discrete and ontologically dissimilar, *while at the same time* offering . . . a coherent and compelling account of the ultimate contingency of any interpretation or description" (53, emphasis in original). In addition, systems theory, like other theoretical approaches with which it shares characteristics, retains a crucial pragmatic dimension, which, as both Wolfe and Bruno Latour in *We Have Never Been Modern* acknowledge, is crucial because of its impact upon not just language and meaning but larger, more encompassing systems that cannot be simply reduced to things like meaning and language.

Similar to N. Katherine Hayles's approach, Wolfe's discussion of systems theory is grounded in the evolution of cybernetics, particularly in the differences between first- and second-order cybernetics. First-order cybernetics is exemplified in the work of cultural anthropologist Gregory Bateson, whose work brings scientific systems theory into a social science context to describe a host of social interactions, including the dynamics of alcoholism, the ecological crisis, schizophrenia, and communication among wolves and dolphins, to name but a few (Wolfe, *Critical Environments* 54). Bateson's systems theory is a radical theoretical shift in that it is "*integrative* and *organizational*, as opposed to analytical and atomistic" (54, emphases in original). The distinction is important here as it signifies a shift from traditional scientific methodologies, which reduce phenomena to interplay of identifiable units that can be examined independently of one another, to a more systems-based approach that focuses on whole systems and problems that cannot be reduced. In other words, Bateson's shift is interested in the system, not in the properties of the system. The system, though, as second-order cybernetics shows, is never objectively observed; the contingency of observation is always in place. Systems theories can be divided generally into two approaches: contextualism (or conventionalism) and a less constructivist and more realist approach Wolfe labels "organicism" (54). Robert Lilienfeld explains the differences to these approaches in this way: "The contextualist uses the category of integrating structures (contexts) to explain experience, but denies to these integrating structures any reality of significance. The organicist maintains that [they] . . . are more numerous, coherent, and 'real' than the contextualist wants to admit" (qtd. in Wolfe, *Critical Environments* 54–55). Simply put, the kind of information one observes is dependent upon the context of the observation (and yes, for me, the use of "information" here is, as per my previous comments about information, highly problematic).

Earlier I noted that systems are not always stable and don't always strive for stability and proposed the possibility of system *as* fluctuation. To amend that claim a bit, and in an effort to begin to initiate systems theories approaches to thinking of writing as complex system, let me add that in conjunction with systemic fluctuation, we must acknowledge, à la Bateson, that systems are self-corrective, that they are "always *conservative* of something" (qtd. in Wolfe, *Critical Environments* 55, emphasis in original). That is, systems, even systems that fluctuate, maintain some form of status quo. Wolfe, citing Bateson's *Steps to an Ecology of Mind*, establishes criteria of system:

> In Bateson's view, the "essential minimal characteristics of a system"—
> be it biological, mechanical, or social—are (1) that the system operates
> upon *difference*, deviations from a norm or baseline that are processed as
> information; (2) that it consists of "closed loops or networks of pathways
> along which differences and transforms of differences shall be transmit-
> ted" (as when a thermostat detects the difference between its setting and
> the room temperature, activating the furnace to restore the total loop
> of room/furnace/thermostat to the desired homeostatic state); (3) that
> "many events in the system shall be energized by the respondent part
> rather than by impact from the trigger part" (a principle most clear,
> perhaps, in phenomena such as color vision, and the various tricks
> and demonstrations, such as the parallax effect, which show how the
> nervous system actively and constructively responds to environmental
> stimuli rather than simply registering them in linear fashion); (4) that
> systems "show self-correctiveness in the direction of homeostasis and/
> or the direction of runaway." (*Critical Environments* 56)

The fourth characteristic always includes recursivity, more familiarly known as the feedback loop, a principle central to Hayles and Hawk.

Within this rubric, we can extract not only a guiding set of characteristics for understanding systems but also a direct implication for thinking of writing as ecologic system. First, of course, we must rewrite characteristic

#2 a bit, nuancing the position to account for Sánchez's critique of information that I have adopted and to reformulate the characteristic in terms of writing. Second, characteristic #2 must be reapplied not as closed loops in which difference and transforms-of-difference are transmitted but, given the ubiquity of writing as system and its relations to other systems, as loops that have a more "open" interconnectivity in which the integration of difference and transform of difference mingle more actively among systems interrelations. That is, because writing-as-system envelops and is enveloped by the kinds of systems that both Wolfe and Bateson envision, a more diffuse process of looping is required. I should mention at this point as well that writing, unlike the systems about which Wolfe and Bateson theorize, interrelates with other systems in ways not yet accounted for in either complex ecology or systems theory, what I describe in the next chapter as an interrelation based upon saturation rather than a simple connection. Part of the agenda of ecocomposition postcomposition must be to work toward a more dynamic systems approach to writing than either complex ecology or systems theory have forwarded or for which they have provided methodologies. This is a claim, problematic as it may seem, that writing is a more complex system than either complex ecology or systems theory imagined as an object of investigation, one requiring even more complex theoretical approaches, an idea derived from Mark C. Taylor's synthesis of complexity theories (see the next chapter), which he describes by way of postmodern architect Frank Gehry as "altogether different levels of complexity" (41). The impetus for such theories grows from, first, postcomposition's attention to writing as an object of study in ways that no other epistemological project has embraced writing as its sole object, one that accounts for a whole of which only limited numbers of its parts have been previously considered, and second, from the fact that systems theories, particularly those informed by cybernetics and informatics, have been entrapped in metaphors like "information," "ideas," and "meaning" as representational transfer. These concepts are necessary for these kinds of projects, but writing is unique in its systemicity in that theorizing it does not require a metaphor to explain what it carries or represents, as what it carries or represents is either not as important as writing itself or else writing does not carry or represent anything beyond or outside itself (see Sánchez).

Characteristic #3 is particularly important because it further adds to the disruption of the web metaphor toward more complex thinking about writing as system. The web metaphor, as it has become employed, contends that the web responds/reacts to contact, to disruption, to movement, but as I have shown, that metaphor assumes the movement or disruption initiates from an external, identifiable agent whose (independent) action works as a trigger mechanism (despite the fact that the construction of the web and the placement of it in the path of the agent probably more accurately describe the catalyst). Characteristic #3, though, provides the possibility that events in the system are not always the result of an external trigger; in fact, we might even read this to suggest that the trigger itself is not to be seen as outside the system but as a place of relational contact within the system. In terms of velocity and interconnectedness, then, characteristic #3, particularly when placed in relation to characteristic #4, provides grounds for considering triggers neither as originators of velocity nor as independent of the system to which the trigger is applied. Without falling prey to metaphors of nodes or conductors (Jean-François Lyotard and Gregory Ulmer), which, again, imply identifiable systemic independence—if only in the moment of assuming the role of trigger or conductor—we might instead think of triggers as points of interactive contact that reinvigorate velocity. That is, the agent does not become triggering agent or even agent until contact is made with the web; it is that place of contact, inherent in the system, which propels writing's velocity. To visualize, this might be thought of as the reaction that occurs when two wires carrying electric current touch; there is no agent to act as trigger other than the result of the contact. This might be thought of in terms of potential and kinetic energies, particularly given the ratio relation of the kinetic to velocity, but I hesitate to suggest this, given the problems that I have already noted when one speaks of complex systems in terms of energy flow and of reducing the dynamics of this kind of catalyst of velocity to such simplistic metaphors.

Characteristic #4 describes the feedback loop, a central tenet of cybernetics in the form of recursivity.[10] Feedback loops occur in two forms, one negative in which the system processes information toward the end of maintaining homeostasis or directionality, and one positive in which systems process information toward the end of destabilization, or Bateson's "runaway." Negative feedback loops are of more interest to second-order cybernetics. Of course, given my dismissal of information as a useful metaphor by way of Sánchez, the feedback loop becomes a problematic concept. However, if we rethink the action of positive and negative feedback loops as a way of describing velocity rather than information transfer, then the idea holds more potential, particularly as a method for thinking about systemic destabilization or fluctuation and even destabilization as a form of directionality. In other words, in a fluctuating system, one inherently disruptive of itself in the ways I have suggested writing-as-system might be, it is through feedback loops that the system maintains internal velocity and directionality; feedback loops are also how the system maintains velocity, in, through, and with relational systems. Because of the importance of the feedback loop concept to complexity theory (which I address more fully in the next chapter), particularly positive feedback, it is important not to issue a dismissal of its embrace of information but to instead rethink the function and flow of feedback loops sans information as the thing transferred in and among loops.

Because the contingency of observation is always at play, Wolfe explains that Bateson's concept of a total loop becomes problematic as there is no way to distinguish the loop from the not-loop, introducing instead what second-order cybernetics postulates as the "strange loop," or the situation of a loop turning back in upon itself. The visual metaphor Wolfe provides to explain this is M. C. Escher's Möbius strip. What the strange loop signifies is an abandonment of the "total 'pattern which connects' on behalf of the contingency of observation" and ultimately signals a direct connection between second-order cybernetic systems theory and other postmodern theories (*Critical Environments* 58). For ecocomposition, this is critical in that the attachment to postmodern/poststucturalist theory is manifest in a move away from Bateson's understanding of feedback loops toward a more Guattarian approach, which I take up in the next section of this chapter. Félix Guattari's *The Three Ecologies* parts company with Bateson at the site of Bateson's "ecology of ideas," which posits that ideas are not contained within an individual but are instead organized in systems not limited to the boundaries of an individual or agent. For Guattari, treating ideas (as well, I would assume information and meaning) as a subsystem identified as "context" is supported by a larger understanding that the systemic "pre-text" can be ruptured. For Guattari, the system cannot be convincingly divided into subsystems in ways that reveal any essential ruptures in the system itself.

But before turning in depth to Guattari, I want to adopt a few more principles from Wolfe as a way of establishing the groundwork for ecocomposition methodologies postcomposition. The first of these is the contingency of observation; Wolfe explains—by way of Huberto Maturana and Francisco J. Valera's *The Tree of Knowledge: The Biological Roots of Human Understanding*—that

> because all contingent observations are made by means of the "strange loop" of paradoxical distinction between inside and outside, x and not-x, "every world brought forth necessarily hides its origins. By existing, we generate cognitive 'blind spots' that can be cleared only through generating new blind spots in another domain. We do not see what we do not see, and what we do not see does not exist." (*Critical Environments* 59)

Second, again borrowing from Maturana and Valera, Wolfe describes a theory of autopoiesis as accounting for systems that can be considered both open and closed, a distinction characterized as a difference between "organization" and "structure." In this theory of autopoiesis ("self-producing"), "organization" is understood as the ordering of a system's components—relations—in order for that system not only to be a particular kind of system but to exist at all. "Structure," on the other hand, refers to the relations of a system's components that form a unity among those components in order for the system to make its organization real (59–60). This innovation in thinking about autopoiesis, which, again, Wolfe attributes to Maturana and Valera, is that it drastically rethinks the conceptual relationship between "*system* (organization + structure) and *environment* (everything outside the system's boundaries)" (60, emphasis in original). What this provides is a way to think about autopoietic systems as closed systems (recall Coe's descriptions) "on the level of *organization*, but *open* to environmental perturbations of the level of *structure*" (60, emphases in original). As Taylor explains, "Autopoietic systems can be members of complex networks comprised of other autopoietic systems. Furthermore, autopoietic systems are not as closed as they appear and, thus, a certain degree of interactivity remains possible" (89–90). Given what I have suggested regarding writing-as-system's interactions/relations with other systems and networks, the theory of autopoiesis and its organization and structural components provide access to thinking about how writing maintains systemic order as a fluctuating system while engaging other systems and networks by way of velocity exchange.

Of course, Wolfe's attention to autopoiesis is much more comprehensive than my gloss here lets on, particularly in terms of how environmental triggers interact with a system and the role of ethics in political systems theory, but my intent here isn't to rehash all of Wolfe's theory; instead, it is to establish its basic tenets as a basis for *why* and perhaps *how* we might begin to elaborate a complex systems theory rhetoric in which to theorize the function of writing independent of the hegemonic rhetorics that have shaped composition theory thus far. Part of the problem with turning to Wolfe in total, however, is that he is bound in his agenda to a social epistemic rhetoric as it works to refigure social scientific systems theory. Wolfe's agenda in *Critical Environments*—like much of his other work, including his landmark book *What Is Posthumanism?*—involves recasting the relation between human and nonhuman, a project that requires deep attention to social/cultural structure. While I am not resistant to such projects, at this moment for postcomposition it seems more useful to direct attention away from foundational constructions like culture and social that have dominated composition theory approaches and denied the contingencies of writing theory's potential. That said, I do believe that Wolfe's turn to social theorists like Ernesto Laclau, Chantal Mouffe, and Slavoj Žižek to invigorate a concept of "antagonism" within systems theory provides one final facet crucial to ecocomposition postcomposition: a way to actively think about disruption. Like Žižek's social antagonism, which promotes an "ethics of confrontation" ("Beyond" 249) as an answer to Jürgen Habermas's claim of relativism and nihilism in complexity and contingency, ecocomposition and postcomposition require engagement in disruption.

An Ecosophy Approach

In the final account, the ecosophic problematic is that of the production of human existence itself in new historical contexts.
—Félix Guattari, *The Three Ecologies*

Current ecological movements certainly have merit, but in truth I think that the overall ecosophic question is too important to be left to some of its usual arcaizers and folklorists, who sometimes deliberately refuel any large-scale political involvement.
—Félix Guattari, *The Three Ecologies*

Providing a step away from Bateson's attachment to subsystems, Guattari's *The Three Ecologies* offers another important posthumanist perspective for ecocomposition postcomposition. Guattari argues that humans are being manipulated by way of the production of a collective, mass-media subjectivity and that there is a need for a mental ecology that accounts for the manner in which "Integrated World Capitalism (IWC)" has achieved social control via mass media as a means of controlling human thought. Part of Guattari's project is, evidently, a defense of subjectivity away from a mediated collective and is a project of social liberation. It is also, without naming it so, a project in posthumanism and postmedia. Guattari contends that there are numerous components that converge to create the sense of who we think we are—subjectivity—but that the singularity of subjectivity is repressed by the dominant mass-media subjectivity and has nothing to do with individuals. This portion of Guattari's argument is crucial as it allows us to argue that the pervasiveness of the writing network/system and the condition of the posthuman are bound with a mediated subject formation to the extent that conditions of subjectivity are of no importance beyond an understanding of the surrounding mechanisms that form the collective, mediated subjectivity. In fact, the fear that Guattari expresses regarding the collective mediated subject we now recognize as having already occurred, or as occurring, in the posthuman world to such an extent that the role of the subject in considering the ecological prevalence of media control (or in the case of postcomposition, the ubiquity of writing) is irrelevant and can be set aside along with any other subject-based inquiry. Instead, what holds promise are Guattari's methods regarding ecological consideration of that which mediates; for Guattari, this requires an ecology that enfolds subjectivity and environment into a single approach. In the case of ecocomposition postcomposition, this is writing.

Guattari proposes an *ecosophy*, or ethico-politico articulation between three "ecological registers": the environment, social relations, and human subjectivity.[11] Of course, these registers are problematic for ecocomposition postcomposition, as I have shown that concepts like "the environment" are floating signifiers whose use is at all times a forwarding of a political agenda; social relations entrap ecocomposition thinking in limiting rhetorics of the social epistemic; and individual human subjectivity is an outdated concept in the posthuman world. However, Guattari's registers can be rethought to fit current needs and be recast to understand environment more broadly as *writing*, social relations as all *relations*, and human subjectivity as *posthuman agents* of a part/whole relation. Ecosophy leads to a reinvention of the examination of the relations of writing systems to networks embodied by posthuman agents. For Guattari, traditional views of environment/culture dualisms oversimplify what amounts to complex relationships. Ecosophy, then, constitutes an attempt at formulating a nonscientific theory of complex ecology. Despite Guattari's social liberation agendas and his links with Marxist philosophies, which generally espouse economic methods couched in economic metaphors, ecosophy proves useful in seeking an ecological rhetoric in which to situate postcomposition theory.[12] Of course, we must also acknowledge that *The Three Ecologies* is an anomalous work for Guattari as its call for systems of interconnectedness seems counter to the resistance to holism that is evident in much of his collaboration with Gilles Deleuze, notably in work regarding difference and multiplicities in theories of rhizomatic structure forwarded in *Anti-Oedipus* and *A Thousand Plateaus*. Nonetheless, *The Three Ecologies* is of use postcomposition.

Guattari works away from individual subjects toward a more complex notion of subjectification, wanting to make explicit the distinction between individuals and subjectivity, exploring what can be clearly termed as a whole-part relation between subjectivity and the concepts that form subjectivity, what Guattari calls "processes of subjectification" (*Three Ecologies* 36). In order to do so, Guattari proposes developing ecological methods that are rid of scientific references and metaphors to instead generate an ecology of ethics. To do so, he proposes what amounts to a posthuman approach to ecological/ethical thinking:

> I want to uproot them from their post-structuralist ties, from a sub-jectivity anchored solidly in the individual and collective past. From now on what will be on the agenda is a "futurist" and "constructivist" opening up of the fields of virtuality. The unconscious remains bound to archaic fixations only as long as there is no investment [*engagement*] directing it toward the future. This existential tension will proceed through the bias of human and even non-human temporalities such as the acceleration of the technological and data-processing revolutions, as prefigured in the phenomenal growth of a computer-aided subjec-tivity, which will lead to the opening up or, if you prefer, the unfolding [*dépliage*], of animal-, vegetable-, Cosmic, and machine-becomings. (38)

While I am less interested in the objective of a better sense of subjectifica-tion that such investigation pursues, this approach does suggest a good deal about the ubiquity of writing—if we take writing to encompass the digital, new media formations to which Guattari alludes—and about the interrela-tions between posthuman agents, writing systems, and relations with the networks with which writing interacts. As Guattari suggests:

> The question of subjective enunciation will pose itself ever more force-fully as machines producing signs, images, syntax and artificial intel-ligence continue to develop. Here we are talking about a reconstruction of social and individual practices which I shall classify under three complimentary headings, all of which come under the ethico-aesthetic aegis of an ecosophy: social ecology, mental ecology, and environmental ecology. (41)

In mapping out these three ecologies, then, Guattari explains that it is crucial to dispense with any pseudo-scientific approaches to established ecologic paradigms. This is because the ecologies of *The Three Ecologies* propose to examine entities that are vastly more complex than those that scientific ecologies examine and because "the three ecologies are governed by a *different logic*" (44, emphasis in original). This is a crucial point in that, like Guattari's entities of measure, when dealing with complexities to the degree found in systems like writing, scientific approaches can no longer provide the degree of complex observation required, nor can the logics of scientific paradigm—or even entrenched rhetoric—provide the needed approaches for considering the ecologies of writing. To borrow from Guattari, then, ecocomposition postcomposition, or what Guattari might call ecological praxes, strives to scout out the potential vectors of writing at the locus of each location of interaction/relation. When linked with systems theory, this recognition becomes crucial to developing ecological rhetorics from/ in which to extend complex theories about writing-as-system.

Part of the objective for ecocomposition postcomposition is not necessarily to formulate writing theories that work toward consensus but instead to cultivate a dissensus (Guattari's term) that perpetually disrupts what we can "know" about writing to the end of an ever-increasingly complex view of writing. Borrowing again from Guattari, these new ecological practices must articulate themselves within tangled and heterogeneous spaces toward the objective of locating and making visible the relations that lend toward writing's velocity across and among integrated systems. As Guattari suggests, this dissensus will inevitably lead to new forms of eco-logics that might be thought of in terms of the proverb "the exception proves the rule," only in the new eco-logic, the "exception can just as easily deflect the rule, or even recreate it" (*Three Ecologies* 52). It is in this type of eco-logic—and echoing Coe's—that writing theory will unfold postcomposition.

Ecology, particularly environmental ecology in its current formation, can "barely begin to prefigure the generalized ecology" that Guattari proposes (*Three Ecologies* 52). Instead, ecology must look to more dynamic aspects of whole systems; in the case of ecocomposition postcomposition, the focus of that investigation is writing. Guattari makes clear that the three registers of ecology proposed are never to be seen as independent but as intricately intertwined, "capable of bifurcating into stratified and deathly repetitions or of opening up processually from a praxis that enables it to be made 'habitable' by a human project" (53). There is no hierarchy here; the essential thing is the potential for fluctuation, the inherent violence of disruption.

6. The Edge of Chaos

> Something else, something different, something *new* is emerging.
> —Mark C. Taylor, *The Moment of Complexity:*
> *Emerging Network Culture*

Interestingly, Cary Wolfe's systems theory in *Critical Environments* looks remarkably like the rudiments of the complexity theories that have begun to creep into the fringes of composition, providing an invigorating and potentially groundbreaking shift in how the field views rhetoric and writing. Much of this renewed vitality emerges in composition theory by way of Mark C. Taylor's *The Moment of Complexity: Emerging Network Culture*, a multidisciplinary philosophical work that posits a theory designed to explain this moment of "unprecedented complexity" in which we live and which has been embraced by a handful of composition scholars over the last few years (3). As Taylor puts it, "Any theory of complexity must . . . also be a theory of systems" (140). Taylor elaborates that though systems theories and complexity theories share some similarities, there are a number of differences that should be considered. "Like general system theory," Taylor explains, "complexity theory attempts to identify common characteristics of diverse complex systems and to determine principles and laws by which they operate" (141). Like systems theories, complexity theories are not limited in their investigations to natural or "scientific" phenomena but are equally as valuable to social, economic, cultural, political, and other areas of critical concern.

In this chapter, I further the ecological approaches to writing I initiated in the previous chapter by way of systems theories, turning to complexity theories as an extension of systems theories and as an area of growing importance to composition studies and postcomposition. Following a detailed examination of Taylor's work, I look to the three primary locations of complexity theory's incursion into writing studies: Byron Hawk's *A Counter-History of Composition: Toward Methodologies of Complexity*, a 2004 special edition of *JAC* devoted to complexity theory edited by David Blakesley and Thomas Rickert, and Margaret A. Syverson's *The Wealth of Reality: An Ecology of Composition*. Following this examination of the possibilities of complexity theory for writing studies as forwarded thus far, I examine the metaphors of network toward the end of further developing network/systems theories of writing in an ecological context while returning to the problems of metaphor I introduced in chapter 2. Part of my agenda is disruptive. While the metaphors of network or system seem to be accepted as a functional way of talking about society, culture, or other complex systems, I am not convinced these metaphors fully address the needs of writing theory as we begin to understand writing as complex system or network. As I noted in the previous chapter, perhaps one of the reasons that metaphors like "information" or even "network" or "system" do not import into writing theories unproblematically, despite the efforts of Hawk, Rickert, Blakesley, Syverson, and others, is that the theories that employ these metaphors—systems theories and complexity theories—do not anticipate the degree or type of complexities that writing embodies. Likewise, no matter how we attempt to *apply* systems theories or complexity theories to writing (or even to culture or to society, as Taylor, Wolfe, and others have), these theories retain particular scientific characteristics of their origins; they are always already methods that attempt to account for mapping processes in the objects to which they are applied. Such methods may not be able to account for characteristics of writing in the same ways that they account for characteristics of differently (or more easily) observed phenomena than writing. What emerges at the end of this chapter is an attempt to make more fluid the inherent rigidity of complexity theories in order to accommodate both writing's different degree of complexity and writing's unique form of relations with other networks and systems. Where I hope this push leads is to one of many potential spaces in which writing theories might evolve free from the limits imposed by the tradition of composition studies research. To borrow from Taylor, this is a push farther to "the edge of chaos," a concept I will explain later in this chapter. It is specifically in spaces at the edge of chaos where the potential postcomposition lies, where spaces of complexity, ecological relations, and posthuman agents begin to expose the dynamic facets of the phenomena of writing. It is in and through such spaces we engage postcomposition's becoming.

The Moment of Complexity

Falling *between* order and chaos, the moment of complexity is the point at which self-organizing systems emerge to create new patterns of coherence and structures of relations.

—Mark C. Taylor, *The Moment of Complexity:*
Emerging Network Culture

Taylor's *The Moment of Complexity: Emerging Network Culture* has been the central source through which complexity theories have begun to creep into composition theory. At its base, Taylor's book resists stability, arguing that this moment of complexity in which we find ourselves appears "betwixt and between" periods of stability in which there seems to be a desire to achieve, once again, stability and equilibrium, if, in fact, these were ever really achieved (3). But stability and the security it implies, Taylor contends, are deceptive, only "eddies in an endlessly complex and turbulent flux" (3). Complexity, then, is inescapable, and what "distinguishes the moment of complexity is not change as such but rather an acceleration of the rate of change" (3). Given the hyper-circulatory nature of writing and the drastic technological shifts we are witnessing regarding the (re)circulation of writing, complexity theory offers a dynamic way to revitalize writing theory and to counter the field's will to stability, inherent in which resides the will to pedagogy and the disciplinary urge to homogenize writing and writing subjects. Just as the pervasiveness of technological development has shed light on the anachronism of subjectivity as a useful way of thinking about the role of the agent within the system—particularly writing-as-system—instead highlighting the posthuman as a more accurate description, Taylor identifies the rapid (and often radical) technological advances of the last half-century as potentially "creating conditions for a revolution as profound and far-reaching as the industrial revolution. Information and telematic technologies are recasting the very social, political, economic, and cultural fabric of life" (4). Inherent in this shift, and what Taylor subtly suggests throughout *The Moment of Complexity*, is a subject that is no longer autonomous but an agent of the system that is neither identifiable as independent from the whole system nor able to be conceptualized in any way non-systemically. The system is the agent; the agent is the system.

For Taylor, information is the central metaphor through which technology, culture, economy, and, in fact, just about everything is explained. Postcomposition, reliance upon this metaphor is highly suspect as it implies that the complex system of writing operates as a representational technology through which information (and again, meaning, knowledge, and so on) is carried and transferred somehow separate or separable from the system. Such reductive assumptions relegate writing and writing's ontology to carrier vessel and suggests that information, agents, and the like can operate outside of writing, independent of the system, even if only for rapid moments of disconnect. As I explained in the previous chapter, writing not only requires systems theories or complexity theories as ways of thinking about writing-as-system but also requires a more complex kind of complexity than has yet been proposed simply because writing systems are a different, more complex kind of system than those complexity and systems theories have worked to engage thus far. In some ways, then, this also poses a methodological problem in that the attempt to *apply* systems theories or complexity theories to systems for which they were not developed risks ensnaring writing in reductive approaches not capable of engaging the intricacies of writing (again, as I explained in chapter 2, one way this might be thought of is as the problem of metaphor). What this implies, more generally, is that using an already developing theory as a way to think about writing is problematic, as seen in composition studies' history of importing theories as ways of thinking about writing that have not provided sustainable access to writing. Yet, this is where we stand. Thus, while Taylor relies on the metaphor of information and information transfer as central to his complexity theory, this facet of complexity theory should be set aside as less than useful in attempts to apply complexity theories to understanding writing-as-system.

Interestingly, Taylor briefly acknowledges the problem of relation between writing and information. In describing how we have come to the "information age," Taylor turns to Michael Hobart and Zachary Schiffman's *Information Ages: Literacy, Numeracy, and the Computer Revolution* to pose one part of the information/writing relationship. According to Hobart and Schiffman, "The invention of writing actually gave birth to information itself" (qtd. in Taylor 104). Writing, in Hobart and Schiffman's model, exists apart from speech, but at the same time "writing functions like a code or program whose quasi-algorithmic operations produce information" (104). The link between writing and information, though, provide what Taylor identifies as a "remarkable conclusion: 'the information revolution born of literacy is all the more stunning and revolutionary when seen in stark relief against an oral world where information did not exist.' Information, in other words, is impossible apart from writing" (104). However, Taylor contrasts Hobart and Schiffman's separation of speech and writing as problematic given that Jacques Derrida's deconstructive analyses work to "expose the far-reaching implications of the traditional distinction between speech and writing" and "demonstrate the untenability of their opposition" (104–5). If, as Derrida argues, speech and writing engage in an "endless play of difference through which all signs are articulated" and if we combine Derrida's argument with Gregory Bateson's argument (see the previous chapter), then, according to Taylor, "information appears to be a function of differential inscription," or, more directly, information appears to be a function of writing, and "if there is such a thing as an information revolution, it must involve *something more* than the mere existence of information" (105, emphasis added). This echoes

Raúl Sánchez's claims regarding writing as always thought of as conveying "something else" and reinforces the notion that the information metaphor is, in fact, inadequate for addressing writing (*Function* 4). Likewise, we must also acknowledge that Taylor's formulation of writing relies on a historical shift from orality to literacy, despite its deep investment in technology's role in network formation. The transition that is missing here is that from literacy to electracy (Ulmer), which then implicates the importance of writing/coding as significantly more important than Taylor lets on.

Tellingly, Taylor abandons his discussion of writing with absolutely no nod to the significance such claims imply about information and writing, instead employing information as a central metaphor as though such difficulty was never acknowledged. This might be read as symptomatic of a pervasive attitude toward developing writing theories in general, one in which writing is simply not taken seriously enough to warrant any detailed conversation; the exception here, of course, is Derrida, who engages writing in depth in nearly all of his work. Instead, there seems to be a general approach that writing can be pointed to offhandedly, as it is by Taylor, without committing any serious or sustained attention to the role of writing. We have to accept Taylor's remarks about the relationship between writing and information as important in our understanding of the complexities of writing and our retrofitting (or hyper-fitting?) of complexity theories to writing, but our acceptance of this aspect does not change Taylor's agenda in explaining complexity theory and the moment of complexity.

The moment of complexity occurs when information in feedback loops becomes more and more complex through exchange between and among systems, accelerating the rate of exchange to a "tipping point," a moment when the rapid increase of information produces *different* information (Taylor 5). What emerges, then, from moments of tipping points is a "new *network culture* whose structure and dynamics we are only beginning to fathom" (5, emphasis in original). Ultimately, with this in mind, Taylor's primary objective is to "develop an interpretation of network culture that will make it possible to understand what is occurring more adequately and to respond more effectively to the challenges and opportunities we face" (5). As the notion of network culture is central to Taylor, the idea of network society is of primary significance to network theorist Manuel Castells's *The Information Age: Economy, Society and Culture* trilogy and his collection *The Network Society: A Cross-Cultural Perspective*. In order to better unpack the complexity of network culture, Castells's definitions of network society become useful when placed in conversation with the view of network culture that Taylor proposes, as the two theories share much in common, beginning with the acknowledgment that the "technological revolution" of the late twentieth century created a moment of radical restructuring of society by way of information technologies, a shift we have come to understand as altering not only societies/culture but the very notion of the human subject.

While I do not extend my reading or critique of Castells here beyond a few introductory remarks in order to focus on Taylor, I do want to note Castells's work as a significant contribution to thinking about network, despite its relative absence in composition studies scholarship. For Castells, the network society is "a society whose social structure is made of networks powered by microelectronics-based information and communication technologies," and social structure is "the organizational arrangements of humans in relation to production, consumption, reproduction, experience, and power expressed in meaningful communication coded by culture" ("Informationalism" 3). This definition mirrors the definition of network culture that materializes throughout Taylor's book. Likewise, the most significant component in understanding both network culture and network society is the pervasiveness of technology "throughout the whole realm of human activity" (Castells, *Rise* 5), a claim that echoes and reinforces the role of the posthuman in network society/culture. For Castells, this acknowledgment is crucial because in network society, "the search for identity, collective or individual, ascribed or constructed, becomes the fundamental source of social meaning" (*Rise* 3). Identity, self, and subjectivity for Taylor are a result of network interaction, as I began to address in chapter 3 and will further address later in this chapter. What transpires for Taylor, then, is a detailed unpacking of how complex thinking reveals the function of the network. This approach conflicts with Castells's reading of complexity theory, and he makes adamant in the first volume of the trilogy, *The Rise of the Network Society*, that "complex thinking should be considered as a method for thinking about diversity, rather than as a unified meta-theory. Its epistemological value could come from acknowledging the self-organizing character of nature and society" (74). While Castells does not dismiss complexity theories out-of-hand, he does leave the work of complexity theories relatively under-considered, though he is clear that the most important aspects of complexity thinking are its links to ecological thinking.[1]

Taylor, on the other hand, develops a detailed theory of complexity that begins with an examination of artistic, theological, and philosophical contributions beginning in the late eighteenth and early nineteenth centuries. Though I do not address it in detail in this book, one of the secondary agendas that emerges for Taylor is the growing relevance of the image. "In a visual culture increasingly governed by electronic media," Taylor explains, "the currency of exchange is image" (9). While I am not convinced of the image's economic position suggested here, it is important to note that theories of the visual and of image hold great potential for future writing theory postcomposition and are crucial to understanding writing as system, particularly when taken as an implicit part of technological coding/writing.[2]

Because "architectural practices both reflect and shape broader social and cultural currents" (20), Taylor examines work by three architects—Mies van der Rohe, Robert Venturi, and Frank Gehry—to address architectural shifts as reference points for the transition from modern industrial society to network culture. Within the discussion of these shifts, Taylor offers a number of useful concepts, beginning with the acknowledgment that "walls, which once seemed secure, become permeable screens that allow diverse flows to become global. What is emerging from these flux and flows is a new *network culture*" (20, emphasis in original). By tracing the work of the three architects, Taylor suggests a trajectory in which "the moment of complexity can be understood in terms of the shift from a world structured by grids to a world organized like networks" (20). Taylor proposes a different structure as the new dominant metaphor: the network. Networks are irreducibly complex; they are neither "autonomous nor complete, but they are deliberately unfinished or even broken" (40). Networks do not simply replace or destroy grids; instead, they incorporate, twist, fold, negate, and warp grids into more complex networks. They impose a "different logic" (41). Order in the network is "emergent and transient" (44). Networks suggest growing complexities that teeter on the edge of chaos, a space, Taylor explains, "where it becomes clear that this moment of complexity is where the action is" (46).

With this framework in place, Taylor offers an insightful critique of three tendencies that have dominated cultural criticism in the past thirty years: Michel Foucault's social constructivism, Jacques Derrida's deconstruction, and Jean Baudrillard's theory of simulation. The critique of these three critical theories is not intended as rejection but as a method for turning these critical theories "back on themselves to detect new lines of analysis, which might overcome the current theoretical impasse" (15). This impasse is described as a lack of theoretical resources through which to account for the moment of complexity. Like in post-theory (and postcomposition), part of the argument here is a demand for more complex theories rather than the simple rehashing of the same exhausted critical theories that have become popular over the last thirty or so years: "At this moment, theory, as it has recently been understood, reaches a dead end" (48). Ultimately, what Taylor's critique leaves us with is the notion that "in a world where screens displace walls, neither map nor territory, code nor substance, information nor matter, image nor reality, virtuality nor actuality, simulacra nor the real is what it had seemed to be when it was the opposite of its presumed other" (72). Instead, as Taylor points out, "something *new* is emerging" (72), but by limiting our critical perspectives to theories that have served well to assess social and cultural issues—Foucault's constructivism, Derrida's deconstruction, and Baudrillard's simulacra—we limit access to how we come to know what that "something new" can be. I take this lesson to be of critical importance when formulating theory postcomposition. Reliance upon theoretical modes and approaches that have served well as explanations of other moments, events, and phenomena are not likely to answer the needs of complex systems, given both unprecedented complexities and departures from logics that dominated earlier moments, events, and phenomena.

  Following the critiques and the call for new approaches to understanding complex networks—what we should understand as work to contextualize the emergence of complexity theories—Taylor turns to Kant's philosophy and Hegel's mechanical logic as a route to unpacking autopoiesis. Like Wolfe, Taylor examines Huberto Maturana and Francisco J. Valera's work as the door to autopoietic systems. In order to elucidate the ideas of open and closed systems, Taylor offers an interesting, if not familiar, reading of René Magritte's paintings. This conversation is set in an address of self-reflexivity in order to, first, link the conversation of autopoiesis to the critiques of Foucault, Derrida, and Baudrillard and, second, examine the concept of the strange loop, a concept also key to Wolfe's systems theory. For Taylor, not unlike Wolfe's remarks about strange loops as Möbius strips, strange loops are "self-reflexive circuits, which, though appearing to be circular, remain paradoxically open." Within strange loops, meaning becomes "undecidable" (75). Strange loops engage in a "weird process of self-engulfing" in which "emerging patterns are not static but repeatedly morph in unexpected ways" (78). These changes and morphs occur when the self-reflexivity creates moments of apparent pause, temporal delays in the system, as though the system hiccups when it becomes self-reflexive. "In this momentary space of this delay," Taylor explains, "patterns appear to organize themselves spontaneously" (78). Strange loops, then, when displayed within the systems' screens,

> display rhythms of network culture. In a world where signs are signs of signs, and images are images of images, all reality is in some sense screened. The strange loops of information and media networks create complex self-organizing systems whose structure does not conform to the intrinsically stable systems that have governed thought and guided practice for more than three centuries. (78)

As Hawk explains it, "Oppositions, then, are polarities caught in these complex relationships in which each side is evolving and changing in relation to the other. One pole does not overtake the other: it changes and thereby changes its opposition. In the end, polarities do not function alone but in complex, co-adaptive relations with other polarities, creating a larger whole" (181). For Hawk, the strange loop is significant because it explains how in any rhetorical system reliant upon oppositional dialectics to establish privilege, the weaker pole may become the stronger. In turn, then, Hawk proposes that this effect changes the way in which we conceptualize rhetorical situations and, ultimately, that "rhetoric becomes a cause, not simply an effect" (*Counter-History* 182).

Given the problematic relationship I have suggested between rhetoric and writing, seeing rhetoric as an attempt to identify parts within a whole, I am less interested in the effects of the strange loop on how we think about rhetoric or rhetorical situations. As I began to elaborate in the previous chapter, first the strange loop provides an ecological approach to considering not just the contingencies of observation but also a framework for seeing writing as a dynamic autopoietic system participating in a perpetual self-reflexivity that generates resistance to its own polarities by engaging in its own weird processes of self-engulfing. It is the pause of these moments that provide the perception that patterns within the system can be observed. However, if we look more carefully at Taylor's language in describing strange loops, we see that there is a desire to understand the pauses inflicted by strange loops not necessarily as moments but as "momentary space of this delay" (78). This link between pause (time) and space seems remarkably like a central facet of occupation (see chapter 2), suggesting that strange loops occupy space within networks/systems (both also spatial metaphors) in such a way that spatial ecologies of systems and networks play a significant role in network formation and fluctuation. That is, if strange loops morph in such a way as to register on a network's screen while at the same time contributing to fluctuation in such a way as to encourage a system to remain open, then perhaps we can begin to formulate strange loops as spatial occupations that reveal systemic anchors rather than recurring patterns, spaces that contribute to the organization of the system. In this way, by shifting the understanding of strange loops from moments to spaces in which self-reflexivity appears to be revealed, we may be able to achieve a more ecologically based view of writing by examining the spaces of strange loops as dynamic spaces in which systems establish internal order and as locations in which interrelations may take hold. Given that strange loops contribute to the openness of autopoietic systems, we must concede that it is in the strange loop space where interrelations with other systems are most likely to occur.

Taylor offers that the often overwhelming abundance of information that characterizes network culture is regularly understood as "noise." It is the interaction of noise and information that "leads to the emergence of increasingly complex structures" (15). By way of communication theory, cybernetic systems, literary criticism, and information theory, Taylor contends that "the relationship between information and noise can clarify recent philosophical and critical debates about interplay between system and structure, on the one hand, and, on the other, otherness and difference" (15). Explaining that the information revolution has essentially displaced the communist revolution, Taylor shows how the economic theories of Karl Marx and Friedrich Engels can no longer account for the complexities of network cultures. In this ongoing call for new modes of inquiry, Taylor investigates the "relationship of information and information theory to complexity and complexity theory," but part of this investigation is the admittance that "we do not really understand what information is and surely do not know what makes it revolutionary" (100). Instead, what we do know about information, Taylor claims, is that there is too much of it, naming the constant bombardment of information by "less and less obvious networks" as "noise": "The buzz of information is the white noise of today's culture" (100). However, both noise and information must be understood as "thoroughly relative; what is noise at one level or in one location is information in another moment or in another location" (110).

There are three key points that these claims render regarding writing postcomposition. The first is that perhaps "information" is not the metaphor that needs to be employed here, particularly, as I have explained, not when considering writing. Second is the idea that information is transferred by systems that are growing less obvious. Inherent in this claim is the suggestion that some systems operate less evidently than others. It is the ubiquity of such systems and their lack of visibility that render them so powerful. Systems become naturalized. It is precisely this kind of less-visible system that drives the posthuman condition: pervasive systems that invisibly engulf, creating the sense that their permeation is a natural condition of existence. But more telling is the idea that writing has perhaps become a less-visible system as its complexity has increased. This is perhaps why writing is disregarded as a system worth investigating: it has been naturalized into the background, less-visible, but pervasive nonetheless. Or, perhaps, the velocity with which writing has changed its methods of (re)circulation and the rapidity with which writing has infused its indispensability into/onto other systems, taking on the role of host system in and through which all other networks and systems emerge, thrive, and evolve, has rendered writing unseeable. As I explain later, this pervasiveness might be thought of as systemic saturation. In this way, writing's ubiquity is overlooked, its role in network culture and society sidestepped in favor of investigation into more readily visible systems, culture or society, for instance. The third point directly affects the disruption of subjectivity postcomposition. The abundance of information and the circumstance of network cultures drastically change how we can think about subjectivity (see chapter 3). As the complexity of networks with which we interact increases and as the speed of network-changes accelerate, the ability to adjust to rapid shift becomes necessary to the point that "those who are too rigid to fit in rapidly changing worlds become obsolete or are driven beyond the edge of chaos to destruction" (Taylor 202). The unprecedented level of noise generated by ever-expanding and proliferating networks inevitably lends to radical changes in the function of the subject within the system.

When information becomes noise, "distinctions, differences, and oppositions that once seemed to fix the world and make it secure become unstable. Lines of separation become permeable membranes where transgression is not only possible but unavoidable" (Taylor 100–101). Polarities shift. Noise, then, is "a sign of the increase in complexity," and "no sign of the current moment is more telling than the increasing complexity created by the noise of information" (103). But what exactly information *is* remains ambiguous. Taylor explains how Hobart and Schiffman's information separates form and matter, leading to an inevitable misunderstanding of information that has plagued many cultural theorists who "interpret the classical distinction between form and matter to imply that information is the *opposite* of matter or, in some cases, energy, and, therefore, can be separated from its 'material substrate'" (105). N. Katherine Hayles addresses this similar problem in terms of embodiment, explaining that information cannot be separated from the material entities that embody it (2), and Taylor embraces the idea that information is "material, and matter is informational," explaining that moves into the "information age" should not be seen "in terms of growing abstraction and increasing dematerialization, but as the complication of the relation between information and the so-called material conditions of life" (106). Ultimately, noise and information are inseparable:

> When information is understood as a process rather than a product, the line separating it from noise is difficult to determine. . . . Life is lived on the shifting margin, boundary, edge between order and chaos, difference and indifference, negentropy and entropy, information and noise. The interplay of noise, which is informative, and information, which is noisy, creates the condition for emerging complexity. (122–23)

Emerging complexity, or emerging self-organizing systems, might be thought of as "complex adaptive systems," a concept Taylor extracts from the extensive work about adaptive social and natural systems coming out of the Santa Fe Institute (156). Emerging complexity occurs when the action of the parts of a system generate the action of the entire system. That is, from the parts, the complexity of the system emerges. Noise, then, "provides the occasion for the emergence of complex order" (136); "order emerges from noise" (137). Complexity, as Taylor explains through the work of Henri Atlan, is "composed of a great number of parts interconnected in multiple ways" (137). According to Taylor, humankind has embraced a will to simplicity, seeking a reduction of the complex to the simple. The idea of emergent complexity, though, suggests that systems move toward complexity, not simplicity; "complexity, we are discovering, is inescapable" (138).

For Taylor, "complexity" means

> "consisting of interconnected or interwoven parts; composite; compound; involved or intricate, as in structure." Etymologically considered *complexity* derives from the past participle of the Latin *complectere*, *complexus*, which means entwine together (*com-*, together + *plectere*, to twine, braid). The stem *plek* (to plait) forms the Latin suffix *-plex*, which means to fold. Complexity, then, is formed by interweaving, interconnecting, and folding together different parts, elements, or components. Complexity not only harbors multiple implications but is actually an intricate process of implication; complication implicates and implications complicate. (138, emphases in original)

Complex adaptive systems are, John H. Holland of the Santa Fe Institute notes, "adaptive nonlinear networks" (qtd. in Taylor 165). Complex adaptive systems include self-organizing systems like "ecologies, immune systems, the development of multicellular organisms, and the processes of evolutionary genetics" (165). Complex adaptive systems "inevitably evolve, or more accurately, coevolve" (156), and they must "evolve the ability to evolve" (171). Subject formation and the humanist subject/object binary evolve from/as complex adaptive systems. Interestingly, Taylor attributes the impact of the rapid spread of technology as contributing to the increasing complexity of human lives; in this way, complexity is inescapable. This argument, though Taylor does not name it so, is a posthumanist argument, identifying the unavoidable shifts in human agency resulting in the ubiquity of increasing technological influence. Seemingly, the moment of complexity is also an inescapable tipping point toward the posthuman.

From the notion of complex adaptive systems, Taylor unpacks a more explicit definition of complexity, beginning with the basic understanding that complexity consist of "interconnected or interwoven parts" (139). Inherent in this definition is a relation between complexity and connection: "As connections or interconnections proliferate, complexity increases" (139). Taylor turns to David Depew and Bruce Weber's *Darwinism Evolving: Systems Dynamics and the Genealogy of Natural Selection* in order to distinguish complex systems from complicated systems:

> A snowflake is complicated, but the rules for generating it are simple. The structure of a snowflake, moreover, persists unchanged, and crystalline, from the first moment of its existence until it melts, while complex systems change over time. It is true that a turbulent river rushing through the narrow channel of rapids changes over time too, but it changes chaotically. The kind of change characteristic of complex systems lies somewhere between the pure order of crystalline snowflakes and the disorder of chaotic or turbulent flow. So identified, complex systems are systems that have a large number of components that can interact simultaneously in a sufficient rich number of parallel ways so that the systems show spontaneous self-organization and produce global, emergent structures. (qtd. in Taylor 142)

Later in this chapter, I return to the distinction between the stability of the crystalline and the chaos of turbulence as a useful way of considering the role of writing in the network of systems that complexity theories and systems theories suggest. For now, though, what this contrast provides is a parameter ranging from the stable to the chaotic as a space in which complexity can be situated.

Taylor sums up complexity by providing seven key characteristics of complex systems:

1. Complex systems are comprised of many different parts, which are connected in multiple ways.
2. Diverse components can interact both serially and in parallel to generate sequential as well as simultaneous effects and events.
3. Complex systems display spontaneous self-organization, which complicates interiority and exteriority in such a way that the line that is supposed to separate them becomes undecidable.
4. The structures resulting from spontaneous self-organization emerge from but are not necessarily reducible to the interactivity of the components or elements of the system.
5. Though generated by local interactions, emergent properties tend to be global.

6. Inasmuch as self-organizing structures emerge spontaneously, complex systems are neither fixed nor static but develop or evolve. Such evolution pre-supposes that complex systems are both open and adaptive.
7. Emergence occurs in narrow possibility space lying between conditions that are too ordered and too disordered. This boundary or margin is "the edge of chaos," which is always far from equilibrium. (142–43)

"The edge of chaos," a term Taylor adopts from John Langton, is particularly revealing when placed in relation to both composition studies and writing. It is from the edge of chaos that order emerges; the will to stability is a conscious retreat from the edge of chaos, away from complexity. Yet, as we have seen, the will to stability is a pipe dream, as complexity is inevitable. At the edge of chaos, systems and networks either "transform or collapse" (214).

Composition Studies and *The Moment of Complexity*

If rhetoric and composition is to move forward and adapt to the coming networked cultures, it can no longer settle, much less strive for, the production of overly simple systems to account for the complexity of writing.
—Byron Hawk, "Toward a Rhetoric of Network (Media) Culture: Notes on Polarities and Potentiality"

As I have said, a few compositionists have begun to take notice of systems theories and complexity theories, primarily by way of the work of Mark C. Taylor. Most notable in this endeavor is Byron Hawk's landmark work both in *A Counter-History of Composition: Toward Methodologies of Complexity*—a book that has obviously been influential in my own thinking postcomposition—and in his contribution, "Toward a Rhetoric of Network (Media) Culture: Notes on Polarities and Potentiality," to the 2004 special issue of *JAC* devoted to complexity theory. Though I do not comment on all of the inclusions in the special issue, primarily because it would be redundant to point out how often the articles fall back into the social constructionist model Hawk warns us about, I should note the importance of the special issue as a primary text in composition studies' initial encounters with complexity theories. It would be unfair (and an inaccurate critique), too, to note that most of the articles in the special issue do not address writing-as-system or even writing at all (especially if we accept my suggested divisions between writing and rhetoric), as the agenda of most of the pieces tends toward further explication of the intricacies of complexity theories. Nor does offering simple summaries of all of the articles and responses in the issue serve any purpose beyond acknowledging their general contribution to the conversation. Nonetheless, this work is commendable, and articles like John Johnston's "Network Theory and Life on the Internet" truly offer insightful components to understanding complex networks while Jennifer L. Bay's "Screening (In)Formation: Bodies and Writing in Networked Culture" and Thomas Rickert's "In the House of Doing: Rhetoric and the Kairos of Ambience" offer some remarkable suggestions about complexity and writing (I address Rickert's work in the section that follows rather than here, as it is particularly useful in a different context).

Hawk's contribution to the *JAC* special issue, which predates the publication of *A Counter-History of Composition* by three years and hints at its rigorous agenda, argues that traditional rhetorical concepts do not work in network culture, particularly given the ubiquity and increased speed of new media influence; instead, it proposes a series of shifts that allow us to reformulate rhetorical concepts to networked logic. Ultimately Hawk's *JAC* article encourages composition studies to realize that rhetoric and writing require more complex understandings than have been granted because, as Hawk notes in his *JAC* essay, in the face of the impending network culture, composition studies cannot continue to articulate writing and rhetoric as simple systems and expect those explanations to account for the complexities of writing as it now stands. To this end, the article functions as an introduction to the basic concepts found in Hawk's book and argues that such concepts are relevant to developing contemporary rhetorical theories while calling for "further inventions in the areas of new media environments and network cultures" (832). Hawk works away from the trappings of social constructionism, noting specifically that familiar rhetorical concepts like "rhetorical situations" emphasize social construction and the idea that situations generate discourse. He provides a series of "compositions or polarities between key terms" in order to "lay some initial groundings for a rhetorical theory based on the topoi of complexity and networks": "Heuristics : Schemata; Dissoi-Logoi : Polarities; Rhetorical Situation : Complex Adaptive Systems; Kairos : Emergence; Logos : Network; Ethos : Screen; Pathos : Affect; Process : Evolution" (832). Hawk does not intend these pairings as a fully developed theory but as an enacting of strange loops in order to "set ideas in motion" (832).

Hawk's article, particularly when taken alongside the more fully developed book, certainly does set ideas about Taylor's version of complexity theory in motion, especially as a method for considering the role of network and system in areas that have become important to composition studies: culture, society, identity, subjectivity, and, even, rhetoric. The difficulty with what Hawk does isn't in his attempt to formulate a new kind of rhetorical theory in light of Taylor's theories but because he does so within the already problematic language of rhetoric and in partnership with his rereading of composition studies by way of vitalism. I don't mean to fault this agenda, particularly given the enlightening counter-history he provides of the field. However, as I extrapolate via Richard Coe in the previous chapter, working with rhetoric as the vehicle through which we attempt to theorize writing defaults to a process of rendering parts of the whole identifiable; that is, rhetoric is a will to simplicity and stability, even if rhetoric is recast in the language of complexity theories. Consider, for instance, how Hawk creates oppositions between "traditional" rhetorical terms and terms more apropos of the language of complexity theory in order to force the emergence of strange loops. In the end, while the rereading of the traditional terms in light of their complex-theory oppositions is certainly interesting and provides a solid series of binaries through which to consider network cultures, the new terms retain the rhetorical mission of simplification, division, and order. That which we call a rhetoric by any other name . . .

Likewise, Hawk bounces between rhetoric, language, and writing as though they are interchangeable ideas. But Hawk is not alone in creating these amalgams; his compatriot Thomas Rickert in his outstanding contribution to the *JAC* special issue, "In the House of Doing: Rhetoric and the Kairos of Ambience," begins to address Taylor's decentering of the subject in writing but then shifts from writing to language as though the two terms are interchangeable. This, of course, has been a primary difficulty for composition studies: the unexplained need to find what Sánchez identifies as alternatives for talking about writing: language, discourse, signification, meaning, information, and so on. Given that Hawk focuses on rhetoric as something to inform writing, a part of writing, and a thing that can be frozen in process, writing itself is then set aside just as Taylor altogether abandons it, in favor of considering the writer as an intrinsic part of multiple networks. In addition, given the disciplinary problems of distinguishing between rhetoric and composition, Hawk does little to show how complexity might address writing itself. Similarly, in the article version, Hawk couches discussions of writing and rhetoric in the familiar traps of the will to pedagogy, explaining, for instance, that "students need to develop their own schemata" and the like ("Toward a Rhetoric" 833). These kinds of moves rely on autonomous student subjects in their formation, even though the article calls for the loss of the subject in complex systems. While such a contextualization certainly works rhetorically to situate the conversation in the familiar landscape of composition studies, it does little to push beyond those confines.

In the penultimate paragraph of the *JAC* article, Hawk briefly acknowledges Margaret A. Syverson's *The Wealth of Reality: An Ecology of Composition* as "perhaps the best example in rhetoric and composition trying to create an encounter with complexity theory." But for Hawk, "Syverson doesn't go far enough" (846). I appreciate Hawk's desire for more from composition studies' encounter with complexity theory and echo his call to go farther, but I think perhaps part of his frustration (or what I read as frustration, what he expresses as worry [846]) is that those who have brought complexity theory to composition studies—or, more specifically, to writing theory— have done so with the same enthusiasm as Hawk but, like Hawk, have run into a number of barriers. In the final section of this chapter, I attempt to go a bit farther, pushing not only for an understanding of writing as complex system that hovers a bit closer to the edge of chaos but also for writing studies to consider writing postcomposition in the ways I have suggested throughout this book that might disrupt the stability of composition studies.

Perhaps one of the speed bumps that has slowed composition studies' engagement with complexity theories—and perhaps one that I have also tripped over—is the reliance primarily upon Taylor as the avenue to complexity. Interestingly, though, a number of the pieces in the *JAC* special issue do not fall prey to what Edith Wyschogrod suggests might be understood as a will-to-Taylor (my term, not hers). That is, contributions to the special issue like those by John Johnston and Wyschogrod don't accept Taylor as the primary (let alone only) source for understanding complexity, instead placing him in conversation with the sources from which Taylor draws his synthesis of complexity theory and with other theorists and philosophers who have influenced the expansion of complexity theories. Wyschogrod's reading of Taylor is sharp; she understands his claims not only as an important galvanizing of complexity theories into a workable, transdisciplinary synthetic but as an act of complexity itself, each of its parts embodying the complexity it depicts (876). I think this is a critical point as we turn to complexity theories and systems theories postcomposition: none of the theories we employ to further develop theories of writing can be taken at face value or independently. Taylor's complexity theory is certainly popular and useful, but that popularity and usefulness seems to emerge from the fact that Taylor has done the difficult work of synthesis for us, extracting the useful bits from the milieu. Works like Wyschogrod's extend the screen, revealing a bit more, displaying a broader picture of complexity theory than we see only through Taylor.

One of the earliest efforts to bring complexity theories into conversation with composition studies comes from Syverson's *The Wealth of Reality*, a book with its feet firmly planted in composition studies' traditions of cognitive studies, student writers, and pedagogy as its realm of inquiry. Its methodologies are anthropological in origin and serve to inform composition studies through cognitive science methodologies. In order to do so, Syverson unpacks complexity theories pre-Taylor, arriving though at similar key concepts as central to complexity, primarily complex adaptive systems, and at the very location of complexity that Taylor finds: at the edge of chaos. Syverson's complexity emerges in three now familiar concepts—distribution, embodiment, and emergence—and a fourth, unique to Syverson's complexity: enaction. These four attributes are not intended as exhaustive of the possibilities for "describing an ecology of composition"; rather, they are described as holding the potential to shed new light "on our understanding of writers, readers, texts, and composing processes" (18). Combining complexity theory with an ecological approach to viewing writer, reader, and text as engaged in a complex ecological system, Syverson opens the doors for a complex ecological approach to writing, though it is hampered by its cognitive methodologies that bind writing to cognitive processes and its implication that writing is (only) an activity of agent, despite its recognition of and resistance to subject privileging.

For Syverson, in complex systems, "processes—including cognitive processes—are distributed, that is, both divided and shared among agents and structures in the environment. . . . Complex systems are also divided across space and time in an ensemble of interrelated activities" (7). Within distribution, Syverson contends that cognition is either distributed or situated:

> *Distributed cognition* refers to the way that cognitive processes are shared, that is, both divided and coordinated among people and structures in the environment. *Situated cognition* refers to the fact that cognitive processes are always embedded in specific social, cultural, and physical-material situations, which determine not only how cognitive processes unfold but also the meanings they have for participants. (9)

This approach to cognition, Syverson argues, holds a number of important implications for composition studies, the most important of which is that "by privileging the individual writer composing in isolation, we have slighted or ignored compelling evidence that writing, like other cognitive processes, occurs in ecological systems involving not only social but also environmental structures that both powerfully constrain and also enable what writers are able to think, feel, and write" (9). Despite the obvious problems of relegating writing to a cognitive process and in doing so creating a dynamic that provides for separation between writer and writing, writer and environment, writing and environment, the basic hypothesis here is extraordinarily insightful in establishing writing as a complex ecological system. If we complicate this claim by folding all of the independent elements (writer, thinking, feeling, environment) into parts indistinguishable from the whole of writing, then the ecological relationships between the parts can be seen as interrelationships within a whole, none of which can be separated from the whole without rendering the parts and whole radically different from itself at the moment of separation. This folding into indistinguishable parts suggests a hyper-interconnectivity that emerges, as I explain in the next segment, as a fluid complexity much further from stability but flowing in distribution currents more dynamically than Syverson suggests.

Syverson's emergence is the same emergence that we see in Taylor and Hawk. It is derived from thermodynamics and refers to "the self-organization arising globally in networks of simple components connected to each other and operating locally" (11). Emergence counters entropy while including it; emergence moves toward self-organization. Emergence can be seen in writing, Syverson posits, in "meaning, genre, irony, style, authority, credibility" (11). For writing, what emergence forces is the recognition that classification systems are "actually open-ended, explanatory theories rather than closed, deterministic containers" (11). Rhetoric, we might say, stands as a prime example.

Like Taylor and Hayles, Syverson identifies embodiment as central to complexity, arguing that "neither writing nor reading can be accomplished without physical activity" (12); embodiment extends beyond conceptual structures and cognitive activities to include a physical materialism of writing. Unfortunately, Syverson's discussion of embodiment lacks any substantial theoretical undertaking. By addressing "Embodiment and the Writers" linked to a case study addressing student collaborative writing and "Embodiment and Readers" linked to a case study about an interdisciplinary computer-mediated discussion group, Syverson identifies three physical/material forces at work on the writing agent: agent as physical being (affected by things like fatigue, illness, headache, and so on), agent as inhabitant of physical environment (affected by things like ambient noise, ambient temperature, light, comfort of furniture, and so on), and agent engaging technology (affected by things like typing speed, computer access, and the like) (97–103). However, embodiment, particularly when addressed in terms of an online discussion group (which Syverson oddly describes as a "'disembodied' discourse arena" [155], as though the text is somehow one step more removed from the body in digital media than in print text), does not ground embodiment in strictly physical experiences; embodiment can also include discursive structures that enforce relationships or create barriers, preventing or allowing access.

Enaction is "the principle that knowledge is the result of an ongoing interpretation that emerges through *activities* and *experiences* situated in specific environments" (13, emphases in original). But enaction is more than simple situated activity. Extrapolating and citing a definition from Huberto Maturana and Francisco J. Varela's *Autopoiesis and Cognition: The Realization of the Living*, Syverson describes enaction as "the principle that 'every act of knowing brings forth a world' and 'all knowing is doing'" (13–14). Writing—or in Syverson's language, composing—brings forth textual worlds; it does not report on preexisting worlds. For Syverson, this is crucial because it opens the doors to examining ecological systems of composing beyond the "reductionist perspective of actual writing situations" that have dominated disciplinary discussions (17).

Ultimately, Syverson's agenda is commendable, for it works against the oversimplification of composing as a result of ingrained disciplinary methodologies and the consequences of not considering significant theoretical insights, like those suggested in providing ecological and complex approaches. Syverson rightly issues a (now familiar) warning: "As contexts and technologies for writing continue to change at an ever accelerating pace, we cannot cling to our familiar, comfortable assumptions about writers, readers, and texts, or we will find ourselves increasingly irrelevant and even obstructive" (27). A decade later, the words, seemingly ignored, still hold true. However, now, as the situation of writing has changed even more dramatically/radically than even Syverson suggests, these changes can no longer hold to models that equate writing and cognition or that rely on pseudo-anthropological case studies as providing insight into the complexities of writing. Instead, such calls are now to be seen as calls postcomposition.

With these synopses of systems theories, complexity theories, and their intercessions into composition studies in mind, I turn now to postcomposition as tipping-point, further critiquing complexity theory toward the end of suggesting a more complex ecological theory of writing, a fully un-formed (though, I hope, not un-informed) theory, standing at the brink of chaos, seeing potential in the chaotic stream and the contingencies it offers. This "theory" is intended as disruptive, as problematic, and as lending itself to spaces beyond composition studies.

Saturation

> There is no simple definition of complexity.
> —Mark C. Taylor, *The Moment of Complexity:*
> *Emerging Network Culture*

> The interactivity of thinking complicates the moment of writing.
> —Mark C. Taylor, *The Moment of Complexity:*
> *Emerging Network Culture*

Earlier in this chapter, I noted that Taylor briefly addresses the problem of writing as representational technology for information, implying that information is, indeed, a function of writing, but then fails to sustain any substantial consideration of writing or what it means to say that information is a function of writing. It is only fair to note that this discussion is not the only address of writing in the book; in addition to the ephemeral, offhanded remarks regarding writing and information, Taylor does take up writing again briefly. The implication of the second discussion about writing assumes that writing is vehicle not only for information transfer but for transfer, circulation, and conveyance of identity as well.[3] In this second discussion, writing serves the network, and the individual writer stands as the screen through which writing is displayed:

> I, Mark C. Taylor, am not writing this book. Yet the book is being written. It is as if I were the screen through which the words of others flow and on which they are displaced. Words, thoughts, ideas are never precisely my own; they are always borrowed rather than possessed. I am, as it were, their vehicle. Though seeming to use language, symbols, and images, they use me to promote their circulation and extend their lives. The flux of information rushing through my mind as well as my body (I am not sure where one ends and the other begins) existed before me and will continue to flow long after I am gone. "My" thought—indeed "my" self—appears to be a transient eddy in a river whose banks are difficult to discern. (196)

For Taylor, then, "all writing is ghostwriting . . . haunted by countless specters," which leaves "*My*" work unwritten and the writing that appears the result of a "colony of writers" (196). All "writing is re-writing"; all writing is screening; all writers are screens and their identities are what appear on those screens (196). Autonomous subjectivity collapses; the posthuman appears. Writing can be found on the edge of chaos, at points taking place *in* the turbulent flow of the river, far from crystalline stability: "The mix swirling in my mind becomes dense and diverse, like some primal soup slowly heating to the boiling point" (197). At times, Taylor even appears to describe writing *as* chaos.

The second address of writing provides two interesting points of departure in considering writing-as-system in light of complexity theories. First, during the second address of writing, Taylor begins to make seemingly uncritical shifts between metaphors of network and metaphors of fluidity, metaphors that do not project writing in the same place as complexity, on the edge of turbulence, instead suggesting that writing is a step beyond complexity further into the swirl of chaos, situated in the turbulence. Writing is in the river, not on its edge. That is to say, there seems to be a desire when addressing writing's role in complexity and network to describe writing in terms more dynamic and complex than the established metaphors of complexity and network provide, metaphors that most often emerge as metaphors of fluidity. This might be read as an unwitting nod to writing as more complex than complexity and the need for a more complex series of metaphors through which to describe writing. This is not to say that the *only* instances in which Taylor employs fluidity metaphors occur when writing is addressed; they do indeed appear sprinkled throughout the book. The increase in frequency of reference to fluidity when addressing writing, though, suggests, perhaps, that it is difficult to write/talk about writing without acknowledging a different kind of flow taking place beyond the node-to-node transmission model, a more fluid dynamic than the flows of networks.

Second, inherent in the networks and the complexity that Taylor—and other complexity and systems theories approaches, as I will show—describes, despite his attempt to show otherwise, is a sense of linearity attached to the transmission and circulation of information. This movement between nodes, though, becomes all but absent when addressing writing, suggesting that writing does not function (or cannot be talked about) as simply operating in a node-to-node dynamic and that, perhaps, writing plays a different role in the relationships between nodes and networks. What I propose, then, is that the greater complexity of writing-as-system demands not a new form of metaphor for describing writing (though it becomes all but impossible to avoid, falling prey to the will to metaphor) but a more complex complexity theory, one that accounts for writing's more turbulent characteristics, one that describes writing in less linear structures, adopting, instead, more fluid understandings of writing. This account of writing relies on the often overlooked facets of complexity and systems theories that evolved from studies in fluid dynamics, hydrodynamics, and other similar areas of research that initially contributed to the development of systems theories. That is, in conjunction with complexity theories, I offer here a perception of writing as a complex "liquid" system.

The rudimentary structure of the complex network involves movement (of information) from one node through or by way of a connection to another node, a unit of transfer that has been accepted as standard and unproblematic in most network theories. According to Taylor:

> Networks consist of interconnected nodes, which are able to communicate with each other. Each node is constituted by its interrelations with

other nodes and its place in the overall network. A node, as the word implies (*nodus*, knot; from *ned*, twist, tie, know), is a knot in a web of relations. Knots function like switches and routers that send, receive, and transmit information throughout the network. (154)

"While the connections of each node ramify throughout the network," the explanation continues, "the relations that are most decisive are relatively localized" (154). Hawk synthesizes nodal construction, explaining that the "basic structure is a set of nodes (or knots) and the relations among these nodes; its basic dynamics are determined by the strengths of the relations that adapt to the nodes around it" ("Toward a Rhetoric" 839). Castells's "Informationalism, Networks, and the Network Society: A Theoretical Blueprint" finds the fundamental node-to-node relation so critical that it foregrounds the entire theory of network society on the idea of the node:

> A network is a set of interconnected nodes. A node is the point where the curve intersects itself. A network has no center, just nodes. Nodes may be of varying relevance to the network. Nodes increase their importance for the network by absorbing more relevant information, and processing it more efficiently. The relative importance of a node does not stem from its specific features but from its ability to contribute to the network's goals. However, all nodes of a network are necessary for the network's performance. When nodes become redundant or useless, networks tend to reconfigure themselves, deleting some nodes, and adding new ones. Nodes only exist and function as components of networks. The network is the unit, not the node. (3)

While information may move among and between multiple nodes along multiple connections within the network congruently, simultaneously, reflexively, recurrently, or transparently, these movements still occur in a node-to-node direction. The basic unit of flow remains constant. Even when paralogic sequences are invoked or the complexities of multiple flows are discussed, we still imagine a kind of node-to-node transfer occurring. In fact, it is specifically this basic unit of information flow that allows for the feedback loop to form as information loops back from and to some specific nodal point in order for the feedback loop to feed back any self-reflexive information. Feedback loops may appear with as few as only one nodal point in the network, but the flow of information can only, then, return to the same nodal point, thus creating a one-directional loop, even if the loop is strange. In many ways, for thinking about writing, this inherent linearity becomes deeply problematic and calls to question thinking of writing as network, as we have come to understand networks to function in this accepted nodal model. This is one of the reasons I have suggested that writing-as-system interrelates with networks rather than suggest writing is itself an identifiable network.

It is specifically this linear network flow, no matter if designated complex or not, that limits how we understand writing in the context of complexity and systems theories; it is also the disruption of the node-to-node linearity that exposes writing's greater complexities than those accounted for by systems theories or complexity theories. Such a move is not, though, a rejection of nodes as components of either systems or networks; instead, it is a reconfiguration of the concept of nodes as they pertain to writing. One distinction in my proposed configuration as opposed to the configuration of nodes in networks and systems as complexity and systems theories have offered thus far is that those theories imply that despite their interconnectivity, nodes can be singled out as nodes, as knots. Certainly, this does not imply that all nodes are knowable but that they are independent formations within the network. Nodes, however, in writing-as-system dissolve into the system, inseparable, unidentifiable. Nodes are less important in this way than they appear to be in the formation of networks. What is important in writing-as-system is the wholeness of the system, the systems as fluctuation, and the points of interaction with networks and the nodes of those networks. In other words, a crucial facet of writing-as-system is that the system functions because of its interaction with other networks. As a further push toward the edge of chaos (or perhaps more appropriately, toward turbulence) and in an attempt to find use for systems theories and complexity theories as means for thinking about writing and through which to develop ecologically based theories of writing postcomposition, I want to suggest that by tempering both systems theories and complexity theories with aspects of fluid dynamics and fluid mechanics—both of which are tied closely with the development of scientific systems theories—we can begin to elaborate a more fluid writing theory than can be provided through systems or complexity theories alone.

In order to develop a more complex, fluid understanding of writing, two key concepts should be considered in relation to complexity theories and writing. The first—*flow*—is often employed by network theorists as a way of talking about (information) transfer along the node-to-node circuit. However, flow is left naturalized, an assumed concept suggesting a particular kind of movement between nodes. Flow, particularly when considered from the standpoint of hydrodynamics, suggests that "flows" are more complex than movement node-to-node. This also hints at questions of space: what characterizes the spaces between nodes, how does the flow itself construct and react to that space, what distinguishes nodal space from the space of flows? "Flow" functions as noun and verb, the verb indicating movement, often associated with smoothness or gliding. In Newtonian calculus, the verb implies continuous increase or diminishment; the key point is the continuity, the unchanging movement in a given direction. As a noun, "flow" refers to an instance of flowing, to that which flows, the mass that is moving. The flow is the opposite of the ebb. Ultimately, what this implies is that flows occur more complexly than is suggested in the node-to-node model and that in the movement between nodal points more is happening than simply an uninterrupted, unaffected, direct transfer of information. In the node-to-node network model, the spaces between nodes are relegated to lesser importance than the nodes themselves, when the spaces in between nodes, as well as what occupies and what occurs in those spaces—characterized as flow—should be considered as critical as the nodes themselves. Flow, then, is understood, too, as the not-node, a space distinguished from nodal space but deeply implicated in the construction of nodal space as the space against which nodes form difference/*différance*. Because of the evident influence of Gilles Deleuze and Félix Guattari's work on their work, we can assume that both Hawk's and Rickert's understanding of flow is swayed by discussions of flow, line-of-flight, and rhizome, an approach that accounts for differing rates of flow, viscosity, and flow disruptions, yet neither Taylor nor the compositionists who turn to his work or other complexity theories have elaborated the ramifications of Deleuzean/Guattarian flow in the network formation. Given the distinction I have made regarding Deleuze and Guattari's rhizomatic multiplicities and Guattari's holistic triple ecological approach, I want to nod to their influence upon my thinking about flow but will not take up their work here in detail, though further considerations of flows in writing-as-system might benefit from such an examination.

The second key concept is derived from Rickert's "In the House of Doing": *ambience*. I want to employ the metaphor of ambience in describing writing's relation to systems and networks; it is an effective metaphor with many implications. For Rickert, ambience serves as a way of thinking about an incarnational network logic, but this logic is employed as a way of talking about information distribution in light of *kairos* and, in turn, as a means for talking about language and the world. Smartly, Rickert points out that "ambience" works differently as a metaphor than does "network," offering the metaphor not as a means for overturning or marking the network metaphor as erroneous. Instead, ambience becomes an additional approach aiding Taylor's argument for collapsing subject. "In short," Rickert explains, "ambience seeks to put place, language, and body into co-adaptive, robust interaction" (904). In this way, the proposal of ambience Rickert offers is one of the smartest disruptions to information, subjectivity, and network I have encountered. Observing that complexity theories' metaphor of network suggests a hardware function to networked cultures, Rickert proposes ambience as the software "logics of being and doing that arise from the network" (904). Ambience, then, is the logic-environment in which networks operate. Ambience, in this context, suggests an encompassing environment, a space in which networks function and evolve, a space more dynamic than the idea of environment suggests. There is a sense of immersion in ambience, that which surrounds, and Rickert works to employ ambience as a way of pushing Taylor's complexity theory a bit further in explaining how complex networks operate. I do not disagree with this concept of ambience, nor with suggesting that it is within an ambient logic that networks evolve; however, in addressing writing-as-system, the presence of writing and its inter/relation to other networks/systems suggests an even greater degree of immersion than an ambient presence, one that might be thought of as *saturation*.

Saturation implies a thorough soaking, which might be better understood as *imbuing with*. Saturation fills, makes a space full. Saturation also suggests a sense of overwhelming (as in saturation bombing) or of completeness. Unlike ambience, which serves as the environment in which network logic emerges, writing saturates networks, interacts with networks by overwhelming the spaces of networks. Saturation is active; ambience is a condition of being. Certainly ambience affects and is affected by that to which it is ambient, but the effect of saturation is more thorough, more active, potentially more violent. Ambience surrounds or, more accurately, networks evolve within ambience; saturation penetrates. Nodes and knots are not merely in an ambient environment; they are saturated by writing. Writing penetrates nodes, knots, and networks, altering and influencing the very makeup of what a node, knot, or network is. Without the saturation of writing, nodes, knots, and networks are not. In the previous chapter, I characterized writing as fluctuation, a system that is both fluctuating and a fluctuation. It is by way of saturation that writing fluctuates, moving through the very networks that emerge from within writing, adjusting to and contributing to changes in networks, filling in new spaces, perpetually permeating all of a network while simultaneously eroding away the very edges of its own boundaries, seeking to expand its space while providing new spaces in and through which networks may move. Its force opens new tributaries, new dimensions of its saturation, often slowly but at times dangerously *rapidly*. Writing fills; writing overflows. Like a river that carves its path over time while engulfing all within its path, flowing over, in, around, and through that which it encounters, reacting to every presence, even retreating and abandoning at times, writing overwhelms the network, saturating every part of the network. Velocity is achieved through the interaction with network; the complexity of the network contributes to writing's flow and velocity. The more complex the network, the greater the velocity writing achieves, at times rushing seemingly out of control, at others eddying in pools of pause. Keep in mind, too, that "fluid" refers not only to liquid but to other matter like gasses and, in some instances, solids (think about sand in an hourglass or plastic). Rickert initiates his explication of ambience in sound, turning to music as a method for explaining ambience. This approach is particularly telling in that sound operates fluidly, in waves, and there is a remarkable sense of fluidity in Rickert's discussion in this segment of the article, one that extends fluidity and flow beyond the liquid.

Flow and saturation are affected by not only the complexity or density of an encountered network but by the very viscosity of writing itself. Viscosity might be thought of as the "thickness" of writing. Viscosity is also a measure of resistance, a degree of flow reactive to resistance to the amalgam of the fluid and that which it saturates. Unlike the node-to-node flow, understanding writing as saturating all of the spaces of a network— between nodes and in nodes themselves—requires that the "thickness" of the saturation be considered because the movement between, among, and within nodes is tempered by that which occupies all network spaces, including those spaces we understand as occupied by nodes and knots. In chapter 2, I invoked Archimedes' Principle of Displacement: any object wholly or partly immersed in a fluid is buoyed up by a force equal to the weight of the fluid displaced by the object. Where the fluidity of writing varies is that in its saturation, writing must occupy the same space as nodes, because without the saturation and flow of writing, the node would not be. The node is formed in and by saturated spaces. This implies that networks rely on writing's flow and saturation not just for circulation but for structural integrity as well. Without writing, the network collapses as nothing, then occupies the spaces between and within nodes, and nothing circulates. Network emerges from writing and depends upon its saturation, its fluctuation, and its mass. Without being saturated by and within writing, the network would neither emerge nor evolve, nor would the connections between nodes and knots serve the network to any degree of circulation. Nodes would degrade without the internal support of saturation and flow and would have no strength of connection to other nodes, their lack of relations eroding their purpose within the network, as we recall that the node's importance grows from its ability to connect with other nodes. Likewise, networks would not be able to interact with other networks absent of saturation.

Writing, I have claimed, is resistance; the degree to which it resists is, in part, a degree of its viscosity in saturation. From a hydrodynamics or rheology (the study of flows) perspective, fluids that have no resistance are known as *ideal* or *inviscid fluids*. Writing is never an ideal fluid; it is always viscid to some degree or another, depending upon both its immediate relation to/ with a network or node in any given space/moment as well as the memory/ residue of its previous interactions with the same or other networks. Residue remaining from one interaction affects the flow of every interaction to follow until that residue is either washed away or diluted to the point of irrelevance. Residue that remains compounds with other residue, contributing to viscosity. Just as Taylor's complexity theory is, in part, a reaction against Newtonian thinking, so too is this complex approach to fluid saturation a step away from Newtonian fluids, a conceptual fluid that remains constant no matter the viscosity or resistance it encounters. Non-Newtonian fluids, like writing, do not flow consistently. Imagine stirring a thick custard, the custard retaining indentations from the stirring utensil, filling in slowly, its flow affected by level of saturation, temperature, speed of stirring, and other conditions weighing on the fluid. A less viscous custard will fill in the indentations at a different rate, contributing to a more rapid velocity of flow and fluctuation. This condition of viscosity is understood as a dynamic viscosity. In this way, too, a dynamic fluid can rupture, torn, as it were, by the utensil or by interactive flow with network. Rupture and resistance, then, are key facets in the flow of writing's saturation. Newtonian fluids reveal no trace of the utensil's intrusion.

Many may read this theory of saturation as being more akin to language than writing, but such a reading would fail to account for what writing has become in the current condition of hyper-circulation. It is not language that lends to the posthuman; it is the prevalence of technological code—which is better understood as writing. Postcomposition, the relationship between writing and language becomes even more complex (and problematic) as the hyper-circulation of writing becomes the fundamental network saturation. Perhaps more important, too, is that as writing saturates, its codes become more universal, or more universally adaptive, as digital writing/electracy might reveal. This globalization of writing distribution creates a tipping point in which writing supersedes language. Such a shift opens dynamic spaces in which to consider the role of writing postcomposition. While I don't claim to be an expert in fluid dynamics or fluid mechanics, I do believe that by reinvigorating discussions of complex and systems theories by way of fluidity, we find a more dynamic way of approaching writing-as-system in light of what complexity and systems theories have thus far provided us regarding thinking about systems and networks. However, in doing so, it must be noted that one of the key objectives in the scientific study of fluid dynamics is flow measurement, or the process of quantifying how fluids move. Like other attempts to bring scientific efforts to writing studies as a measure of the function of writing, flow measurement and other scientific methodologies cannot simply be applied to writing-as-system, even if we accept my proposal of writing as dynamic fluid system. Likewise, flow of writing quite simply can't be quantified. Instead, what hydrodynamics offers is a way of *thinking about* writing as a more complex system than complex systems theories have accounted for, pushing writing theory a bit closer to the edge of chaos.

7. Pedagogy

> Disorder does not merely destroy order, structure, and organization, but is also a condition of their formation and transformation.
>
> —Mark C. Taylor, *The Moment of Complexity:*
> *Emerging Network Culture*

> If writing has a point, it is to leave everyone and everything forever unsettled.
>
> —Mark C. Taylor, *The Moment of Complexity:*
> *Emerging Network Culture*

The mantras of composition studies have worn thin, no longer offering answers that satisfy emerging questions about writing in its networked, hyper-circulatory condition. Questions now linger, unanswered by composition studies' dominant inquiries of the last forty years: How is writing learned? How do students write? How do students learn to write? Can writing be taught? These inquiries, perhaps, have served composition studies well, but they offer little toward future investigation, theory. The current circumstance of writing elicits a new attention away from the student subject, away from subjectivity, and toward writing as complex system and the complex systems that writing saturates. This new theoretical endeavor, as I hope I have shown, evolves not as a restoration or re-invigoration of composition studies but as a step beyond the limit-situation of composition studies into the possibilities found at the edge of chaos. Possibilities for better understanding writing emerge with a new focus on the spatial qualities of writing, considering that production in the emerging condition of writing no longer refers simply to the making of writing (or any *thing* else for that matter—goods—as economic thinking has led us to understand) but to the production of space itself. Theorists like Michel Foucault, Henri Lefebvre, Edward Soja, Gaston Bachelard, Georges Perec, Julian Murphet, and others have alerted us to the possibility that we now occupy a historical period characterized by the production of space. As Murphet puts it, "Space is at once the *field* of production and the ultimate *goal* of production"

(203, emphases in original). New theories, then, emerge from this spatial awareness, making urgent new ways of thinking about writing that account not just for spatiality but for ecologic relationships within space and the circulation and saturation of and by writing in space. My proposals for developing theories that conceive of writing in spatial, ecological, complex, networked approaches are intended to shift the very ground from which writing has been primarily theorized in composition studies. This shift is intended to leave behind the subject, the student subject, the writing-subject, and subjectivity as outmoded ways of thinking about the production of writing. Instead, considerations of the posthuman agent operating non-autonomously in complex networks, not as producers, or even conductors, of writing but as indistinguishable from writing itself, now drive writing theory postcomposition.

This book does not work toward resolution; it is intentionally a moment of resistance, of violence, that does not anticipate or desire answers. It is a nudge toward a much-needed tipping point, toward what we have come to oversimplify as a "paradigm shift." To initiate this moment of tipping, postcomposition, à la Frantz Fanon, requires a total revolution, one of "absolute violence" (37), because, according to Fanon, violence purifies; it is a cleansing force. Fanon's postcolonial revolution was to end categories of white and black, a revolution of much greater significance and importance than my application of violence to mere disciplinary matters of an elitist academic function, and I do not mean to diminish Fanon's violence by applying it to composition studies. Yet, the call to violence and disruption seems right-minded.[1] The difficulty is that throughout *Postcomposition* I have employed the word "violence" to suggest disruption, but the term carries too much baggage. It is spread thinly through our lexicon, and to suggest doing violence to composition studies is to unintentionally, though unavoidably, invoke an understanding of violence that lends to real suffering. And so, while it doesn't, ahem, pack the same punch, I clarify here that by "violence" I intend "disruption" because I'm generally not in favor of exploiting those who take punches. *Postcomposition* is a pedagogy of disruption, a pedagogy of what Mark C. Taylor, borrowing from Le Corbusier, calls "creative destruction" (28), a concept that suggests wiping the slate clean and starting anew. Of course, there is little possibility or need to decimate composition studies and start from a completely blank slate; we can't really be free of our past, nor do we want to be. As I made clear in chapter 1, postcomposition is not anti–composition studies, not opposed to composition studies; it is a measure of composition studies; it is buttressed up against composition studies. Instead, the destruction of composition studies occurs not as an evident or sudden wiping out but as a deliberate, slow reinscription of the objectives of the field and the spaces composition studies occupies. This is composition studies' becoming, not its end. Postcomposition is a re-categorization, a mutation into a different form.

As we have seen, disruption/violence is enmeshed with becoming, mutually generative, not destructive but productive, creating possibilities. Gilles Deleuze, in *Nietzsche and Philosophy*, for instance, argues that violence does not devastate that which it is enacted upon but instead reveals and generates opportunities for new possibilities. For Deleuze, the destruction of idols, as I discussed regarding the conversations of wpa genealogies, offers a productive separation from entrenched traditions of thought. Likewise, Deleuze's Bergsonian violence (see *Bergsonism*) suggests a violence that forces subjects beyond limit-situations and opens the possibility of new lines of flight. As I hope I have shown throughout this book, it is this possibility of disruption that postcomposition embraces, the opportunity, à la Foucault, to think "differently" about writing than disciplinary limits have previously allowed or encouraged. In this way, not only is composition studies' becoming violent, but it becomes violent because of its relation to systems of writing. Writing, as I have suggested, is itself violent, disruptive. Writing that persuades or informs engages in the violence of changing the ways we think about things. Ernesto Laclau, for instance, talks about discursive force, or violence, saying that all argumentation, if it is successful, does violence to those persuaded—the violence of *changing a mind* (see Drew, "Politics of Persuading"). Sound argument and effective persuasive writing, the becoming of persuasion through the recursivity of writing, is a productive violence. Postcomposition's violence is a pedagogy of mind changing.

We learn from Slavoj Žižek that protest validates that which is protested. This is not to suggest that composition studies requires postcomposition (or any other resistant position) for validation but an acknowledgment that postcomposition's protest, its violence, stands as measure and affirmation of the importance of composition studies/writing studies. I do not want to get trapped by his dependence upon Jacques Lacan, but Žižek's understanding of violence offers a straightforward explanation of the two types of violence. According to Žižek's book *Violence: Big Ideas/Small Books*, we most often focus on subjective violence, acts like murder, war, assault, and the like, but there are two types of objective violence that must be addressed: "symbolic" violence and "systemic" violence. Symbolic violence is "embodied in language and its form" (1). Symbolic violence not only is at work in the obvious, well-studied "cases of incitement and of the relations of social domination reproduced in our habitual speech forms" (1–2) but also is tied to the "universe of meaning" (2). Systemic violence is the "often catastrophic consequences of the smooth functioning of our economic and political systems" (2). Subjective and objective violence, though, cannot be "perceived from the same standpoint: subjective violence is experienced as such against the background of a non-violent zero-level. It is seen as a perturbation of the 'normal,' peaceful state of things" (2). Objective violence, on the other hand, is "invisible since it sustains the very zero-level standard against which we perceive something as subjectively violent" (2). Systemic violence, then, is to be thought of as "invisible," something like "dark matter," "the counterpart to an all-too-visible subjective violence" (2). Though "invisible," it must be accounted for in order to make sense of what might seem to be "'irrational' explosions of subjective violence" (2). Postcomposition engages violently, objectively and subjectively, seeking to actively disrupt and to alter by way of the universe of meaning. Postcomposition embraces violence as its pedagogy.

The term "postpedagogy" is most often understood as pedagogies that evolved to account for postmodern situations or, more specifically, pedagogy that teaches within postmodernity (see, for instance, McCracken). The original thought behind the idea of postpedagogy was that because postmodern theory revealed fundamental shifts in sources of articulation, forms of expression, and possibilities of expectations, there was a need for a new rhetoric of education, one that presented new forms of pedagogies to account for these shifts. We find, postcomposition, the need for another rhetoric to account for disciplinary shifts away from pedagogy, a rhetoric that emerges fully postpedagogy. Postpedagogy implies two aspects of the shift postcomposition. The first might be thought of, borrowing from Žižek's categorizations of violence, as symbolic, as identifying a disciplinary shift away from research agendas bound to composition studies' pedagogical imperative. In this way, "postpedagogy" suggests a new mantra for writing studies: stop talking about teaching. This new mantra urges researchers to step beyond the limits of thinking about writing in terms of classroom application and observation, calling instead for research that begins to tear down the very boundaries of the field in order to develop more useful, accurate theories of writing. The second implication of postpedagogy is that of pedagogical violence, of the disruptive pedagogy of postcomposition. This pedagogy is not to be read as a new way of teaching students how to write or in any literal classroom understanding of pedagogy. Instead, it should be understood as how we teach ourselves about our discipline, about our object of study.

Part of my argument throughout *Postcomposition* is an argument of survival and validation. Certainly, composition studies will linger in its academic function, providing writing instruction to institutions that see such instruction to be of value; as I have said, institutionally, composition studies is a juggernaut and will protect its safe places. The discipline will continue to produce research about teaching students, engaging new technologies for doing so and resisting institutional mechanisms that intervene into the spaces the field considers its own occupied territories. The discipline and the academy will continue to (minimally) reward the field for this production. Yet, little of this research is likely to provide us any further insight into how writing functions. It may offer new, exciting observations about the teaching of writing, student subject formation, and labor/institution politics, but little more. Because writing saturates and affects lives beyond the lives of students and their teachers in American college classrooms, we need to study and theorize the function of writing beyond classrooms. Because writing permeates every facet of all lives—human, posthuman, animal, cyborg, and so on—composition studies has an ethical responsibility to no longer limit its work in ways that it has over the last forty-plus years, ascribing writing to a very small, elite population. Composition studies is the discipline best positioned to invigorate writing studies, to occupy new intellectual spaces that test the very frontiers of the field, seeking new, useful directions that reveal more about how writing works. We see such shifts, such border expansions, beginning to happen on the fringes, often in engagement with information technologies, but just as often these efforts are encumbered by the bonds to classrooms, teaching, and student writers. *Postcomposition* is a call to resistance, to a rewriting of what *We* do, of how *We* think about writing and about how *We* define the spaces We occupy. Postcomposition might be thought of as Leibnizian possible, in that there are more possibles than actuals.[2] Possibles emerge on the edge of chaos, and the difficulty comes in the willingness to step a little closer into chaos. Possibles strive toward becoming actuals, but without engaging possibles, we stand little chance of altering the conditions of composition studies' actuals.

Composition studies suffers from what might be likened to Paulo Freire's "narration sickness": an adherence to a particular narrative that is reinscribed as master narrative. Narration sickness is what, in Freire's terms, banks. We have accepted composition studies' histories as indicative of the field's only futures. The past happened, but it is over. Many of our narratives can no longer account for new conditions of writing. Postcomposition steps away from those histories and narratives, looking to the contingent frontiers of writing studies.

Postscript: On the Very Idea of Post-ness

> As boundaries become permeable, it is impossible to know when or where this book began or when it will end. Since origins as well as conclusions forever recede, beginnings are inevitably arbitrary and endings repeatedly deferred.
>
> —Mark C. Taylor, *The Moment of Complexity: Emerging Network Culture*

> The "post-" indicates something like a conversion: a new direction from the previous one.
>
> —Jean-François Lyotard, "Note on the Meaning of 'Post-'"

> In the beginning, in principle, was the post, and I will never get over it.
>
> —Jacques Derrida, *The Post Card*

This was written first, and so it comes last.

This postscript is problematic, both in its placement and its argument. What unfolds here is an exploration of the idea of "post." It is an unpacking of the term that I engaged early in this project in order to better understand what it might mean to suggest that something might occur postcomposition. It is, then, my justification for the "posting" of composition studies. But it is also problematic in that this unpacking reveals nothing new. The very idea of *Postcomposition* is grounded in tired metaphors: "post" and "beyond." A "new vision" of composition studies that finds its footing in well-worn concepts is likely to be limited by those very metaphors. The prefix "post" carries decades of baggage from other contexts. I recognize the problems in this reliance, in trying to find use in old ideas rather than in making new ideas to accommodate a new theoretical need. What follows is an attempt to explain why I have opted to chain composition studies' disruption to an overworn marker. The works I cite here are intentionally to be read out of context in order to accentuate the very idea—or, rather, ideas—of post, ideas that helped frame my thinking about the field of composition studies in ways that brought me to this point of disruption. This, then, is a survey of why *Postcomposition* embraces post.

Postcomposition suggests a composition that is based in other posts: postmodernism, poststructuralism, postcolonialism, post-theory, posthumanism, and other post-theories. *Postcomposition* intentionally evokes links with the postmodern, with the kinds of theoretical works that postmodernity has encouraged. In doing so, *Postcomposition* examines the very post-ness of composition studies in its current formation(s), representations, subjectivities, and systems and its lack of subjectivities and systems. Ultimately, *Postcomposition* argues that composition studies must radically change its functions, identities, and cultural capitals and enter into a position postcomposition, a space in which composition studies is no longer composition studies as many came to understand what that term of disciplinary demarcation identified it as being. That is, composition studies, as its histories, narratives, and even meta-narratives have until now defined it, did end already (more than once) and has been reconceived in many postcomposition formations. These changes have gone unnoticed, or at least unacknowledged, by many, likely because such changes are necessarily fluid, often naturalized. As with history, the demarcations are always artificial and can be codified and named, set apart from what came before, only after the change has become practice and, perhaps, after additional changes have contributed. Disciplinary changes have also been resisted by more than a few, and part of my agenda has been to address this resistance and composition studies' disciplinary conservatism. Likewise, part of my agenda has been to examine a historical narrative that has constructed an "identity" of a young field and to explore a new variation of that formation in its newest—and certainly not last—incarnation, *postcomposition*. Postcomposition is a historical moment, or a moment to be historicized, in which composition studies has shifted—or, more to the point, *should* endlessly shift—its disciplinary focus from student writers to the act of writing in general, and more specifically to the phenomena of writing itself. Postcomposition is a space of theorizing writing. Postcomposition is, as I hope to have made clear, a *tipping point*.

To be explicit, however, in making such a claim, I do not identify an end to composition studies, to the teaching of writing, or to students of writing. I do not make a Hegelian teleological argument that triumphs at the coming end of composition studies. I do not suggest an epistemological break separating early composition studies and a "new" composition studies in the way that, say, Louis Althusser suggests a break between early Marx—the ideological Marx—and the later, scientific Marx (see *For Marx*). That is, while some postmodernist thinkers such as Jürgen Habermas

specifically identify postmodernism as a direct rejection of modernist thinking, a rejection Habermas opposes (see "Modernity vs. Postmodernity," for
instance), others, like Jean-François Lyotard, do not cast postmodernism as
a radical departure from (high) modernist thought or periods and do not
afford postmodernism a complete break from modernism (see "Answering
the Question," for instance).[1] So, just as Lyotard claims that postmodernism is "undoubtedly part of the modern" (79), so too is postcomposition
undoubtedly part of composition studies. Modernism, often cast as the par-
ent/precursor to postmodernism, is not overthrown and eliminated; postmodernism is not somehow the "better" theoretical position, just the new
or different position, a position that has grown to permeate contemporary
thinking more than its parent now does. This might be thought of, too, in
terms of Thomas Kuhn's now familiar idea of scientific revolutions, a useful
way of understanding discursive/disciplinary change, particularly in terms
of its insistence on pragmatic concerns as the initial catalyst: current para-
digmatic thinking and vocabulary no longer serve to address the questions
that need to be asked—indeed, the questions themselves cannot even be
formed within the normal discourse—and (over time) the paradigm shifts.

Edward Soja's magnificent book *Thirdspace: Journeys to Los Angeles and
other Real-and-Imagined Places* addresses the forms in which postmodern
critiques of modernisms have limited the kinds of critiques that can be leveled
against modernism. *Thirdspace* identifies that postmodernism is "reduced
here to anti-modernism, to a strategy of annihilation that derives from modernism's demonstrated epistemological weakness and its presumed failures
to deal with pressing problems of the contemporary world" (4). Postcomposition is not cast as the mortician of composition studies, seeking a particular
end to the discipline, though it does question composition studies' ability to
address numerous epistemological weaknesses. Postcomposition becomes
not an overthrowing paradigm for composition studies but rather a marker
through which composition studies itself is measured. Composition studies, then, is measured in postcomposition in the same ways in which Marie
Louise Pratt's "Modernity and Periphery: Toward a Global and Relational
Analysis" identifies that postmodernism serves as a strong measure not of a
postmodern era but specifically of modernism. For the most part, this is the
same service postcomposition provides composition studies: primarily as a
way of thinking about (and beyond) the scope of composition studies. Joe
Marshall Hardin's *Opening Spaces* makes a similar argument: "The postmodern perspective, then, is the critical moment of self-reflection when modernity
recognizes its ethical pretense in a moment of self-reflexive critique" (66).
What *Postcomposition* works toward, then, is the hope that what grows from/

in postcomposition is the same sort of self-reflection and critical moment in which composition studies recognizes not just its ethical pretenses but its departure beyond—not from—the scope of composition studies.

None of this is to suggest in any way that composition studies has been or should be "defeated" by postcomposition; rather, this is a recognition that postcomposition is becoming. Hal Foster, in *The Anti-Aesthetic: Essays on Postmodern Culture*, makes the crucial claim in reference to the relationship between postmodernism and modernism that "this state of affairs suggests that if the modern project is to be saved at all, it must be exceeded" (ix). It is in this statement that I see the promise of postcomposition. If composition studies is to succeed, then it must be exceeded. Likewise, Kwame Anthony Appiah identifies that "postmodernism can be seen . . . as a retheorization of the proliferation of distinctions that reflects the underlying dynamic of cultural modernity, the need to clear oneself a space" (346). It is this kind of retheorization and clearing of space that holds the potential for post-composition to exceed, and the work of spatial theory will greatly drive the attempt at that theorization as it is specifically composition studies' attempt to clear a space for itself that has piloted (prodded) composition studies (in) to the need for postcomposition.

Scholars working in areas of postcolonialism have been particularly attentive to the idea of post, and it is from their work that *Postcomposition* begins to develop an understanding of post in postcomposition. Perhaps most influential, Homi K. Bhabha's discussion of posts in *The Location of Culture* identifies that the move to a state of "post" is an attempt to move into a location of "beyond." For postcolonialism, such a move provides opportunity for examining the idea of colonialism, to some degree antagonistically; postcomposition adopts a similar critical eye. What Bhabha makes clear is that the postcolonial is still very much colonial; we might think, then, of the postcolonial as a "later period" of colonialism if we imagine a future historical view of this present as past. It is in this way of looking ahead to look back at postcomposition that we see more clearly the intended relationship between postcomposition and composition studies.

Anne McClintock's "The Angels of Progress: Pitfalls of the Term 'Post-Colonial'" questions the very idea of postcolonialism's post-ness, explaining that if postcolonial theory "promises a decentering of history in hybridity, syncreticism, multi-dimensional time, and so forth, the *singularity* of the term effects a re-centering of global history around the single rubric of European time. Colonialism returns at the moment of its disappearance" (86). McClintock goes on to clarify that "the word 'post,' moreover, reduces the cultures of peoples beyond colonialism to *prepositional* time. The term confers on colonialism the prestige of history proper; colonialism is the determining mark of history" (86). What this suggests, then, is that posts are really discursive demarcations more than anything else; posts mark a period in which conversations initiate about not only what we have been doing but what we are still very much currently doing. This conversation occurs in a reflexive, critical way that was not possible during the period prior to the post. This is what is hopeful about the post: the possibility of seeing and knowing the effects of that which is posted becomes greater. While this vision doesn't guarantee any sort of reform or improvement, it holds promise for critical work without truncating movement into "eras," instead recognizing the fluidity of discursive/disciplinary shift. In this way, then, composition studies becomes the historical marker for postcomposition, and as it does so, composition studies becomes the measure of postcomposition and postcomposition the measure of composition.

From each of these discussions, we begin to see possibilities for understanding postcomposition. In particular, Bhabha identifies that any move to the post—postmodernism, postfeminism, and in particular postcolonialism—is a move into the "beyond." The notion of exceeding falls specifically into this category. For Bhabha, the location of the beyond is a powerful place: "'Beyond' signifies spatial distance, marks progress, promises the future; but our intimations of exceeding the barrier or boundary—the very act of going beyond—are unknowable, unrepresentable, without a return to the 'present' which, in the process of repetition, become disjunct and displaced" (4). The explanation continues: "Postcoloniality, for its part, is a salutary reminder of the persistent 'neo-colonial' relations within the 'new' world order and the multi-national division of labour. Such a perspective enables authentication of histories of exploitation and the evolution of strategies of resistence" (6). "Being in the 'beyond,' then," Bhabha explains, "is to inhabit an intervening space, as any dictionary will tell you. But to dwell 'in the beyond' is also . . . to be part of a revisionary time, a return to the present to redescribe our cultural contemporaneity" (7). With this understanding in mind, postcomposition intervenes in the beyond. Like Friedrich Nietzsche's beyond, and Jean Baudrillard's to follow, the beyond of composition studies' "post" is no longer composition studies itself but remains *within* composition studies. Postcomposition moves beyond its own condition of composition studies to transcend its own capability and position. According to Bhabha, to move into the beyond, to turn the present into the post, is to "touch the future on its hither side" (19). Postcomposition, then, is understood, à la Lyotard, not to be composition studies at its end but composition studies in a constant nascent state of becoming beyond.

Like Bhabha, Gilles Deleuze and Félix Guattari offer us the opportunity to look toward horizons and develop a hermeneutics of the future. In addressing planes—particularly in the discussions of planes of immanence—Deleuze and Guattari, in *A Thousand Plateaus*, look toward understanding how planes might be traversed. Planes are unseen designs that provide organization and development; planes are at once both the "structural plan(e) of organizations with their developments" and the evolutionary development of those organizations (265). Planes, though, should be looked beyond:

> Precisely because the plane of immanence is prephilosophical and does not immediately take effect with concepts, it implies a sort of groping experimentation and its layout resorts to measures that are not very respectable, rational, or reasonable. These measures belong to the order of dreams, of pathological processes, esoteric experiences, drunkenness, and excess. We head for the horizon, on the plane of immanence, and we return with bloodshot eyes, yet these are the eyes of the mind. (*What Is Philosophy?* 41)

Drawing from Deleuze and Guattari, Michael Hardt and Antonio Negri also situate their analysis of empire within a framework of horizon, arguing that there needs to be "a new scenario of different rational acts—a horizon of activities, resistances, wills, and desires that refuse the hegemonic order, propose lines of flight, and forge alternative constitutive itineraries" (48). Horizons, though, we must acknowledge, are illusions, a trick of perspective.

Deleuze and Guattari, furthering the concepts of planes and horizons, offer the concept of becoming that drives a vision of postcomposition. Becoming, they explain,

> is certainly not imitating, or identifying with something; neither is it regressing-progressing; neither is it corresponding, establishing corresponding relations; neither is it producing, producing a filiation or producing through filiation. Becoming is a verb with a consistency all its own; it does not reduce to, or lead back to, "appearing," "being," "equaling," or "producing." (*Anti-Oedipus* 239)

Deleuze and Guattari situate the concept of becoming as becoming-animal, as movement from human to animal, but it is clear that becoming is not limited to such a transition. All things can become all other things. What is crucial to postcomposition is both the potential of becoming and the idea that not only becoming can lead to an endless array of new forms but anything can spark the becoming: "We can be thrown into a becoming by anything at all, by the most unexpected, most insignificant of things"

(292). A becoming, Deleuze explains in *Bergsonism*, persists. Identifying becoming in the work of Henri Bergson, Deleuze illustrates that a becoming is a "transition," a "change," and that a becoming endures; it is a "change that is substance itself" (37). Becoming, Deleuze and Guattari identify in *A Thousand Plateaus*, "lacks a subject distinct from itself" (238), and the self is "only a threshold, a door" to becoming (249). There is no logic to the process or order of becoming, no way to anticipate or demarcate what will become, what will result from the becoming. There is potential in the becoming, but of what, we cannot say. The paralogical nature of becoming may seem uncontrolled, unstable, potentially disruptive; but it is precisely in this disruption that becoming holds promise. Becoming is boundless, endless in its potential. Disruption is crucial.

Embedded in becoming is a sense of violence, a violence that permeates Deleuze and Guattari's work—both as collaborators and individually. Violence, however, is not seen as a destructive force; rather, it is cast as productive, creating possibilities. Specifically in Deleuze's writing about Nietzsche and in his *Cinema 2*, violence is a way of disrupting controlling systems and making evident the traditions of thinking that give power to those very systems. Deleuze's objective (in *Bergsonism*) in enacting productive violence is to produce victims, to intentionally act upon subjects (and objects), as Michael Vastola's "The Rhetoric of the Cold War in the Age of Terror: Toward a Deleuzean Pedagogy of Violence" explains, with a violence that "drags its victims beyond the conventional and safe limits of thought in order to potentiate new imaginings." In *Cinema 2*, such violence encourages the subject to become more fully aware of its own temporality, of its own mortality; the subject itself becomes a "revealer of the deadline" (15), cognizant of its own deadline, its own passing. Acknowledgment of the primordial recognition of the subject's own death is a necessary part of the violence, encouraging the subject to destroy hegemonic ontological formations that enforce limits upon the subject. It is specifically this disavowal of conventional limits that allows postcomposition's becoming to exceed itself. Violence is necessary.

Similarly, Paulo Freire's concept of limit-situation suggests a need to look beyond; in analyzing a "universe of themes," Freire explains,

> the *themes* both contain and are contained in *limit-situations*; the *tasks* they imply require *limit-acts*. When the themes are concealed by the limit-situations and thus are not clearly perceived, the corresponding tasks—people's responses in the form of historical action—can be neither authentically nor critically fulfilled. In this situation, humans are

> unable to transcend the limit-situations to discover that beyond these situations—and in contradiction to them—lies an *untested feasibility*. (83)

It is precisely this untested feasibility, the potential for contradiction to historical action, to which postcomposition looks. While *Postcomposition* does not mean to cast Bhabha's beyond, Deleuze and Guattari's horizon and becoming, and Freire's limit-situations as homologous, it does read these four ideas as offering possibilities for the transition postcomposition. Past the limit, over the horizon, and in the beyond, possibility is immeasurable and subjectivity drastically recast, as we shall see; the untested potential for theorizing writing becomes boundless, and the role/position/location of what might be done postcomposition, too, is inestimable.

This move beyond composition studies, then, is not a look toward the end of composition studies or the start of some new or different study since, as Baudrillard identifies, "the whole problem of speaking about the end . . . is that you have to speak of what lies beyond the end and also, at the same time, the impossibility of ending" (*Illusion* 110). Postcomposition is a move past the limit-situation of composition studies, a move beyond the disciplinary identities that composition studies has attempted (and often failed) to assume and the identities that have been foisted upon it by other institutional and cultural powers, and most specifically the identities that composition studies itself has (often uncritically) embraced and to which it has consigned itself/its selves. Postcomposition, to paraphrase and borrow from Baudrillard, is the end of composition studics' linearity. It is the end of its history and its future, for without a future it cannot end (10).

Interestingly, postmodern sociologist Zygmunt Bauman's *Liquid Modernity* and *Postmodern Ethics* contend that postmodernism stepped in when modernism failed in its ability to answer critical questions—particularly ethical questions—thereby resulting in modernity's self-dismantling. Bauman argues that modernity's inability to engage in self-critical reflection resulted in a need for critical questioning of modernity's motives. As I quoted Hardin earlier, postmodernism is, then, the critical moment when modernity recognizes its own self-reflexive critique (66). Though I do not intend to adopt Richard Rorty's notion of systematic philosophy by equating the move postmodern with the move postcomposition, I do find Bauman's account interesting and am willing to suggest that the need for the move postcomposition specifically grows from composition studies' necd to engage in radical critical self-examination in ways that allow/encourage composition studies to consider itself trapped by institutional and cultural identities and boundaries in such a way that has forcibly stagnated the work in composition under rubrics of student (subjectivity) and classroom (administration). Resistance to such work limits self-reflection (even using the full-length mirror provides only a one-dimensional reflection) and will inevitably lead to composition studies' own self-dismantling by way of confining the discipline to a service position in the academy. I am not opposed to that dismantling, nor to the (Deleuzean) violence that such dismantling demands.

Postcomposition is a step away from and beyond composition studies. Walter Benjamin has explained that "dialectics at a standstill" (*Dialektik im Stillstand*) occurs when all events come to a standstill in anticipation of the end. For Benjamin, of course, that anticipation is that of the arrival of the Messiah; composition studies, too, seems to be waiting for some sort of messianic arrival—an event that liberates composition from its stagnation. Composition studies has come to a standstill: in its research, in its goals, in its progress. Postcomposition addresses how that stagnation has led to composition studies' dialectical standstill, perhaps in anticipation of its own end. That end, when it will (again) occur, will come as illusion, as all horizons do, and will come for the simple fact that composition studies has shunned its horizons in the movement of theory, maintaining a conservative grasp of a teleological binding to classrooms (administration) and students (subjectivity). Composition will not, however, end in a spectacular flash, its dramatic death throes suggesting a proud glory worthy of an end of times; rather, it waits complacently while the American university confirms that current times will continue as they have, and safely so, in "a state of frozen animation" such as Slavoj Žižek describes in *Welcome to the Desert of the Real* (8).

Composition studies marches on as a zombie: animate but empty. Like Bhabha explains of cultural difference: "It is the problem of how, in signifying the present, something comes to be repeated, relocated and translated in the name of tradition, in the guise of a pastness that is not necessarily a faithful sign of historical memory but a strategy of representing authority in terms of the artifice of the archaic" (35). And, so, *Postcomposition* works to disrupt that pastness, embracing the beyond of composition studies, since, to turn again to Baudrillard, "we are encircled by our own end" (*Illusion* 119) and, to paraphrase Soja, whether one likes it or not, postcomposition is a state of things (*Thirdspace* 92).

As I have said, the idea of *Postcomposition* rests in the ideas of the beyond, the horizon, the becoming, and the limit-situation. While these ideas are central to understanding postcomposition, it is also useful to examine all of the implications of "post" in order not to be trapped by the conventional uses of "post" as it serves in prefixes to postmodernism, poststructuralism, post-Marxism, postfeminism, and so on. As Soja puts it, "The affirmedly prefixed 'post-' seems literally to signal the irrevocable 'end of' all progressive modernist projects rather than their potentially advantageous reconstitution and renewal" (93). I want to suggest a further/ farther understanding of "post" that flirts with multiple uses of the word/ prefix. Of course, my play(ing) with the idea of post is directly influenced by Derrida's play with the term in *The Post Card*. "The Glossary" in Alan Bass's "Translator's Introduction" to *The Post Card* explains Derrida's "post" (I quote at length):

> *Poste* derives from the Latin *ponre*, to put, to place. It is therefore linked to *position* (also derived from *ponre*), and to the entire topic of "thesis," the singular position (and the "athesis" . . .). *La poste* is "mail," with all of its resonances of position and relay; *le poste* is "post" in the sense of the position to be held, like a soldier's post. . . . *Les postes* is the usual expression for the French postal system, the government agency once called the *P.T.T.* (*Postes, Télégraphes, et Téléphones*), and now called the *P. et T.* (*Postes et Télécommunications*). A post office is a *bureau de postes* or *la poste*. *Le poste* can also mean a station, as in *poste de police*, police station. Derrida exploits every possible play on "post": *imposteur* (imposter), *imposture* (imposture), "poster," in the English sense, especially with the resonance of "wanted poster" (leading to posse and to bounty, reward). There is also an etymological link between *poser* (to pose, to position) and *pauser* (to pause). *Poser* and *pauser* are homonyms, and the idea of stopping, halting, pausing, is intrinsic to the idea of the thesis, to being set in place at a post which one guards . . . : thus Derrida calls the great philosophers masters of the post, interns of theses that bring things to halt; but this immediately implies post in the sense of sending. The ambiguity inherent in "to post"—to station and to send—is played throughout. Derrida states several times that the "Envois" are a satire (farce) of the two basic forms of literature, the detective novel and the epistolary novel, which both depend upon *postes*. In "Le facteur," nore 6, there is a quote from Littré, who wrote in his dictionary: "Le poste ne diffère de lat poste que par le genre," i.e. "Post—in the sense of position—differs from post—in the sense of mail—only by gender." Finally, there is the play on *postérieure*, which is the same in French and English ("posterior" . . .), posterity, etc. (xxv–xxvi)

As I have already suggested, "post" is more often than not understood to mean "after." Too frequently, however, that same post-ness is read to mean "anti" or "against": postmodernism as antimodernism; post-theory as anti-theory.

Certainly, in some cases these posts are anti. There is no definitive approach to post. Post can be after and can serve as a marker by which the thing, idea, concept, phenomenon, era that has been placed before the post is measured: postcolonialism as measure of colonialism, post-theory as measure of theory, posthumanism as a measure of humanism. However, what often happens is that if the thing measured is found wanting, the mechanism for measuring is dubbed "anti" or is itself criticized as lacking the ability to accurately measure. To assume that postcomposition—which, like other posts, is a discursive moment that allows for a doubling-back, a reflective, critical view—is anticomposition is essentially an ad hominem argument, flawed and defensive and unable to address the critique itself without acknowledging its validity.

"Post" also implies following, that which is *after*. Postcomposition is both after composition studies chronologically and after composition studies in that it follows after composition studies, is a follower of composition studies, a devotee of composition studies. It *is* against composition studies as it is buttressed up against composition studies; it abuts composition. It *is not* against composition studies as an opposition to composition studies. It is a marking of composition studies. Though, some possibilities arise in that postcomposition in its measure of composition studies may critique composition studies and thus be seen as against (opposed to) composition studies, and, to follow the potential of Freire's limit-situation, postcomposition may offer contradictions to composition studies. This is the easy part of post. This is the easy part of postcomposition. But there is more than the easy part. The multiplicities of post should be considered.

Between you, me, and the post (actually a derivative of the bedpost, indicating intimacy), the post is the stout timber that serves as foundation. To play the metaphor game, the post is the first part of the construction, the outline of the foundation, post construction. We set posts to give framework. Postcomposition theory stands not as foundational but as the ideas on which we compose the new composition studies beyond. Posts are the figures of support. Posts are also set as boundary markers, identifying where borders begin and end; they surround a field, fencing its boundaries, keeping occupants in and the unwelcome out. Posts are disciplinary. Posts are strategic. Posts serve as landmarks, marking sites of interest and importance; they may be placed as monuments, reminding us of what has transpired in a given place and time, marking cultural and historical locations of note. Posts are sites of exchange: trading posts.

These understandings of post, as well as Derrida's play in *The Post Card*, move postcomposition into the realm of the spatial. Posts are positions, foundations, markers of territory. Posts position; posts place. Posts are thesis, are topics, are *topos*: the very spaces and places of writing. It would be short-sighted, then, to address postcomposition without an eye toward the spatial (see chapter 2).

Posts may be set to display public messages and notices. The poet of the post is the writer who makes his or her writing public. We know that it was common to set posts by the doors of offices of authorities both as emblematic of the power of those who lived/worked inside and as the site through which those authorities made their proclamations and announcements public. These posts were also the location of waiting for audience with the authority; they identify a place of pause, of waiting, just as a solider or guard is to stand at his post, to remain in position, in place, alert, unless he receives orders to abandon post. Posts mark the start and end of a race, the position of beginning and end. One need not run from pillar to post to begin to consider post as spatial. Just as we each fill a post—fill multiple posts, occupy multiple positions—so too does postcomposition work to fill its post in the American university. It is given official post.

In the first week of September 1666, London burned. In the time before the Great Fire, the space allocated for foot traffic was demarcated by rail and post. Upon these posts, bills of announcement were attached (*placed*), providing both public announcements and theatrical placards. Posting-bills became *posters*, transferring from the act of posting to the thing that is posted by shifting to the anthimeria (or is it polyptoton?) *ers* ending (apologies to Orwell).

For those of us of the nautical mind, sternposts are the timbers on which rudders are hung, the mechanism for steering a boat or ship—and the derivation from which the term the "stern" of the boat originates: the "end" of the boat. Posts, then, not only mark positions, locations, or ends (a historical/ideological position) but may act as the very mechanism by which objects/subjects are steered into those positions, by which spaces and places are navigated. Posts navigate; posts negotiate.

Tavern keepers kept accounts and tabs—and sometimes scores of competitions—notched in doorposts. From this the idea of post-writing grows. The tavern post was a post of reckoning, of making good, of account(ability), and of score. Posts were for keeping tabs (on), for measuring, and accounting for (from which the post-book is derived). To post an account, then, is to give it order, to *place* it in context. To post is to make public, to *place* in a public sphere, to situate and make available. To post is to make visible, to be seen, to inform. To post is to publish. To be well-posted in a subject is to be thoroughly informed.

Of course, "post" evokes the postal system, a system by which mail (read: letters) is assigned. Postal systems began in the sixteenth century when men and horses were placed along post roads at specified posts, called post-stages. Each man and horse, when urgent news was to be delivered, was to ride from his post to the next as fast as possible—posthaste—to transfer the message to the next rider. Riders later began to carry letters (quite literally carrying letters, an arrangement of symbols in alphabetic writing to make words, to give meaning) and when arriving at post transferred to new horses, allowing them to ride through post, expediting the delivery of letters. Establishing such routes of delivery was to lay posts, to set a route and determine the paths of transmission, the direction and circulation of information. Posts were, at first, temporary, shifting as territories and geopolitical boundaries shifted. Later, in the seventeenth century, as routes of information transfer became more stable, posts were made permanent and were given over to keepers of the post: post masters, the precursor to contemporary postmasters who oversee local post offices, where postal work, workers of the post, from time to time "go postal," enacting violence against the post and the keepers of the post—a metaphor that many have adopted, including Lynn Worsham, as a manner of understanding pedagogic violence (see Worsham, "Going Postal"). The post(al) becomes central for Derrida's post:

> Want to write and first to reassemble an enormous library on the *courrier*, the postal institutions, the techniques and mores of telecommunication, the networks and epochs of telecommunication throughout history—but the "library" and the "history" themselves are but "posts," sites of passage or of relay among others, stases, moments or effects of *restance*, and also particular representations, narrower and narrower, shorter and shorter sequences, proportionally of the Great Telematic Network, the *worldwide connection*. What would our correspondence be, and its secret, the indecipherable, in this terrifying archive?
>
> The wish to vanquish the postal principle: not in order to approach you and finally to vanquish you, to triumph over distancing, but so that by you might be given to me the distancing which regards me. (*Post Card* 27)

Grounded in the idea of the postcard and its transmittal of information, Derrida's post becomes a post of possibility, a disruption of the pause of posts. In French, *poste restante* refers to remaining at post—literally at the office of the post—until summoned. Postal services worldwide accept posts (letters) that remain housed in the post office until they are called for. In some instances, such as in the British system, letters remain at post only for a limited time until they are returned to the writer.

Post is derived from the Latin *positus*, to position, place, or arrange (*pono posi positum*: to lay place, put, set, post, station). Post is seen also in light of the Greek *meta*, which refers to a change or a transformation. *Meta* carries implications of beyond and becoming in that the change it denotes is a transformation to higher levels. As Soja explains: "In Greek, *meta-* carries the meaning of both something beyond or after (akin to the Latin *post-*), and also (related to the Latin *trans-*) a change of place or nature, i.e. to transport and/or transcend (as in the roots to the word 'metaphor')" (33). Soja also explains in a footnote to the discussions of "post" that "were it not for the Greco-Roman impurity, the term 'postmodernity' (and related usages) might better be translated as 'metamodernity' to capture the more complex meanings of the Greek versus the Latin prefix: not simply coming after but moving beyond, in the sense of transporting and transcending, moving modernity to a different place, nature, meaning" (33n). Soja, turning to Henri Lefebvre's discussion of meta-philosophy in *The Production of Space*, cites Lefebvre: "The term meta-philosophy then is not the abolition of philosophy. To the contrary, it opens up a sphere of reflexion and meditation in which philosophy appears in all its fullness but also with all its limitations" (qtd. in *Thirdspace* 34). Meta-philosophy exposes philosophy; postcomposition exposes composition studies. To be exposed makes one vulnerable. Composition studies, though always vulnerable, needs its soft white underbelly prodded a bit, its position questioned and re-posted.

The end of composition studies may or may not be nigh, but news of its demise or survival will not be headlining in the *Saturday Evening Post*, *Denver Post*, or *Washington Post*. To speak of such things is not to invoke a postapocalyptic or postpartum rhetoric; though it may signify my own post-traumatic stress disorder. I may have noted the passing of composition studies on my Post-it Notes but did so post hoc and postoperatively. Perhaps Emily Post will provide me with some information as to how to act appropriately in the time of postcomposition.

We stand at the doorpost of postcomposition, posting an entry into the beyond.

To kiss the post is analogous to kissing the hare's foot, to being too late. And though it may be too late for composition studies, there is not yet a need to conduct a postmortem examination of composition studies as its heart still beats; stagnation may be setting in, but it is not yet stiff as a post. That argument, you may criticize, is merely to run one's head against the post. Yet composition studies seems to have developed an a posteriori approach to writing as a methodology and in doing so has trapped itself in its own post, leaving little room to maneuver *post factum*. Postcomposition stands to disrupt the pause at post, leaving composition studies the opportunity to find itself on the right or wrong side of the post. But before we celebrate and tear down the goalposts, there is much to be done to call composition studies to the post.

So as not to postpone my argument any longer and to end this dreadful comp-post, I move on.

Post-Theory

This is not the first time that Theory has been reported dead.
This is not the first time that Theory has been reported dead.
This is not the first time that reporting the death of Theory has been reported dead.
This is not the first time that reporting the death of Theory has been reported dead.
. . .
It will come as no surprise to learn that the "post" in "post-theory" is not to be taken unequivocally—which immediately begs the question of how it *is* to be taken. Common sense is only too happy to witness the passing of Theory. It was only a matter of time before we outgrew what had only ever been an irritating fad, just a phase we were all going through. Theory has no shortage of opponents waiting for the chance to say I told you so. Not that this distresses Theory. If resistant Blimps did not exist, Theory would have to invent them. The monolith of Common Sense has always been a fantasy of Theory, and a gratifying and sustaining one at that. Relegating resistance to an external reactionary force is always a profoundly comforting strategy.
In any case, Theory itself is only too happy to witness the passing of Theory. Nothing stimulates the production of Theory like the proclamation of its own death, regardless of who makes the proclamation.
—Martin McQuillan, Graeme MacDonald, Robin Purves, and Stephen Thomson, "The Joy of Theory"

I want to know where Theory is buried, so I can go and dance on its grave.
—Thomas H. Benton, "Life after the Death of Theory"

The idea of postcomposition is also heavily modeled upon and derived from post-theory, from investigations into what comes/chases "after theory." Post-theory expresses not a resistance to theory—the anti position—but a frustration or impatience with theory and a wish for theory to (re)direct in more productive undertakings. While few post-theorists agree precisely as to what new productive directions theory should take, most do identify a criticism of the theory movement of the 1960s through 1990s as lacking. Post-theory, Martin McQuillan, Graeme MacDonald, Robin Purves, and Stephen Thomson identify, "rejects the dead hand of a self-satisfied and hypostasised 'Theory,' a theory in love with and, finally, indistinguishable from its own rhetoric. It rejects the sclerosis of theoretical writing, the hardening of Theory's lexical and syntactical arteries" (xi–xii). Yet, post-theory does not take the anti-theory stance so many in composition studies have taken. Post-theory's theory wars are not composition studies' theory wars. Post-theory's reaction against—and here, again, I do not mean "anti"; I mean *against* as in "buttressed up against"—is not the anti-intellectual reactions of Wendy Bishop, Maxine Hairston, and others against theory in composition studies. As Stefan Herbrechter and Ivan Callus's introduction to *Post-Theory, Culture, Criticism* puts it, post-theory is not "understood in its facile and improbable sense of a condition 'after theory,' 'theory overcome' or even 'without theory,' but rather as an undertaking (without, necessarily, any of an undertaker's duties)" (8). Postcomposition, then, is ante-theory, not anti-theory.

Much of post-theory can be traced to questions about the role of theory as posed by Jacques Derrida, Paul de Man, and Terry Eagleton, though McQuillan, Purves, and MacDonald's *Post-Theory*, Michael Payne and John Schad's *life.after.theory*, Thomas Docherty's *After Theory*, Wendell Harris's *Beyond Poststructuralism*, Judith Butler, John Guillory, and Kendall Thomas's *What's Left of Theory?*, and Stefan Herbrechter and Ivan Callus's *Post-Theory, Culture, Criticism* all galvanize post-theory projects. None of these works proclaims the end of theory as the indication of the start of post-theory. They herald, however, the passing of theory, the posting of theory in all that those gerunds might evoke. As McQuillan, MacDonald, Purves, and Thomson explain, "'Post-Theory' must be a Theory which comes before and after itself" (xv):

> Post-Theory then is not just a Theory which is not present but is potentially so, rather it is a theory (an experience of thought) which cannot be fully activated even potentially. Post-Theory is a state of thinking which discovers itself in a constant state of deferral, a position of reflexivity and an experience of questioning which constantly displaces itself in the negotiations with the aporias of Theory. Post-Theory promises that "Theory" will only take place when one can "finally see sight." (xv)

Post-theory is an intervention into the state of theory, into the statehood of theory. Post-theory is a theory of posts. "In a certain sense," McQuillan, MacDonald, Purves, and Thomson submit, "'Post-Theory' is a Theory 'yet to come'" (xv). For Herbrechter and Callus, post-theory, first, is an undertaking that involves "theory's task in theorising its own institutionalisation and internationalism; and secondly it envisages a critical return upon theory's 'others' (its repressed, its excluded, its unthought) in terms of a theory 'yet to come'" (8). Post-theory expands the horizons of theory, moves theory into the beyond. For McQuillan, MacDonald, Purves, and Thomson, the future of post-theory, and in turn the future of theory, lies in the hands of new theorists whose task, they claim, is "not to re-enact old paradigms and operations, no matter how comforting and familiar. They must be in a state of constant rediscovery of the conditions of Post-Theory: thinking through the aporias of the institution and resisting a disengagement with theoretico-political events. As such, we are already in the Post-Theory condition" (xvi). Herbrechter and Callus are also clear that "theory can only reinvent itself as worthwhile 'post-theory' through its own critical self-revaluation" (9).

As I have said, one of the most detrimental (in)activities of composition studies has been its overall failure to participate in substantial critical self-reflexive rediscovery that amounts to anything more than an ongoing self-validation in which old paradigms may be recast in new clothing but still remain as they always have. Or as Antonio Negri cites Marx, it's "all the same old shit" (219). I have attempted to explain how such disciplinary paradigms have become comforting and safe, providing an illusion of freedom. It is in these very simulacra of freedom that composition studies has burrowed itself into a comfortable place in the American university—and it is this safe place, this free place, that has become composition studies' cage. "We 'feel free' because we lack the very language to articulate our unfreedom," Slavoj Žižek would say (*Welcome* 2). Instead, composition studies has corralled what it identifies as composition theory into a role of servitude, serving its subject (student) and administrative (pedagogy) agendas. Throughout this book, then, I pay a good deal of attention to the role theory plays in composition studies in an attempt to articulate a need for a more rigorous kind of work for composition theory and for the slowly evolving theoretical work that moves in such a direction. For now, I want to note that the growing critical work that is being forwarded in composition theory is indeed what allows me to say, echoing McQuillan, MacDonald, Purves, and Thomson, that we are already in a postcomposition condition. Like postcomposition is to composition studies, post-theory is a state of theory in its becoming.

Post-theory, like postcomposition (or is it the other way around?), encounters other post theories: poststructuralism, postmodernism, and so on. But, ultimately, post-theory is about posts. As Nicholas Royle explains through Robert Young:

It must be at once theory about posts (about all kinds of sending and tele-phenomena) and about post-theories. But there is perhaps also something new, uncertain, exciting and even frightening that is intimated in the word "post-theory," a sense perhaps that we are again getting to a point where (to quote Young's more recent essay again) "Suddenly it becomes apparent that poststructuralism's abstract theorising, apparently divorced from the social and from history, in fact catches most accurately the forms of certain contemporary political and social situations relevant to the new radical democratic movements" . . . and where the energies or allergies of a new generation of academics are starting to announce themselves in the thought of other spaces and times: post-theory. (4)

Much of the post-theory movement grows not *from* but *in response to* an ongoing anti-theory position that blames theory for changes in contemporary academia. Post-theorists (and many theorists) argue that questions of theory should not be directed toward a disavowal of theory but instead toward a consideration of the role of theory. As David Carroll's introduction to *The States of "Theory"* asks:

But what is this strange thing called "Theory" that seems to be the source of so many problems in so many different disciplines and that appears to provoke such violent reactions? What has it actually done to provoke such reactions, and is the bad reputation it has in the eyes of many in any way deserved? Most important, are the changes it has helped bring about really to be denounced, and should they be, can they be reversed? What is at stake in these questions is the future: not just the future of the various disciplines and the research done within them, but a certain relation to the possibility of (necessity of) movement, reevaluation, transformation in general, the future not as the logical outgrowth of the past and present but as the indication of and relation to what has not been anticipated or programmed. (2)

This question of the reaction to theory echoes de Man's query in *The Resistance to Theory*:

What is it about literary theory that is so threatening that it provokes such strong resistances and attacks? It upsets rooted ideologies by revealing the mechanics of their workings; it goes against a powerful philosophical tradition of which aesthetics is a prominent part; it upsets the established canon of literary works and blurs the borderlines between literary and non-literary discourse. By implication, it may also reveal the links between ideologies and philosophy. All this is ample reason for suspicion, but not a satisfying answer to the question. (11)

Though Carroll does not use the term "post-theory," the work is nonetheless a critical component of the post-theory movement in that it identifies that it is time to get beyond the arguments over enclosure, exclusion, and repression that theory must confront and instead "get on with the difficult task of keeping theory an active, critical endeavor (or making it one, if it is not already)" (2). For Carroll, this means raising not only questions that are theoretical but questions about theory itself. These are the kinds of self-reflexive assessments that post-theory depends upon in order to push theory into the beyond, into the unanticipated. Postcomposition takes this kind of work to be of the utmost importance.

Post-theory is about theory that does not yet exist, the theories-to-come. Post-theory is not about theory but about what Derrida might call a *countersignature* of theory, a counter-theory (see *"As If"*). From this idea of countersignature, postcomposition looks to countersign composition studies, not overwrite composition studies, not promulgate composition studies as dead and postcomposition its successor, for composition studies, like theory, dies and ends continuously. As Geoffrey Bennington says of deconstruction and Derrida's *"As If* I Were Dead" echoes, so too can we say of composition studies: nothing seems so clearly to indicate the vitality of composition studies as announcements of its imminent demise, of its passing. And so when misinformed, anti-intellectuals such as *Chronicle of Higher Education* columnist Thomas H. Benton (the pseudonym of an assistant professor of English at a midwestern college) praise the death of theory, as Benton rants in his *Chronicle* column "Life after the Death of Theory," it is a passing of theory that I instead applaud, choosing to read *life* in the light of Payne and Schad's *life.after.theory* as chasing after theory, something Benton misses in his choice of words for his title.

It is a passing of composition studies into which postcomposition works. Postcomposition is the surpassing and overtaking of, the moving beyond the limits of, composition studies. It is the passing *of* one discourse to another; it is the passing *from* one discourse to another. Postcomposition is both a contingent temporal moment and a place of passing, the passing (as in head off at the pass). Would somebody please pass the composition studies? Postcomposition moves forward, not bound by rethinking, reassessing, or reworking the past but by looking to new frontiers for composition theory.

Traditionally, in composition studies, theory has been employed not to understand writing but instead primarily to explain the discipline of composition studies, to explain pedagogies, particularly pedagogies of writing. That is not to say that theories of writing have not been forwarded, but generally speaking, those theories do not come from composition studies. *Postcomposition* recognizes instead, as Raúl Sánchez explains, "*theory as a function of writing*" (3). Postcomposition, in turn, does not focus on traditional binaries between theory and practice but transcends current understandings of theory as a mechanism of explanation and instead sees theory as one of many apparatuses that evolve from with/in writing. Theory is not pursued for the sake of theory but rather as a platform through which to better understand writing, not by (necessarily) theorizing writing but by understanding how theory comes to be through writing, how the function of theory is itself a function of writing.

Postcomposition navigates along the same course as post-theory, working to demand more of composition studies, of theory, and specifically of composition theory, or more specifically of writing theory. Postcomposition is of post-theory and embraces many of its agendas in its push toward more critical theories of writing. Postcomposition questions composition studies' allergic disposition toward theory, its resistance to theory and theorizing. Terry Eagleton's *After Theory* is clear that "if theory means a reasonably systematic reflection on our guiding assumptions, it remains as indispensable as ever. But we are living now in the aftermath of what one might call high theory, in an age which, having grown rich on the insights of thinkers like Althusser, Barthes, and Derrida, has also in some ways moved beyond them" (2). It is time for composition studies to move into this beyond, to work toward developing theories of writing beyond classrooms, beyond students. As Eagleton explains, when it comes to theory, "we are still trading on the past" (2). Composition studies' theory has been tied down by its histories, by its temporality, and that temporality as it relates to composition studies' anti-theoretical positioning. Postcomposition moves forward, away from composition studies' past(s).

NOTES
WORKS CITED
INDEX

Notes

1. Disrupting Composition Studies

1. I should note, too, that part of Smit's resistance to research is a cynicism regarding the motives of researchers in composition:

> Also noteworthy is the increasing amount of research and scholarship in the field, much of it based on the history of rhetoric, the sociology of the profession, or critical theories currently popular among literature faculty, much of it only tangentially related to the teaching of writing per se. This trend raises the suspicion that a great deal of the research and scholarship in composition is not conducted primarily to promote our understanding of the nature of literacy and how people become literate; rather, it is conducted as a means of professional advancement. (6–7)

2. While the UNESCO study covers enrollments from 1999 through 2004, the UN global population estimates are made every five years. Thus, I'm fudging these numbers a bit by comparing the 2004 estimated world tertiary enrollment against the 2005 estimated world populations. So my numbers may be a bit inaccurate as a statistical measure, but they are close enough to make the point. See also UNESCO Institute for Statistics, "African Students Most Mobile in the World," 23 Jan. 2007, http://www.uis.unesco.org/ev.php?ID=6513_201&ID2=DO_TOPIC (accessed 26 Apr. 2007), and United Nations Population Division, "World Population Prospects: The 2008 Revision Population Database," http://esa.un.org/unpp/p2kodata.asp (accessed 26 Apr. 2007).

3. The question of composition studies' identity and its location in the American academy has been a central conversation within the field. This conversation has produced a number of disciplinary canonical texts, including Stephen M. North's *The Making of Knowledge in Composition: Portrait of an Emerging Field*, Louise Wetherbee Phelps's *Composition as a Human Science: Contributions to the Self-Understanding of a Discipline*, Susan Miller's *Textual Carnivals: The Politics of Composition*, Lester Faigley's *Fragments of Rationality: Postmodernity and the Subject of Composition*, Robert J. Connors's *Composition-Rhetoric: Backgrounds, Theory, and Pedagogy*, Sharon Crowley's *Composition in the University: Historical and Polemical Essays*, Hephzibah Roskelly and Kate Ronald's *Reason to Believe: Romanticism, Pragmatism, and the Possibility of Teaching*, Bruce Horner's *Terms of Work for Composition: A Materialist Critique*, Geoffrey Sirc's *English Composition as a Happening*, and Lisa Ede's *Situating Composition: Composition Studies and the Politics of Location*.

4. See Smit, p. 6, for more on the use of the term "field" as opposed to "profession" or "discipline."

2. The Space of Writing

1. Throughout this chapter, I refer to "space" in the singular, while many of the theorists I cite refer to the plural "spaces," suggesting multiple spaces. Given that part of my definition of space, and its distinction from place, is that space is infinite, I attempt to avoid the problem of talking about multiple infinite spaces, since the overlap of multiple, infinite, and spaces seems to be problematic. That is not to say, though, that I disagree with the idea of multiple spaces; instead, I account for such multiplicities and overlaps as conditions of place, not space. Thus, as a matter of consistency, my reference to space remains in the singular as an attempt to emphasize the contingency and totality of space as distinctly different from place, which is imbued with meaning.

2. Granted, while on many campuses all the humanities are hit hard in these assessment/self-supporting days, composition studies is often in a better position to defend itself in terms of the "practicality" of its work for students' material needs. While we might lament such an approach to education as skills-training, compositionists are often in a better position on campus to defend and promote what they do in the language of business and skills than are literature faculty. In this way, we should acknowledge one way in which composition studies maintains some power greater than literature; there are many intersecting, overlapping, and contradictory forms of power within English studies.

3. One of the problems with relying on these sources, though, is that they are old, which is not to say they are not still relevant, but the university setting has changed remarkably since they were written. Drastic changes in availability of resources and political/public pressures on academics to defend what they do as important to students and the twenty-first century economy create a very different context for composition studies. Likewise, these histories address writing from a different perspective, one not able to account for the technological shifts in writing's hyper-circulation, changing the very landscape not only of what writing is but of its value in the university.

4. I feel obligated to note the problem with the phrase "the nature of" as used in this and other instances in that it reduces the object of the preposition to an alignment with "nature" as an unquestionable position.

5. Here I'm not thinking of "life" in a biological sense but question the very idea of life as it is bound with the very idea of theory, as do Michael Payne and John Schad in their book *life.after.theory*.

6. Admittedly, I make this distinction out of disciplinary convenience; in addressing space from rhetorical and philosophic positions, it is easier to make connections to issues pertaining to writing and composition studies–specific arguments (and, to be honest, I just don't have the background to appropriately address things like quantum field theory). While work in the space of

mathematics and physics is certainly crucial in informing philosophies and rhetorics of space, those positions are difficult to "translate" into the kinds of arguments I wish to make. Likewise, I must note that my approach to space here is distinctly Western.

7. I should note, too, that the Hebrew *makom* is likely linguistically related to the Arabic *makôm*, a word that indicates a holy place, but given that Arabic did not develop a system of writing until the seventh century A.D. (Jammer 27), it is difficult to play out that relationship fully.

8. See my essay "Writing Takes Place."

9. Here I intentionally use the term "position"—the place where a thing is located—to indicate that the definitions of "occupation" themselves occupy a particular epistemological space within this chapter and within an understanding of space.

10. *Species of Spaces* does not follow through with the exercise at this point in the discussion by then identifying the function of the space of, say, the bed, as defined by the (to borrow from Soja) second space of the bed and its occupation.

11. While making this criticism is crucial, I must own up to the fact that I am guilty of participating in/forwarding such conversations as much as anyone else is. I do not mean to imply that having the conversation about composition studies' "identity" is an inappropriate conversation to have.

12. In saying that Crowley's book is a spatial argument, I mean to suggest that it is an argument about occupation, about how FYC occupies a given space within the American university system.

13. "Minnesota," "Florida," and "Brodkey" all refer to "events" during which forces from beyond the boundaries of composition studies intervened in places thought to be composition studies' safe places and forcefully altered how those places were occupied. In the cases of the University of Minnesota and the University of Florida, upper administrations took control of writing programs with little or no consultation with composition studies faculty in order to impose their own views of what a writing class should accomplish. Linda Brodkey lost her job at the University of Texas specifically because she attempted to create a curriculum within a space she thought to be safe but that was ultimately controlled by stronger administrative forces.

3. Beyond the Subject of Composition Studies

1. The term "transhuman" derives from thinking that in order to achieve a condition of the posthuman, a figure must have at one time been human. In this thinking, because the posthuman is yet to come, or by some accounts only hypothetically may become posthuman, the condition of the transhuman is the state between being human and being posthuman. For those who see the posthuman as either inevitable or hypothetical, the transhuman represents a current condition in which we have moved beyond humanity but not yet achieved posthumanity.

2. See the postscript at the end of this book for more about post-theory.

3. I should note that in the early 1990s, composition studies took a growing interest in Foucault's work. Interestingly, though, the import of Foucault's work to composition studies was limited in its focus primarily to Foucault's address of power, institution, and discourse. Little attention was paid—perhaps strategically or conveniently—to Foucault's questioning of the subject, and Foucault's claims about the historical construction of "man " were overlooked entirely, likely because such claims undermine the mission of composition studies. Foucault himself was concerned that his work would be approached in such a way, writing in the afterword to Hubert L. Dreyfus and Paul Rabinow's *Michel Foucault: Beyond Structuralism and Hermeneutics*—later reprinted as "The Subject and Power" in *Critical Inquiry*—that the goal of his work was not "to analyze the phenomena of power" (777). "My objective, instead," he writes, "has been to create a history of the different modes by which, in our culture, human beings are made subjects" (777). Foucault does not deny that he has been attentive to power, but only as a matter of trying to understand the complex relationships in which the human subject is placed. In fact, much of "The Subject and Power" is devoted to the question "Do we need a theory of power?" (778). But embedded in his detailed response to this question is an intricate uncertainty with the subject. However, Foucault's uncertainty with the subject and what amounts to his posthumanist critique is, as Wolfe's *Critical Environments* clarifies, "more often than not accompanied . . . by a dystopianism that imagines that the end of the humanist subject is the beginning of the total saturation of the social field by power, domination, and oppression" (41).

4. Monsanto, I should explain, is one of the largest bioengineering corporations in the world. It is the largest distributor of the herbicide glyphosate, which it sells under the brand name Roundup. Monsanto is also the world's largest distributor of genetically modified seed, holding 70–100 percent of the world market for some seeds. Monsanto is also the world's leading developer and distributor of bovine growth hormone, which is produced both synthetically and via recombinant DNA technology. Monsanto has a reputation for engaging in assertive lobbying and legal actions. Its global presence makes it a visible target for anti-globalization activism.

5. "Mechanosphere" refers to Deleuze and Guattari's concept of the real as a material stratum.

6. See also Haraway's chapter "A Cyborg Manifesto: Science, Technology, and Socialist-Feminism in the Late Twentieth Century" in *Simians, Cyborgs, and Women*, especially pages 151–55.

7. Please keep in mind that economic and ecologic approaches are closely tied both in metaphor and method. However, their distinctions suggest a manner of looking at system (ecologic) over management (economic).

8. This argument is fully explored in Eric Havelock's *Preface to Plato*.

4. Beyond the Administration of Subjects

1. Granted, much of the bureaucratic history of writing program administration was important in composition studies' academic development. I do not mean to cast this history as entirely negative; composition studies could not have achieved its institutional position without this work, nor could it have developed the research it has thus far about writing, teaching writing, and writing-subjects. Nor, for that matter, would I be able to locate a position from which to make an argument about and conceive of something called postcomposition.

2. As a matter of consistency and clarity, I will use the capitalized WPA to indicate the organization of the Council of Writing Program Administrators and the lowercased wpa to refer to the individual position of a writing program administrator. When I use these acronyms in this way, however, I do not mean to merely identify one as an organized body and the other as an individual body; rather, I mean to imply a more politicized understanding of the WPA as an institutional purveyor of capital, as the mechanism through which and by which writing program administrators seek to maintain a control over the very act of administration over writing programs through a system of homogenization, assimilation, and legitimation. My references to the WPA, then, are to be read as critical. My references to the wpa are to be read not as references to an individual administrator but to the role that individual administrators play in the larger institutional power of the WPA and as the very idea of writing program administration. The wpa is the occupied body used—not empowered—by the WPA. The WPA, then, is constituted by multiple wpa bodies giving subjectivity and authority over to the WPA.

3. Notice that I'm not exempt and that I'm perpetuating that conversation.

4. My apologies to all geeks; I mean nothing by it.

5. In their discussion of "Becoming-Animal" in *Kafka: Toward a Minor Literature*, Deleuze and Guattari explain deterritorialization as a process in which "the animal proposes to the human by indicating ways-out or means of escape that the human would never have thought of" alone (35). In many ways, I like to think of deterritorialization as opening possibilities of ways-out and escape for wpas not yet thought of. Deterritorialization is inherently a posthuman approach, applied here in pursuit of becoming posthuman wpas.

6. A somewhat pedantic note: I find it interesting that this construction of forewarning in writing relies on metaphors of time—now and later, moments— when in fact the writing itself is reliant not on time but on space. I do, in fact, return to the issue at hand several pages deeper into the text; the time of when I return is insignificant and actually not a characteristic of the writing. As per chapter 2, these types of metaphoric understandings of writing have corralled our understanding of writing in terms of chronology.

7. Parenthetically, Bousquet does note that "of course, this equivalence could easily come about by the frightening but very real possibility—evidenced by

clear statistical trends—that labor patterns in other disciplines will become more like those in composition, rather than the other way around" (502).

8. Bousquet capitalizes "WPA" here, but his intention is to refer to a more generic sense of administrator/administration. As I point out in note 2 to this chapter, I have used the capitalized WPA to refer specifically to the professional organization the Council of Writing Program Administrators. I have italicized Bousquet's *WPA* to embed my call against the WPA organizational and imperial push as well. This was never Bousquet's intent.

5. Ecocomposition Postcomposition

1. I do want to make a distinction here between ecocomposition and work in environmental rhetoric or cultural studies approaches that examine the nature/culture binary. Though environmental rhetoric—particularly works like M. Jimmie Killingsworth and Jacqueline S. Palmer's *Ecospeak: Rhetoric and Environmental Politics in America*, Carl G. Herndl and Stuart R. Brown's *Green Culture: Environmental Rhetoric in Contemporary America*, and Sidney I. Dobrin and Sean Morey's *Ecosee: Image, Rhetoric, Nature*—has been particularly influential in the development of early ecocomposition, particularly in maintaining both philosophic and political bonds between composition studies and rhetoric, that research has been more about content and politics than about writing per se.

2. The idea of disrupting ecocomposition may seem a bit odd simply because ecocomposition is so incredibly new (or should we say, ahem, green) to composition studies that many may say it has not yet had the opportunity to establish itself in any way substantive enough to warrant disruption and that disruption so early risks extinction. For many, in fact, ecocomposition may be so new and unfamiliar that disrupting it might seem premature, like beating up the new kid in school before getting to know him (and then beating him up). In addition, many in composition studies have resisted ecocomposition as simply just another special interest to a few in the field and not offering anything substantial to the field writ large.

3. Many may look askance at my disruptive agenda as somewhat odd given that I have spent the past ten years writing about and working to establish ecocomposition as a significant area of studies within composition studies. To these questions, I offer that it is precisely through this disruption that I look to solidify ecocomposition as a critically necessary part of postcomposition theory. I also offer that my position here might seem drastically different from the arguments I have made in other works about ecocomposition; it does, in fact, argue specifically against some of my own previous work, particularly ecocomposition efforts hampered by composition studies' pedagogical imperative. I acknowledge these shifts and point to transitional moves others in composition studies have made over the course of their writing, notably the dynamic shifts Patricia Bizzell made, manifest in the compilation of her essays in *Academic*

Discourse and Critical Consciousness. In other words, in many ways, when it comes to ecocomposition, I've changed my mind.

4. This is certainly not to imply that work that investigates the construction of nature is not significant. In fact, given the possibilities suggested by work in a posthuman era, questions regarding the formations of concepts like "nature" and "human" are crucial, and I pursue these issues elsewhere. But, this kind of work is not work about phenomena of writing, which is the work to which postcomposition must attend.

5. For more about postprocess, see Dobrin, Rice, and Vastola, *Beyond Post-Process.*

6. Zebroski distinguishes between Theory with a capital *T* and theory with a lowercase *t* in the final chapter of *Thinking through Theory: Vygotskian Perspectives on the Teaching of Writing,* "The End(s) of Theory," which he uses to indicate the grand theories of poststructuralist theory and postmodern theory. He uses this same distinction in "Toward a Theory of Theory for Composition Studies."

7. In a note to this claim, Zebroski identifies that readers may attribute his use of "ecology" to a continuation or critique of Louise Wetherbee Phelps's use of the term in her works "Practical Wisdom and the Geography of Knowledge in Composition" and *Composition as a Human Science,* works Zebroski claims to have been "rudely and radically under-appreciated " and "just about the only work in composition that I would be tempted to label brilliant" ("Toward a Theory" 47 n. 1). But Zebroski is clear that his ecology is not Phelps's ecology:

> Our work inhabits two virtually unrelated universes of discourse. Phelps does Phenomenological theory; I see my work as critical theory. Phelps is concerned with knowledge, I with social relations and the circulation and distribution of power. Phelps finds value in Aristotle; I prefer to go with what is left of Heraclitus. Phelps tries to think ahead of the status quo. I try to think around it, that is, to resist it. Phelps, I believe, though I have not consulted her about this, sees her work as being broadly centrist, if it can be said to be political in any sense, while I, a scholar to the left, would argue that Phelps's work has serious potential import for the political right of the future, of the twenty-first century. (47 n. 1)

I do not take up Phelps's ecology here primarily because it focuses on the "ecology of curricular contexts in which any teaching decision is embedded" ("Practical Wisdom" 867) and works to unpack further the theory-practice division in composition studies, an issue I believe I have covered in detail in earlier chapters and in my book *Constructing Knowledges: The Politics of Theory-Building and Pedagogy in Composition* (though not by way of Phelps).

8. I borrow this structure of "flirt[ing] with the 'systemness'" from Bernard C. Patten, "Why 'Complex' Ecology?" (xiv).

9. I want to be cautious, here, too in explaining that by "writing system" or "writing as system," I do not mean to invoke Saussure's "system of signs,"

because as Derrida's *Of Grammatology* shows, "there is no *writing* as long as graphism keeps a relationship of natural figuration and of some resemblance to what is not the *signified* but represented, drawn, etc." (32, emphases in original).

10. For more on recursivity and the history of cybernetics' epistemological transformations, see Hayles, *How We Became Posthuman.*

11. Ecosophy is thought to have two origins, one of which, as I discuss here, is that forwarded by Félix Guattari. The other is forwarded by Arne Næss, founder of the deep ecology movement. Næss defines ecosophy as

> a philosophy of ecological harmony or equilibrium. A philosophy as a kind of sofia (or) wisdom, is openly normative, it contains both norms, rules, postulates, value priority announcements and hypotheses concerning the state of affairs in our universe. Wisdom is policy wisdom, prescription, not only scientific description and prediction. The details of an ecosophy will show many variations due to significant differences concerning not only the "facts" of pollution, resources, population, etc. but also value priorities. (Næss, "Shallow" 8)

Næss's definition and ties to deep ecology suggest an inherency of value in nature and emphasize the value of nature over culture (particularly Western culture). Næss's ecosophy is a philosophy of fundamental binary between nature and culture. In no way do I intend my use of "ecosophy" to reflect Næss's use of the term.

12. Interestingly, in *The Three Ecologies*, Guattari writes, "Although Marx's own writings still have great value, Marxist discourse has lost its value" (43).

6. The Edge of Chaos

1. In fact quite the opposite, as he acknowledges the work of the Santa Fe Institute as important (the Santa Fe Institute, as we shall see, is a central source for *The Moment of Complexity*).

2. While I do not address image or visual in this project, much of my other work focuses on the role of image and writing. See, for instance, *Ecosee* (with Sean Morey).

3. Thomas Rickert takes up Taylor's second address of writing quite smartly in "In the House of Doing."

7. Pedagogy

1. In her response to Lynn Worsham and Gary A. Olson's 1999 *JAC* interview with Ernesto Laclau, Julie Drew makes a compelling argument against violence as power and, simultaneously, for the necessity of discursive violence. While I do not consider her counter-theory here, I acknowledge it as an important possibility for thinking about pedagogical violence differently than I propose it.

2. I adopt the term "Leibnizian possibles" from Deleuze's *Bergsonism.*

Postscript

1. Of course, one of Habermas's primary arguments is that modernism can be recovered. Rejecting the work of thinkers like Adorno, Derrida, Foucault, Nietzsche, Heidegger, and Horkheimer, Habermas works to defend and continue the project of modernity through his "theory of communication." For Habermas, modernity is an "incomplete project" with remaining potential. For me, composition studies has also always been an incomplete project, but I see little benefit in attempting to reclaim, reconsider, or reinvent composition studies.

Works Cited

Althusser, Louis. *For Marx*. 1965. Trans. Ben Brewster. London: New Left Books, 1996.

———. "Ideology and Ideological State Apparatuses (Notes towards an Investigation)." *Lenin and Philosophy and Other Essays*. Trans. Ben Brewster. New York: Monthly Review Press, 1971. 127–86.

Appiah, Kwame Anthony. "Is the Post- in Postmodernism the Post- in Postcolonial?" *Critical Inquiry* 17 (Winter 1991): 336–57.

Bachelard, Gaston. *The Poetics of Space*. Trans. Maria Jolas. Boston: Beacon, 1994.

Badiou, Alan. *Being and Event*. New York: Continuum, 2007.

Badmington, Neil. "Theorizing Posthumanism." *Cultural Critique* 53 (2003): 10–27.

Barthes, Roland. *Image, Music, Text*. Trans. Stephen Heath. New York: Hill and Wang, 1977.

Bartholomae, David. "What Is Composition and (if you know what that is) Why Do We Teach It?" *Composition in the Twenty-First Century: Crisis and Change*. Ed. Lynn Z. Bloom, Donald A. Daiker, and Edward M. White. Carbondale: Southern Illinois UP, 1996. 11–28.

Bass, Alan. "Translator's Introduction." *The Post Card: From Socrates to Freud and Beyond*. By Jacques Derrida. Trans. Alan Bass. Chicago: U of Chicago P, 1987. vii–xii.

Bateson, Gregory. *Steps to an Ecology of Mind*. New York: Ballantine, 1972.

Baudrillard, Jean. *Fatal Strategies*. Trans. Philip Beitchman and W. G. J. Niesluchowski. New York: Semiotext(e), 1990.

———. *The Illusion of the End*. Trans. Chris Turner. Stanford, CA: Stanford UP, 1994.

———. "Photography, or the Writing of Light." *ctheory.net*. 12 Apr. 2000. www.ctheory.net/articles.aspx?id=126 (accessed 19 Dec. 2005).

———. *Simulacra and Simulation*. Trans. Sheila Faria Glaser. Ann Arbor: U of Michigan P, 1994.

Bauman, Zygmunt. *Liquid Modernity*. Cambridge, UK: Polity, 2000.

———. *Postmodern Ethics*. Cambridge, MA: Blackwell, 1994.

Bay, Jennifer L. "Screening (In)Formation: Bodies and Writing in Networked Culture." *JAC* 24.2 (2004): 929–46.

Bazerman, Charles. "The Case for Writing Studies as a Major Discipline." *Rhetoric and Composition as Intellectual Work*. Ed. Gary A. Olson. Carbondale: Southern Illinois UP, 2002. 32–38.

Bennington, Geoffrey. "Inter." *Post-Theory: New Directions in Criticism.* Ed. Martin McQuillan, Robin Purves, and Graeme MacDonald. Edinburgh: Edinburgh UP, 1999. 103–19.

Benton, Thomas H. "Life after the Death of Theory." *Chronicle of Higher Education* 29 Apr. 2005: C1, C4.

Berland, Jody. "Angels Dancing: Cultural Technologies and the Production of Space." *Cultural Studies.* Ed. Lawrence Grossberg, Cary Nelson, and Paula Treichler. New York: Routledge, 1992. 38–55.

Berlin, James. "Contemporary Composition: The Major Pedagogical Theories." *College English* 44 (Dec. 1982): 765-77.

Bhabha, Homi K. *The Location of Culture.* London: Routledge, 1994.

Bizzell, Patricia. *Academic Discourse and Critical Consciousness.* Pittsburgh: U of Pittsburgh P, 1993.

Blakesley, David, and Thomas Rickert, eds. *Complexity Theory.* Spec. ed. of *JAC* 24.4 (2004): 805–1038.

Bloom, Lynn Z., Donald A. Daiker, and Edward M. White, eds. *Composition in the New Millennium: Rereading the Past, Rewriting the Future.* Carbondale: Southern Illinois UP, 2003.

———. *Composition in the Twenty-First Century: Crisis and Change.* Carbondale: Southern Illinois UP, 1996.

Bousquet, Marc. "Composition as Management Science: Toward a University without a WPA." *JAC* 22.3 (2002): 493–526.

Brereton, John C. *The Origins of Composition Studies in the American College, 1875–1925: A Documentary History.* Pittsburgh: U of Pittsburgh P, 1995.

Brooke, Collin Gifford. *Lingua Fracta: Towards a Rhetoric of New Media.* Cresskill, NJ: Hampton, 2009.

Bruffee, Kenneth. "Collaborative Learning." *College English* 43 (1981): 745–46.

Burke, Kenneth. *A Rhetoric of Motives.* Berkeley: U of California P, 1969.

Butler, Judith, John Guillory, and Kendall Thomas. *What's Left of Theory: New Work on the Politics of Literary Theory.* New York: Routledge, 2000.

Calvino, Italo. *Cosmicomics.* New York: Harcourt Brace, 1965.

———. *If on a Winter's Night a Traveler.* New York: Harcourt Brace Jovanovich, 1979.

Carey, Kevin. "A Matter of Degrees: Improving Graduation Rates in Four-Year Colleges and Universities." A Report by the Education Trust, May 2004. http://www.cherrycommission.org/docs/Resources/Completion/A%20Matter%20of%20Degrees.pdf (accessed 8 Dec. 2010).

Carroll, David. *The States of "Theory": History, Art, and Critical Discourse.* New York: Columbia UP, 1990.

Carter, Michael. *Where Writing Begins: A Postmodern Reconstruction.* Carbondale: Southern Illinois UP, 2003.

Casey, Edward S. *The Fate of Place: A Philosophical History.* Berkeley: U of California P, 1997.

Castells, Manuel. *End of Millennium*. 2nd ed. Malden, MA: Blackwell, 2010. Vol. 3 of *The Information Age: Economy, Society and Culture*. 3 vols.

———. "Informationalism, Networks, and the Network Society: A Theoretical Blueprint." *The Network Society: A Cross-Cultural Perspective*. Ed. Manuel Castells. Northampton, MA: Elgar, 2004. 3–45.

———, ed. *The Network Society: A Cross-Cultural Perspective*. Northampton, MA: Elgar, 2004.

———. *The Power of Identity*. 2nd ed. Malden, MA: Blackwell, 2004. Vol. 2 of *The Information Age: Economy, Society and Culture*. 3 vols.

———. *The Rise of the Network Society*. 2nd ed. Malden, MA: Blackwell, 2000. Vol. 1 of *The Information Age: Economy, Society and Culture*. 3 vols.

Cicero. *On Duties (De Officiis)*. Trans Walter Miller. Vol. 30. Cambridge: Harvard UP, Loeb Classical Library, 1913.

Cixous, Hélène. *Three Steps on the Ladder of Writing*. New York: Columbia UP, 1994.

Clark, Andy. *Natural-Born Cyborgs: Minds, Technologies, and the Future of Human Intelligence*. New York: Oxford UP, 2003.

Clark, Romy, and Roz Ivanic. *The Politics of Writing*. New York: Routledge, 1997.

Coe, Richard M. "Eco-Logic for the Composition Classroom." *CCC* 26.3 (1975): 232–37.

———. "Rhetoric 2001." *Freshman English News* 3.1 (1974): 1+.

———. "'Rhetoric 2001' in 2001." *Composition Studies* 29.2 (2001): 11–35.

Connors, Robert J. "Composition History and Disciplinarity." *History, Reflection, and Narrative: The Professionalization of Composition, 1963–1983*. Ed. Mary Rosner, Beth Boehm, and Debra Journet. Stamford, CT: Ablex, 1999. 3–21.

———. *Composition-Rhetoric: Backgrounds, Theory, and Pedagogy*. Pittsburgh: U of Pittsburgh P, 1997.

Cooper, Marilyn. "The Ecology of Writing." *College English* 48.4 (1986): 364–75.

———. "Foreword: The Truth Is Out There." *Ecocomposition: Theoretical and Pedagogical Approaches*. Ed. Christian R. Weisser and Sidney I. Dobrin. New York: State U of New York P, 2001. xi–xvii.

Corbett, Edward. "A History of Writing Program Administration." *Learning from the Histories of Rhetoric*. Ed. Theresa Enos. Carbondale: Southern Illinois UP, 1993. 60–74.

Crowley, Sharon. *Composition in the University: Historical and Polemical Essays*. Pittsburgh: U of Pittsburgh P, 1998.

———. "A Letter to the Editors." *Writing Theory and Critical Theory*. Ed. John Clifford and John Schilb. New York: MLA, 1994. 319–26.

De Certeau, Michel. *The Practice of Everyday Life*. Berkeley: U of California P, 1984.

Deleuze, Gilles. *Bergsonism*. New York: Zone, 1991.

———. *Cinema 2: The Time-Image*. Minneapolis: U of Minnesota P, 1989.

———. *Nietzsche and Philosophy*. Trans. Hugh Tomlinson. Minneapolis: U of Minnesota P, 1983.

Deleuze, Gilles, and Félix Guattari. *Anti-Oedipus: Capitalism and Schizophrenia*. Minneapolis: U of Minnesota P, 1983.

——. *Kafka: Toward a Minor Literature*. Trans. D. Polan. Minneapolis: U of Minnesota P, 1987.

——. *A Thousand Plateaus*. Minneapolis: U of Minnesota P, 1987.

——. *What Is Philosophy?* New York: Columbia UP, 1994.

De Man. Paul. "The Epistemology of Metaphor." *Critical Inquiry* 5.1 (Autumn 1978): 13–30.

——. *The Resistance to Theory*. Minneapolis: U of Minnesota P, 1986.

Derrida, Jacques. "*As If* I Were Dead: An Interview with Jacques Derrida." *Applying: To Derrida*. Ed. John Bannigan, Ruth Robins, and Julian Wolfreys. New York: St. Martin's, 1996. 212–26.

——. "Khōra." *The Derrida Reader: Writing Performances*. Ed. Julian Wolfreys. Lincoln: U of Nebraska P, 1998. 231–62.

——. *Of Grammatology*. Trans. Gayatri Chakravorty Spivak. Baltimore: Johns Hopkins UP, 1976.

——. *The Post Card: From Socrates to Freud and Beyond*. Chicago: U of Chicago P, 1987.

——. "The *Retrait* of Metaphor." *The Derrida Reader: Writing Performances*. Ed. Julian Wolfreys. Lincoln: U of Nebraska P, 1998. 102–29.

——. "Scribble (Writing-Power)." Trans. Cary Plotkin. *Yale French Studies* 58 (1979): 116-47.

——. "White Mythologies: Metaphor in the Text of Philosophy." *New Literary History* 6.1 (Autumn 1974): 5–74.

——. *Writing and Difference*. Trans. Alan Bass. Chicago: U of Chicago P, 1978.

DeVoss, Dànielle Nicole, Heidi A. McKee, and Richard (Dickie) Selfe. *Technological Ecologies and Sustainability*. Computers and Composition Digital Press. Web. May 2009 (accessed 11 Aug. 2010).

Didur, Jill. "Re-embodying Technoscientific Fantasies: Posthumanism, Genetically Modified Foods, and the Colonization of Life." *Cultural Critique* 53 (2003): 98–115.

Dobrin, Sidney I. "A Problem with Writing (about) 'Alternative' Discourses." *Alt Dis*. Ed. Helen Fox, Christopher Schroeder, and Patricia Bizzell. Portsmouth, NH: Heinemann Boynton/Cook, 2002. 45–56.

——. *Constructing Knowledges: The Politics of Theory-Building and Pedagogy in Composition*. Albany: State U of New York P, 1997.

——. "Writing Takes Place." *Ecocomposition: Theoretical and Pedagogical Approaches*. Ed. Christian R. Weisser and Sidney I. Dobrin. Albany: State U of New York P, 2001. 11–25.

Dobrin, Sidney I., and Sean Morey, eds. *Ecosee: Image, Rhetoric, Nature*. Albany: State U of New York P, 2009.

Dobrin, Sidney I., J. A. Rice, and Michael Vastola. *Beyond Post-Process*. Logan: Utah State UP, 2011.

Dobrin, Sidney I., and Christian R. Weisser. "Breaking Ground in Ecocomposition: Exploring Relationships between Discourse and Environment." *College English* 64.5 (2002): 566–89.

———. *Natural Discourse: Toward Ecocomposition*. Albany: State U of New York P, 2002.

Docherty, Thomas. *After Theory*. Edinburgh: Edinburgh UP, 1997.

Drengson, Alan, and Yuichi Inoue, eds. *The Deep Ecology Movement: An Introductory Anthology*. Berkeley: North Atlantic, 1995.

Drew, Julie. "The Politics of Persuading: Ernesto Laclau and the Question of Discursive Force." *JAC* 19.2 (1999): 292–97.

———. "The Politics of Place: Student Travelers and Pedagogical Maps." *Ecocomposition: Theoretical and Pedagogical Approaches*. Ed. Christian R. Weisser and Sidney I. Dobrin. New York: State U of New York P, 2001. 57–68.

Eagleton, Terry. *After Theory*. New York: Basic, 2003.

"Ecocomposition." *Wikipedia*. http://en.wikipedia.org/wiki/Ecocomposition (accessed 19 Sept. 2008).

Edbauer, Jenny. "Unframing Models of Public Distribution: From Rhetorical Situation to Rhetorical Ecology." *Rhetoric Society Quarterly* 35.4 (2005): 5–25.

Ede, Lisa. *Situating Composition: Composition Studies and the Politics of Location*. Carbondale: Southern Illinois UP, 2004.

Faigley, Lester. *Fragments of Rationality: Postmodernity and the Subject of Composition*. Pittsburgh: U of Pittsburgh P, 1992.

Fanon, Frantz. *The Wretched of the Earth*. New York: Grove, 2005.

Foster, Hal. *The Anti-Aesthetic: Essays on Postmodern Culture*. Port Townsend, WA: Bay, 1983.

Foucault, Michel. *The Archaeology of Knowledge and the Discourse on Language*. New York: Pantheon, 1972.

———. "Of Other Spaces." *Diacritics* 16 (Spring 1986): 22–27.

———. *The Order of Things: An Archaeology of the Human Sciences*. New York: Vintage, 1994.

———. Preface. *Anti-Oedipus*. By Gilles Deleuze and Félix Guattari. Minneapolis: U of Minnesota P, 1998. xi–xiv.

———. "The Subject and Power." *Critical Inquiry* 8 (1982): 777–95.

Fox, Tom. "Working Against the State: Composition's Intellectual Work for Change." *Rhetoric and Composition as Intellectual Work*. Ed. Gary A. Olson. Carbondale: Southern Illinois UP, 2002. 91–100.

Freire, Paulo. *Pedagogy of the Oppressed*. New York: Continuum, 1995.

Fukuyama, Francis. *Our Posthuman Future: Consequences of the Biotechnology Revolution*. New York: Farrar, 2002.

Fulkerson, Richard. "Foreword: Preparing the Professors." *Preparing College Teachers of Writing: Histories, Theories, Programs, Practices*. Ed. Betty P. Pytlik and Sarah Liggett. New York: Oxford UP, 2002. xi–xiv.

———. "Four Philosophies of Composition." *CCC* 30.4 (1979): 343–48.

Grego, Rhonda C., and Nancy S. Thompson. *Teaching/Writing in Thirdspaces: The Studio Approach*. Carbondale: Southern Illinois UP, 2007.

Guattari, Félix. *The Three Ecologies*. Trans. Ian Pindar and Paul Sutton. New Brunswick, NJ: Athlone, 2000.

Gunner, Jeanne. "Among the Composition People: The WPA as English Department Agent." *JAC* 18 (1998): 153–65.

———. "Ideology, Theory, and the Genre of Writing Programs." *The Writing Program Administrator as Theorist*. Ed. Shirley K. Rose and Irwin Weiser. Portsmouth, NH: Heinemann Boynton/Cook, 2002. 7–18.

Habermas, Jürgen. "Modernity vs. Postmodernity." *New German Critique* 22 (Winter 1981): 3–14.

Halberstram, Judith, and Ira Livingston. "Introduction: Posthuman Bodies." *Posthuman Bodies*. Ed. Judith Halberstram and Ira Livingston. Bloomington: Indiana UP, 1995. 1–19.

Hall, Stuart. "Cultural Studies and Its Theoretical Legacies." *Cultural Studies*. Ed. Lawrence Grossberg, Cary Nelson, and Paula Treichler. New York: Routledge, 1992. 277–86.

Hand, Sean. "Translating Theory, or The Difference between Deleuze and Foucault." *Foucault*. Ed. Gilles Deleuze. Trans. Sean Hand. New York: Continuum International, 1996.

Hansen, Mark. *Embodying Technesis: Technology beyond Writing*. Ann Arbor: U of Michigan P, 2000.

Haraway, Donna J. *Simians, Cyborgs, and Women: The Reinvention of Nature*. New York: Routledge, 1991.

———. *When Species Meet*. Minneapolis: U of Minnesota P, 2007.

Hardin, Joe Marshall. *Opening Spaces: Critical Pedagogy and Resistance Theory in Composition*. Albany: State U of New York P, 2001.

———. "Writing Theory and Writing the Classroom." *Don't Call It That: The Composition Practicum*. Ed. Sidney I. Dobrin. Urbana: NCTE, 2005. 35–42.

Hardt, Michael, and Antonio Negri. *Empire*. Cambridge: Harvard UP, 2000.

Harris, Joseph. "Meet the New Boss, Same as the Old Boss: Class Consciousness in Composition." *CCC* 52.1 (2000): 43–68.

———. "The Rhetoric of Theory." *Writing Theory and Critical Theory*. Ed. John Clifford and John Schilb. New York: MLA. 1994. 141–47.

———. *A Teaching Subject: Composition since 1966*. Upper Saddle River, NJ: Prentice Hall, 1997.

Harris, Wendell V. *Beyond Poststructuralism: The Speculations of Theory and the Experience of Reading*. University Park: U of Penn State P, 2004.

Hassan, Ihab. "Prometheus as Performer: Toward a Posthumanist Culture." *Performance in Postmodern Culture*. Ed. Michel Beramou and Charles Caramello. Madison: U of Wisconsin P, 1977. 201–17.

Haswell, Richard H. "NCTE/CCCC's Recent War on Scholarship." *Written Communication* 22.2 (2005): 198–223.

Havelock, Eric. *Preface to Plato*. Cambridge: Harvard UP, 1963.

Hawk, Byron. *A Counter-History of Composition: Toward Methodologies of Complexity*. Pittsburgh: U of Pittsburgh P, 2007.

———. "Reconnecting Post-Process: Toward a Theory of Posthuman Networks." *Beyond Post-Process*. Ed. Sidney I. Dobrin, J. A. Rice, and Michael Vastola. Logan: Utah State UP, 2011. 75–93.

———. "Toward a Rhetoric of Network (Media) Culture: Notes on Polarities and Potentiality." *JAC* 24.4 (2004): 831–50.

Hawthorne, Nathaniel. *Tales and Sketches*. New York: Library of America, 1982.

Hayles, N. Katherine. "Afterword: The Human in the Posthuman." *Cultural Critique* 53 (2003): 134–37.

———. "Building Dwelling Thinking." *Basic Writings*. Ed. David Farrell Krell. New York: Harper Collins, 1993. 344–63.

———. "Foreword: Clearing the Ground." *Embodying Technesis: Technology beyond Writing*. By Mark Hansen. Ann Arbor: U of Michigan P, 2000. v–ix.

———. *How We Became Posthuman: Virtual Bodies in Cybernetics, Literature, and Informatics*. Chicago: U of Chicago P, 1999.

———. "The Posthuman Body: Inscription and Incorporation in *Galatea 2.2* and *Snow Crash*." *Configurations* 5.2 (1997): 241–66.

———. "The Question Concerning Technology." *Basic Writings*. Ed. David Farrell Krell. New York: Harper Collins, 1993. 307–41.

———. *Writing Machines*. Cambridge: MIT P, 2002.

Herbrechter, Stefan, and Ivan Callus. "Introduction: Post-Theory?" *Post-Theory, Culture, Criticism*. Ed. Ivan Callus and Stefan Herbrechter. New York: Rodopi, 2004. 7–21.

———, eds. *Post-Theory, Culture, Criticism*. New York: Rodopi, 2004. Herndl, Carl G., and Stuart R. Brown. *Green Culture: Environmental Rhetoric in Contemporary America*. Madison: U of Wisconsin P, 1996.

Hesse, Doug. Foreword. *The End of Composition Studies*. By David W. Smit. Carbondale: Southern Illinois UP, 2004.

Horner, Bruce. *Terms of Work for Composition: A Materialist Critique*. Albany: State U of New York P, 2000.

Jameson, Fredric. *The Political Unconscious: Narrative as a Socially Symbolic Act*. Ithaca: Cornell UP, 1981.

Jammer, Max. *Concepts of Space: The History of Theories in Space and Physics*. 3rd ed. Mineola, NY: Dover, 1994.

Jarratt, Susan C. "New Dispositions for Historical Studies in Rhetoric." *Rhetoric and Composition as Intellectual Work*. Ed. Gary A. Olson. Carbondale: Southern Illinois UP, 2002. 65–78.

Johnston, John. "Network Theory and Life on the Internet." *JAC* 24.4 (2004): 881–99.

Jørgensen, Sven E. "Complex Ecology in the 21st Century." *Complex Ecology: The Whole-Part Relation in Ecosystems*. Ed. Bernard C. Patten and Sven E. Jørgensen. Upper Saddle River, NJ: Prentice Hall, 1995. xvii–xix.

Kant, Immanuel. *Basic Writings*. Ed. Allen W. Wood. New York: Modern Library, 2001.

Kent, Thomas, ed. *Post-Process Theory: Beyond the Writing-Process Paradigm*. Carbondale: Southern Illinois UP, 1999.

Killingsworth, M. Jimmie, and Jacqueline S. Palmer. *Ecospeak: Rhetoric and Environmental Politics in America*. Carbondale: Southern Illinois UP, 1991.

Laclau, Ernesto. *Emancipations*. London: Verso, 1996.

————. Preface. *Post-Theory: New Directions in Criticism*. Ed. Martin McQuillan, Robin Purves, and Graeme MacDonald. Edinburgh: Edinburgh UP, 1999. vii.

Latour, Bruno. *We Have Never Been Modern*. Cambridge: Harvard UP, 1991.

Lefebvre, Henri. *The Production of Space*. Cambridge, MA: Blackwell, 1991.

————. *The Survival of Capitalism: Reproduction of the Relations of Production*. Trans. Frank Bryant. London: Allison and Busby, 1976.

L'Eplattenier, Barbara, and Lisa Mastrangelo, eds. *Historical Studies of Writing Program Administration: Individuals, Communities, and the Formation of a Discipline*. West Lafayette, IN: Parlor, 2004.

————. "Why Administrative Histories?" *Historical Studies of Writing Program Administration: Individuals, Communities, and the Formation of a Discipline*. Ed. Barbara L'Eplattenier and Lisa Mastrangelo. West Lafayette, IN: Parlor, 2004. xvii–xxvi.

Lessing, Gotthold Ephraim. *Laocoon: An Essay upon the Limits of Painting and Poetry*. Trans. Ellen Frothingham. New York: Noonday, 1957.

Lindemann, Erika. "Three Views of English 101." *College English* 57 (1995): 287–302.

Lyall, Laurence Hayden. "A Comment on 'The Ecology of Writing.'" *College English* 49 (1987): 357–59.

Lyotard, Jean-François. "Answering the Question: What Is Postmodernism?" *The Postmodern Condition: A Report on Knowledge*. Minneapolis: U of Minnesota P, 1984. 71–82.

————. "Note on the Meaning of 'Post-'." *The Postmodern Explained: Correspondence 1982–1985*. Minneapolis: U of Minnesota P, 1992. 64–68.

————. *Peregrinations: Law, Form, Event*. New York: Columbia UP, 1988.

————. *The Postmodern Condition: A Report on Knowledge*. Minneapolis: U of Minnesota P, 1984.

McClintock, Anne. "The Angels of Progress: Pitfalls of the Term 'Post-Colonial.'" *Social Text* 31/32.1 (Winter 1994): 84–98.

McCracken, Tim. *Between Language and Silence: Postpedagogy's Middle Way: Part I The Text*. New Jersey: NJP, 1989. Retrieved 13 Apr. 2008 from http://www.eric.ed.gov/ERICWebPortal/contentdelivery/servlet/ERICServlet?accno=ED307630.McLemee, Scott. "Deconstructing Composition." *Chronicle of Higher Education* 21 Mar. 2003. http://chronicle.com/free/v49/i28/28a01601.htm (accessed 21 June 2009).

McLeod, Susan. *Writing Program Administration*. West Lafayette, IN: Parlor/ WAC Clearinghouse, 2007.

McQuillan, Martin, Graeme Macdonald, Robin Purves, and Stephen Thomson. "The Joy of Theory." *Post-Theory: New Directions in Criticism*. Ed. Martin McQuillan, Robin Purves, and Graeme MacDonald. Edinburgh: Edinburgh UP, 1999. ix–xx.

McQuillan, Martin, Robin Purves, and Graeme MacDonald, eds. *Post-Theory: New Directions in Criticism*. Edinburgh: Edinburgh UP, 1999.

Melville, Herman. "Bartleby, the Scrivener: A Story of Wall-Street." *Great Short Works of Herman Melville*. New York: Penguin Classics, 2004. 19–38.

Miller, Richard E. "The Arts of Complicity: Pragmatism and the Culture of Schooling." *College English* 61 (1998): 10–28.

———. *As If Learning Mattered: Reforming Higher Education*. Ithaca: Cornell UP, 1998.

———. "'Let's Do the Numbers': Comp Droids and the Prophets of Doom." *Profession 1999*: 96–105.

Miller, Susan. "Composition as a Cultural Artifact: Rethinking History as Theory." *Writing Theory and Critical Theory*. Ed. John Clifford and John Schilb. New York: MLA, 1994. 19–32.

———. "The Feminization of Composition." *The Politics of Writing Instruction: Postsecondary*. Ed. Richard Bullock and John Trimbur. Portsmouth, NH: Heinemann Boynton/Cook, 1991. 39–53.

———. *Rescuing the Subject: A Critical Introduction to Rhetoric and the Writer*. Carbondale: Southern Illinois UP, 1989.

———. "Technologies of Self?-Formation." *JAC* 17.3 (1997): 497–500.

———. *Textual Carnivals: The Politics of Composition*. Carbondale: Southern Illinois UP, 1991.

———. "Writing Studies as a Mode of Inquiry." *Rhetoric and Composition as Intellectual Work*. Ed. Gary A. Olson. Carbondale: Southern Illinois UP, 2002. 41–54.

———. "Writing Theory: Theory Writing." *Methods and Methodologies in Composition Research*. Ed. Gesa Kirsch and Patricia A. Sullivan. Carbondale: Southern Illinois UP, 1992. 62–83.

Miller, Thomas P. *The Formation of College English: Rhetoric and Belles Lettres in the British Cultural Provinces*. Pittsburgh: U of Pittsburgh P, 1997.

Mitchell, W. J. T. *Iconology: Image, Text, Ideology*. Chicago: U of Chicago P, 1986.

Murphet, Julian. "Grounding Theory: Literary Theory and the New Geography." *Post-Theory: New Directions in Criticism*. Ed. Martin McQuillan, Robin Purves, and Graeme MacDonald. Edinburgh: Edinburgh UP, 1999. 200–208.

Næss, Arne. "The Shallow and the Deep, Long-Range Ecology Movement: A Summary." *The Deep Ecology Movement: An Introductory Anthology*. Ed. Alan Drengson and Yuichi Inoue. Berkeley: North Atlantic, 1995. 3–10.

Negri, Antonio. "Constituent Republic." *Radical Thought in Italy: A Potential Politics*. Ed. Paolo Virno and Michael Hardt. Minneapolis: U of Minnesota P, 1996. 212–21.

North, Stephen M. *The Making of Knowledge in Composition: Portrait of an Emerging Field*. Portsmouth, NH: Boynton/Cook, 1987.

Odum. E. P. "The New Ecology." *BioScience* 14 (1964): 14–16.

Ohmann, Richard M. *English in America: A Radical View of the Profession*. Middletown, CT: Wesleyan UP, 1996.

Olson, Gary A. "The Death of Composition as an Intellectual Discipline." *Rhetoric and Composition as Intellectual Work*. Ed. Gary A. Olson. Carbondale: Southern Illinois UP, 2002. 23–31.

———. "Ideological Critique in Rhetoric and Composition." *Rhetoric and Composition as Intellectual Work*. Ed. Gary A. Olson. Carbondale: Southern Illinois UP, 2002. 81–90.

———, ed. *Rhetoric and Composition as Intellectual Work*. Carbondale: Southern Illinois UP, 2002.

Patten, Bernard C. "Why 'Complex' Ecology?" *Complex Ecology: The Whole-Part Relation in Ecosystems*. Ed. Bernard C. Patten and Sven E. Jørgensen. Upper Saddle River, NJ: Prentice Hall, 1995. xiii–xv.

Payne, Michael, and John Schad, eds. *life.after.theory*. New York: Continuum, 2003.

Pepperell, Robert. *The Post-Human Condition*. Bristol, UK: Intellect, 1997.

Perec, Georges. *Species of Spaces and Other Pieces*. Trans. John Sturrock. New York: Penguin, 1999.

Phelps, Louise Wetherbee. *Composition as a Human Science: Contributions to the Self-Understanding of a Discipline*. New York: Oxford UP, 1988.

———. "Practical Wisdom and the Geography of Knowledge in Composition." *College English* 53 (1991): 863–85.

Plato. *Timaeus. Plato: The Complete Works*. Ed. John M. Cooper. Indianapolis: Hackett, 1997. 1224–91.

Popken, Randall. "The WPA as Publishing Scholar: Edwin Hopkins and the Labor and Cost of the Teaching of English." *Historical Studies of Writing Program Administration: Individuals, Communities, and the Formation of a Discipline*. Ed. Barbara L'Eplattenier and Lisa Mastrangelo. West Lafayette, IN: Parlor, 2004. 5–22.

Pratt, Marie Louise. "Modernity and Periphery: Toward a Global and Relational Analysis." *Beyond Dichotomies: Histories, Identities, Cultures, and the Challenge of Globalization*. Ed. Elisabeth Mudimbe-Boyi. Albany: State U of New York P, 2002. 21–47.

Reither, James A. "Writing and Knowing: Toward Redefining the Writing Process." *College English* 47 (1985): 620–28.

Reynolds, Nedra. "Composition's Imagined Geographies: The Politics of Space in the Frontier, City, and Cyberspace." *CCC* 50.1 (1998): 12–35.

———. *Geographies of Writing: Inhabiting Places and Encountering Difference.* Carbondale: Southern Illinois UP, 2004.

Rice, Jeff. "Conservative Writing Program Administrators (WPAs)." *The Writing Program Interrupted: Making Space for Critical Discourse.* Ed. Donna Strickland and Jeanne Gunner. Portsmouth, NH: Boynton/Cook, 2009. 1–13.

Rickert, Thomas. "In the House of Doing: Rhetoric and the Kairos of Ambience." *JAC* 24.2 (2004): 901–27.

Ridolfo, Jim, and Dànielle Nicole DeVoss. "Composing for Recomposition: Rhetorical Velocity and Delivery." *Kairos* 13.2 (2009): n.p.

Rose, Shirley K., and Irwin Weiser, eds. *The Writing Program Administrator as Theorist: Making Knowledge Work.* Portsmouth, NH: Boynton/Cook/Heinemann, 2002.

Roskelly, Hephzibah, and Kate Ronald. *Reason to Believe: Romanticism, Pragmatism, and the Possibility of Teaching.* Albany: State U of New York P, 1998.

Royle, Nicholas. "Déjà Vu." *Post-Theory: New Directions in Criticism.* Ed. Martin McQuillan, Robin Purves, and Graeme MacDonald. Edinburgh: Edinburgh UP, 1999. 3–20.

Sánchez, Raúl. *The Function of Theory in Composition Studies.* Albany: State U of New York P, 2005.

———. "The Ideology of Identity and the Study of Writing." Conference on College Composition and Communication Convention. New York. 24 Mar. 2007.

Saussure, Ferdinand de. *Course in General Linguistics.* Boston: McGraw Hill, 1965.

Schad, John. "What Are We After?" *life.after.theory.* Ed. Michael Payne and John Schad. New York: Continuum, 2003. ix–xi.

Schwanitz, Dietrich. "Systems Theory and the Environment of Theory." *The Current in Criticism: Essays on the Present and Future of Literary Theory.* Ed. Clayton Koelb and Virgil Lokke. West Lafayette, IN: Purdue UP, 1987. 265–94.

Simon, Bart. "Introduction: Toward a Critique of Posthuman Futures." *Cultural Critique* 53 (2003): 1–9.

Sirc, Geoffrey. *English Composition as a Happening.* Logan: Utah State UP, 2002.

Smit, David W. *The End of Composition Studies.* Carbondale: Southern Illinois UP, 2004.

Soja, Edward W. *Thirdspace: Journeys to Los Angeles and Other Real-and-Imagined Places.* Malden, MA: Blackwell, 1996.

Syverson, Margaret A. *The Wealth of Reality: An Ecology of Composition.* Carbondale: Southern Illinois UP, 1999.

Taylor, Mark C. *The Moment of Complexity: Emerging Network Culture.* Chicago: U of Chicago P, 2001.

Trimbur, John. "Changing the Question: Should Writing Be Studied?" *Composition Studies* 31.1 (2003): 15–24.

Tuan, Yi-Fu. *Space and Place: The Perspective of Experience.* Minneapolis: U of Minnesota P, 1977.

Ulmer, Gregory L. *Heuretics: The Logic of Invention*. Baltimore: Johns Hopkins UP, 1994.

———. *Internet Invention: From Literacy to Electracy*. New York: Longman, 2003.

UNESCO. "Public Reports: Education." http://stats.uis.unesco.org/ReportFold-ers/reportFolders.aspx (accessed 26 Apr. 2007).

Vastola, Michael. "The Rhetoric of the Cold War in the Age of Terror: Toward a Deleuzean Pedagogy of Violence." Unpublished paper. Cited by permission.

Vitanza, Victor J. "Three Countertheses: Or, A Critical In(ter)vention into Composition Theories and Pedagogies." *Contending with Words: Composition and Rhetoric in a Postmodern Age*. Ed. Patricia Harkin and John Schilb. New York: MLA, 1991. 139–72.

Waldby, Catherine. *The Visible Human Project: Informatic Bodies and Posthuman Medicine*. London: Routledge, 2000.

Weisser, Christian R. "Ecocomposition and the Greening of Identity." *Ecocomposition: Theoretical and Pedagogical Approaches*. Ed. Christian R. Weisser and Sidney I. Dobrin. Albany: State U of New York P, 2001. 81–95.

White, Edward M. Preface. *Historical Studies of Writing Program Administration: Individuals, Communities, and the Formation of a Discipline*. Ed. Barbara L'Eplattenier and Lisa Mastrangelo. West Lafayette, IN: Parlor, 2004. xiii–xiv.

Wieseltier, Leon. *Against Identity*. New York: Drenttel, 1996.

Wolfe, Cary. *Critical Environments: Postmodern Theory and the Pragmatics of the "Outside."* Minneapolis: U of Minnesota P, 1998.

———. *What Is Posthumanism?* Minneapolis: U of Minnesota P, 2010.

Worsham, Lynn. "Coming to Terms: Theory, Writing, Politics." *Rhetoric and Composition as Intellectual Work*. Ed. Gary A. Olson. Carbondale: Southern Illinois UP, 2002. 101–14.

———. "Going Postal: Pedagogic Violence and the Schooling of Emotion." *JAC* 18.2 (1998): 213–45.

———. "Writing against Writing: The Predicament of Ecriture Féminine in Composition Studies." *Contending with Words: Composition and Rhetoric in a Postmodern Age*. Ed. Patricia Harkin and John Schilb. New York: MLA, 1991. 82–104.

Worsham, Lynn, and Gary A. Olson. "Hegemony and the Future of Democracy: Ernesto Laclau's Political Philosophy." *JAC* 19.1 (1999): 1–34.

Wyschogrod, Edith. "Networking the Unpredictable: The Lure of Complexity." *JAC* 24.4 (2004): 871–79.

Zebroski, James Thomas. *Thinking through Theory: Vygotskian Perspectives on the Teaching of Writing*. Portsmouth, NH: Boynton/Cook, 1994.

———. "Toward a Theory of Theory for Composition Studies." *Under Construction: Working at the Intersections of Composition Theory, Research, and Practice*. Ed. Christine Farris and Chris M. Anson. Logan: Utah State UP, 1998. 30–48.

Žižek, Slavoj. "Beyond Discourse-Analysis." *New Reflections of the Revolution of Our Time.* By Ernesto Laclau. London: Verso, 1990. 249–60.

———. *Violence: Big Ideas/Small Books.* New York: Picador, 2008.

———. *Welcome to the Desert of the Real: Five Essays on September 11 and Related Dates.* London: Verso, 2002.

Index

Sidney I. Dobrin is an associate professor in the Department of English at the University of Florida, where for ten years he directed the writing program. Dobrin has authored and edited more than sixteen books and numerous articles. His current research engages posthumanisms; visual rhetorics, cultures, and literacies; and ecological methodologies.